4895 Marshall Avenue
Erie, Pennsylvania
June 4, 193-

Dear Althea:

Just a line to say that we are leaving
for Kentucky next Thursday morning. Max says
we can take an hour or two for a visit with you
and Morris. We can't possibly reach your place
until late in the afternoon. I'm eager for a
visit with you, for this is likely to be my only
opportunity to see you for some months.

When I see you, I'll tell you all the news
I do not have time to write now. Until Thursday.

Sincerely yours

Margaret

Miss Althea Graham
530 Walnut Street
Greenfield, Ohio

(*Strokes, 425; Words, 83*)

Style Letter No. 5—Personal Letter with Inside Address
Typed in Semi-formal Letter Style

[75]

Exercise 42

DIRECTIONS: Set the marginal stops so as to give a margin of an inch and a half at the left and at the right. Set the tabular stops for the major indentations. Use single spacing with a triple space between the main heading and the first division of the outline. Center the exercise vertically. Center the main heading horizontally and type it in capitals.

READINGS IN AMERICAN HISTORY

I. Reconstruction of the Southern States.

    A. Federal policy toward South. Dual problem:
        1. Reconstruction of Southern States.
        2. Provision for welfare of emancipated negro.

    B. Nature of problem of reconstruction.
        1. Two possible agencies of reconstruction.
        2. Theories of status of Southern States.
            a. Southern theory.
            b. Presidential theory.
            c. Sumner's theory of "state suicide."

Exercise 43

DIRECTIONS: Set the marginal stops for a sixty-space line. Set the tabular stops for the major indentations. Use single spacing with a triple space between the main heading and the first division of the outline. Center the exercise vertically. Center the main heading horizontally and type it in capitals. Note that in this outline only one space is used after each period following the number and letters.

READINGS IN AMERICAN HISTORY

I. NATIONAL READJUSTMENT AFTER THE CIVIL WAR (1865-1877).

    A. Diplomatic adjustments under Johnson.
        1. French in Mexico and their expulsion.
        2. Purchase of Alaska.
        3. Settlement of difficulties with England.
            a. Johnson-Clarendon Convention.
            b. Sumner's statement of American claims.
            c. Treaty of Washington (1871).
            d. Deliberations at Geneva; the award.

    B. Financial reorganization.
        1. State of national finances.
        2. Sources of opposition to revision of
           financial system.

II. OPENING OF THE MODERN ERA (1877-1898).

    A. Development of the West (1860-1890).
        1. Progress of settlement.
        2. Transcontinental railroads.
            a. Provisions of creating acts.
            b. Rivalry over eastern terminus.
            c. Completion.
        3. Relations with western Indians.

Personal Letters

The form of personal letters differs slightly from that of business letters. Since personal letters are not usually typed on letterheads, a complete return address must be given in the letter. The inside address may be omitted. When the inside address is given, it may be placed at the left margin after the body of the letter. See Style Letter No. 5 on page 75.

Exercise 44

DIRECTIONS: Set the marginal stops for a forty-five-space line. Use double spacing. Type Style Letter No. 5 exactly as it is given on page 75. Type the heading two inches from the top of the paper.

NOTE: When a letter is typed on plain paper, the heading should include the complete return address. The first line should give the number and the name of the street; the second line should give the city and the state, separated by a comma; and the third line should give the date. When typing a letter on plain paper, type the date line two inches from the top of the page.

An explanation of the addressing of envelopes and the folding of letters is given on pages 85 and 86. Students who will not continue in the typewriting course should study this discussion in order that they can properly address envelopes and fold letters in their personal correspondence.

Exercise 45

DIRECTIONS: Follow the directions given for Exercise 44. Instead of using double spacing, however, use single spacing.

1843 Hewitt Avenue Springfield, Ill. Dear Ted: Vacation begins next Friday afternoon at 3:45. I'm hitting the trail for your home early Saturday morning and should be there by noon. If you'll be ready, we can start for the camp right off. (P) I have all my camp equipment ready now. Don't forget to have the tent repaired and the canned goods bought. Saturday can't come too soon for me. Here's hoping it doesn't rain. Sincerely yours (Dick) Mr. Theodore Stone 143 Center Street Hannibal, Mo. *(389–67)*

Optional Exercise 45

DIRECTIONS: Follow the directions given for Exercise 44. Instead of using double spacing, however, use single spacing.

2947 Summit Street San Diego, Calif. Dear Henry: I am settled for the winter, I suppose. Yesterday I enrolled in a private school for boys. It is too late in the semester for me to begin work in the high school. In this private school each fellow works as fast as he can. It is a sort of individual or honor plan. (P) My old Portable is coming in handy. It is a lot better than my illegible scrawl—faster, too. (P) You will hear from me again soon. In the meantime, write me all the news. Sincerely yours (Larry) Mr. Henry McMaster 469 Capitol Street Salt Lake City, Utah *(466–87)*

Exercise 46

DIRECTIONS: This is a timed writing exercise which is to be written for ten minutes. If your teacher cannot time you, use a watch with a second hand and time yourself. Set the marginal stops for a seventy-space line. Set the tabular stop for an indentation of five spaces. Use double spacing. Do not type the heading.

You Can Too— But Will You?

		STROKES
Paragraph 1	Do you ever get worn out, discouraged, just "weary with well	64
(Measurement Paragraph)	doing"? If you do, hear the tale of Demosthenes, a citizen of	131
	Athens who lived a few hundred years before the time of Christ.	197
Syllable intensity, 1.25	The story goes that his was an excellent family of great wealth,	263
	but from the very first he was marked by fate. When he was	324
	but a child, he lost both of his parents. He was then sent to a	390
	relative who was to look after him and the large estate which	452
	was to be held in trust for him. The man proved to be quite un-	518
	worthy of the trust and, through misuse of the funds, made the	581
	boy almost penniless. *(603)*	603

DIRECTIONS: Set the left marginal stop three inches from the left edge of the paper. Set the tabular stop three inches from the left marginal stop. This will give the correct placement of the two columns. Use single spacing with a triple space between the heading and the columns. Center the exercise vertically. Center the heading horizontally and type it in capitals.

NOTE: In typing Arabic numerals, keep the figures at the right even. While it is permissible to maintain an even left margin in typing Roman numerals, it is better to follow the practice of keeping an even right margin in typing figures. The left margin should therefore be reset when Arabic numerals representing tens, hundreds, and thousands are to be typed. When typing the Roman numerals, back-space the required number of times to place the numerals correctly.

ARABIC AND ROMAN NUMERALS

NOTE: Instead of resetting the left marginal stop, you can type outside the left margin by depressing and holding the marginal-release key (No. 26) and back-spacing the necessary number of spaces. If you are using the Underwood typewriter, you must depress the special margin release (B) and back-space the required number of spaces.

NOTE: If you are using a typewriter having decimal tabulator keys, it is not necessary to back-space to place the numerals correctly. Depress the decimal key to type I, the 1 key to type II, the 10 key to type III, etc.

Arabic	Roman
1	I
2	II
3	III
4	IV
5	V
6	VI
7	VII
8	VIII
9	IX
10	X
11	XI
12	XII
13	XIII
14	XIV
15	XV
16	XVI
17	XVII
18	XVIII
19	XIX
20	XX
30	XXX
40	XL
50	L
60	LX
70	LXX
80	LXXX
90	XC
100	C
200	CC
300	CCC
400	CCCC
500	D
600	DC
700	DCC
800	DCCC
900	CM
1000	M
2000	MM

Paragraph 2	The loss of his wealth in itself would seem rather crushing,	666
Syllable	but Nature, too, had been more than hard on the little orphan.	730
intensity, 1.26	His body was deformed and awkward; one shoulder was higher	790
	than the other. At times his face was grotesque; he had a nerv-	856
	ous disease, and when he was excited, his face twisted into all	920
	sorts of queer shapes. When he tried to talk, he lost his breath.	988
	He had a weak voice; he stammered; he could not pronounce the	1051
	letter "r." He was just a poor boy with an amazing number of	1116
	handicaps; yet there was that in his mind and heart and soul	1177
	which bade him rise above all handicaps. *(615)*	1218

Paragraph 3
Syllable
intensity, 1.27

When Demosthenes knew that his wealth was gone, he vowed | 1278
he would never rest until he had gained justice. Now, one would | 1344
hire the best lawyer he could get, and the case would go through | 1409
our courts of law; in those days, there was no such procedure, for | 1476
a man pleaded his own cause before the public. On stated days | 1540
the citizens of Athens gathered to discuss civic questions and to | 1607
vote upon them. It was the custom for those who wished a hear- | 1672
ing to catch the public ear and to sway opinion through the | 1732
power of speech. The handicapped boy was to vie for public | 1793
attention with expert speakers. *(607)* | 1825

Paragraph 4
Syllable
intensity, 1.28

The men of Athens were used to the best in public speaking. | 1888
It was an exacting group which Demosthenes chose to be the | 1949
judge of his cause. At his first appearance, his hearers were | 2013
much amused. They stood laughing at the young man whose | 2071
gasping breath made him hard to understand and whose plea | 2129
was quite without appeal. It was after this that Demosthenes | 2193
set about his training in earnest. That pleasures might not tempt | 2261
him from his aim, he shaved the hair from one side of his head | 2324
and let it grow long on the other side. He knew that if his | 2386
ambition should fail him, fear of ridicule would hold him firm. | 2450
Thus began the amazing course of self-schooling. *(675)* | 2500

Paragraph 5
Syllable
intensity, 1.29

Demosthenes read the talks of famed orators and tried to | 2559
learn to do just as well as they. He built a hidden room, where, | 2626
alone, he practiced gestures and exercised his voice. Before | 2689
a mirror, he learned to curb the twitching of his face. He tied a | 2757
large stone to one shoulder to equalize its height with that of | 2821
the other. To strengthen his voice that it might soar above the | 2887
noise of the crowd, he took his stand by the sea and forced him- | 2952
self to make tones that could be heard above the roar of the | 3013
waters. To correct his stammering, he made himself talk clearly | 3079
with his mouth filled with pebbles. He even mastered his diffi- | 3145
culty with the letter "r." *(674)* | 3174

Paragraph 6
(Measurement
paragraph)
Syllable
intensity, 1.25

Once more, when he felt that he was ready, he went before | 3234
the Athenian public. They laughed at him. To the eye, he was | 3300
untouched by their scorn. Just what heartbreak he experienced, | 3365
we are not told. But we do know very well that he would not | 3427
recognize defeat. After a period of study, he appeared for a | 3490
third time, and success was his. Under the spell of his words, | 3555
his hearers laughed when he wished them to do so; when he | 3613
willed it, they wept. He had conquered his handicaps and the | 3676
men of Athens. For more than two thousand years, he has been | 3740
looked upon as the greatest of orators. Could he speak to us | 3803
now, he would say, "You can too, but will you?" *(680)* | 3854

Exercise 39

DIRECTIONS: Set the marginal stops for a forty-space line. Use double spacing. Triple-space between the heading and the first line of the exercise. Center the exercise vertically on a full sheet of paper. Center the heading horizontally and type it in capitals. *(Total strokes, 680)*

NOTE: Copying from a rough draft requires an understanding of the meaning of the words to be typed. Corrections are not always clearly indicated; context must often be the guide. Read the copy before attempting to type it. This is a simple problem in typing from a rough draft. More difficult problems will be given later. The typed lines will not be the same as the lines in the exercise.

MIRRORS

I have ~~known~~ seen mirrors of rare beauty.
In the ~~fresh~~, clear water of Baxter's
Creek that ran at the foot of the hill
just below our house, I have seen mirrored,
in inverted fashion, the trees swaying
lazily overhead. In the ballroom of the
William Penn Hotel, walls of mirrors catch
gleams of pure diamond-like beauty from
the prisms of the chandeliers. A few books
that mirror life and reflect something of
great understanding and great love are
now mine. I know, too, an old man whose
quiet eyes mirror the richness of a life
well lived and the eager interest of a
soul who views his numbered days without
fear. *Yes, I have seen mirrors of rare beauty.*

Exercise 40

DIRECTIONS: Set the marginal stops for a forty-space line. Use double spacing. Triple-space between the heading and the first line of the exercise. Center the exercise vertically on a full sheet of paper. Center the heading horizontally and type it in capitals. *(Total strokes, 529)*

NOTE: This exercise illustrates the development of the paragraph. Copying from penwritten material is often required in personal typing as well as in office work. The typed lines will not be the same as the lines in the exercise.

Rain

Quick flashes of lightning zig-zagged into the jet blackness of the night. There was a rustle of leaves and a swaying of branches as the wind lightly brushed the trees. All the sounds of night were stilled, like a frightened child with held breath, unexpectedly alone in an unlighted room. As the big drops of rain spattered against the ground, I leaned far out the window and saw, by the light of the great streaks of lightning, the bed of wilted tulips lift their petals to the cool freshness of the rain.

PART II

Office Problems

INSTRUCTIONAL BLOCK VI
THE BUSINESS LETTER

Business letters are the personal representatives of the company by which they are mailed. They tell the sales story, record the complaint, bargain over prices, and close business transactions. They do more, too; they reveal something of the standards of the office from which they come. If business letters are well arranged and accurately typed, they may be effective representatives of the company; if they are poorly placed on the page and carelessly typed, they may be unconvincing and their mission may be unsuccessful. The message is the important part of the letter, of course; but correct punctuation, spelling, syllabication, capitalization, and arrangement will help to make the message effective. It is the dictator's responsibility to say what the message shall be; it is the typist's responsibility to see that it is accurately typed and correctly placed.

In Instructional Block IV, you learned the set-up of the single-spaced and the double-spaced business letters. You may need to review the detailed instructions given on pages 56 to 59. Study also the following information.

Attention Line

Company letters, addressed to the company, may be called to the attention of a particular individual through the use of the *attention line*.

The attention line is a part of the address. It should be typed two single spaces below the last line of the address proper and before the salutation. In order that the attention line may attract immediate attention, and thus insure prompt reference to the individual whose attention is requested, double-space both before and after the special line. The attention line may be (1) centered, (2) indented five spaces from the left margin, or (3) typed flush with the left margin.

Subject Line

If the word *Subject* is printed on the letterhead, type the subject of the letter on the same line. If the word *Subject* is not given on the letterhead, but this information is to be included in the letter, type the subject two single spaces below the salutation; then double-space before typing the first paragraph.

Salutation

As a rule, the more familiar the letter, the shorter the salutation. The word *dear* is not capitalized when preceded by the word *My*. In a letter carrying the company's signature alone, that is, a letter without the personal penwritten signature of the dictator, the *My* is omitted from the salutation. Never use any abbreviation in the salutation except *Mr., Mrs.,* or *Dr.*

Placement of the Letter

The reader of a letter senses the appearance even before he knows the content. If the letter is accurately arranged and pleasing in appearance, it will tend to create a favorable attitude in the mind of the reader. Attention to arrangement is worth while. You may not be responsible for the contents of the letter, but the arrangement of the letter is definitely your responsibility. Accurate placement is vitally important.

The placement chart suggested for use in typing the letters given in this text is discussed on page 58 and shown on page 59. Other ways of determining the correct marginal adjustments for letters may be used. The stenographer judges the correct placement of the letter by estimating the approximate number of lines. The ability to estimate length of material comes with experience. Begin now to develop judgment in the placement of your letters. As soon as you have had considerable practice in placing letters, you should type them without reference to the placement chart.

In determining marginal adjustments, you should make allowance for any unusual features in the letter, such as tabulated material, long quotations, and extra lines in the inside address. Letters without a company signature or an official title will require either wider spacing between the date line and the inside address or shorter lines of writing. Such adjustments must be made in the use of any placement chart.

Exercise 37

DIRECTIONS: Type this exercise on a sheet of paper 8½ x 11". Use double spacing with a triple space between the heading and the first line of the exercise. Center the exercise vertically, and center each line horizontally. Type the heading in capitals.

The problem of centering is not new to you. A centering drill and rules for centering are given on pages 32 and 33. When centering, determine the center of the paper; then place half the letters and the spaces of the line to be centered to the left of the center of the paper and half to the right of the center of the paper. In the work of this instructional block, omit the exercise number when you type a problem.

COURSES IN COMMERCIAL EDUCATION = 15

Business English = 8

Junior Business Education = 12

Economic Geography = 9

History of Commerce = 9

Commercial Law = 7

Economics = 4

Salesmanship = 6

Business Organization = 10

Commercial Arithmetic = 10

Bookkeeping = 6

Typewriting = 5

Shorthand = 4

Office Practice = 7

Exercise 38

DIRECTIONS: Type this exercise on a sheet of paper 8½ x 11". Use double spacing with a triple space between the heading and the first line of the exercise. Center the exercise vertically, and center each line horizontally. Type the heading in capitals.

VALUABLE TRAITS FOR SECRETARIES = 15

Accuracy = 4

Responsibleness = 7

Dependability = 6

Intelligence = 6

Courtesy = 4

Initiative = 5

Judgment = 4

Tact = 2

Personal Pleasantness = 10

Personal Appearance = 9

Interest in Work = 8

Speed = 2

Reticence = 4

Adaptability = 6

Businesslikeness = 8

Neatness = 4

Memory = 3

Good Breeding = 6

Poise = 2

Self-confidence = 7

Summary of the Set-Up of the Business Letter

A. Letterhead.
1. Standard page, 8½ x 11".
2. Average depth of heading, 2".

B. Date Line.
1. On letterhead paper, type the date two single spaces below the city and the state line.
2. The date line may be
   a. Centered under the city and the state.
   b. Indented five spaces to the right of the beginning of the city name.
   c. Begun under the first letter of the city.
   d. Placed so that it will end at approximately the right margin of the letter. This plan is followed if the letterhead is unusual in its arrangement.
3. In the date line, spell the month in full.
4. When the month, day, and year are given in one line, indicate the day by figures separated from the year by a comma, and indicate the year by figures.

C. Spacing Between Date Line and Address.
This is determined largely by the length of the letter. Six single spaces between the date line and the first line of the address will usually give a satisfactory placement of letters of average length. Regardless of the length of the letter, always have at least three single spaces between the date line and the inside address.

D. Address.
1. The official title in the address should be placed at the beginning of the second line, that is, before the company name, and should be followed by a comma. If the second line is very long, however, the official title may be typed on the first line, just after the personal name, separated from the name by a comma and a space.
2. The first line of the address is typed even with the left margin.
3. In the indented style of letter, the second line of the address is indented five spaces from the left margin, and the third line, ten spaces.
4. Double-space between the last line of the address and the salutation.
5. Spell *Street* and *Avenue* in full, unless abbreviations are required in order to secure balance in the address.

E. Attention Line.
1. This is typed two single spaces below the last line of the address and before the salutation.
2. In the indented form, the line is either centered or begun at the paragraph point. In the block form of letter, the attention line is typed even with the left margin.

F. Salutation.
1. This is always typed even with the left margin, two single spaces below the address or the attention line.
2. In the business letter, the salutation is followed by a colon.
   In the use of open punctuation, some writers extend the principle by omitting the colon after the salutation and the comma after the complimentary close.

3. Have two single spaces between the salutation and the subject line or between the salutation and the first line of the body of the letter.

G. Subject Line.
1. The subject is properly a part of the body of the letter. Unless the printed letterhead indicates the position of the subject, type the subject two single spaces below the salutation.
2. Long subjects should be arranged in two lines.
3. The subject is treated as a manuscript heading and is not followed by a period.

H. Body of Letter.
1. Letters which are single-spaced require double spacing between paragraphs.
2. Paragraphs are usually indented five spaces when the indented form is used. Ten-space indentations are permitted, though not generally used.

I. Complimentary Close.
1. The first word only is capitalized.
2. In the indented and modified block letter styles, the complimentary close usually begins at 30 or 35, or slightly to the left of the center of the letter. The longest of the closing lines of the letter must not extend beyond the right margin.

J. Company Signature.
1. This is typed in capital letters, two single spaces below the complimentary close.
2. In the indented form of letter, indent the company signature five spaces from the beginning of the complimentary close.
3. In the block form of letter, the company signature begins even with the complimentary close.

K. Official Title.
1. The official title is typed four single spaces below the company signature.
2. In the indented form of letter, the official title is indented five spaces from the beginning of the company signature, or it may be spaced so that it will end at the right margin of the letter.
3. The official title is typed in small letters, each word of the title beginning with a capital.
4. If an official title is not used, the dictator's name may be typed in the position usually given to the official title.

L. Reference Initials.
1. The reference initials include the initials or the name of the dictator and the initials of the stenographer.
2. Reference initials are typed flush with the left margin of the letter, two single spaces below the official title.
3. If the letter does not carry an official title, the reference initials are typed four single spaces below the company signature.
4. If the letter has neither a company signature nor an official title, type the reference initials six to eight single spaces below the complimentary close.

M. Enclosure.
1. *Enclosure* is typed at the left margin, two single spaces below the reference initials.
2. More than one enclosure is indicated by the correct figure typed after the word *Enclosures*.

Alphabetic Sentence Drill

Liza quickly mixed the very big jar of new soap.

Bezique was the card game often played to vex Jake.

John Zilbandy saw the quick vamp fixing the trapeze.

The bad major will fix a quiet cozy nook for the vexed gypsy.

Pairs of lazy, knowing oxen came by, quietly evading the big jam.

Galaxies of quaint larkspur blew jocundly above the garden maze.

Juxtaposition of ruby and emerald quickly crazed the extravagant wife.

So woebegone a deportment of the wizen extra quickly rejoiced Yvonne.

Jack's perplexed, puzzled physiognomy blinked quietly in full view.

Quizzically juggling extraordinary matters helped Black win favor.

Jacques, the valedictorian, amazed big Frank with explanatory zeal.

Xantippe quickly judged Socrates' quizzical habit of musing was vain.

Bizarre Frenchmen were extremely prejudiced against quick revolution.

Prosceniums of Chekhovian stages utilized well every bequeathed jinx.

Bismarck proved equally just when excluding her from the Zollverein.

Easy Sentence Drill

STROKES FOR
EACH LINE

The first element of success is the determination to succeed.   63

Initiative is doing what should be done without being told to.   64

Every failure will teach a man something if he will learn from it. 68

It is what we think and what we do that makes us what we are.   63

There is nothing either good or bad, but thinking makes it so.   64

The best work of which I am capable every day: this is my pledge. 69

Check-Up on Centering

This check-up of your knowledge of how to center will indicate the review necessary in order that you may accurately arrange your work on the page.

DIRECTIONS: On a separate sheet of paper, write the answers to the incomplete statements given below. Do not write in the text.

1. A vertical inch has_____lines.
2. A horizontal inch has_____spaces.
3. Paper 8½ x 11″ has_____lines.
4. Paper 8½ x 5½″ has_____lines.
5. An 8½″ line has_____spaces.
6. A 5 x 3″ card has_____lines.
7. A 5″ line has_____spaces.
8. The vertical center of an 8½ x 11″ page comes at line_____.
9. The horizontal center of an 8½″ line is
_____.
10. If 8½ x 11″ paper is used, a double-spaced center-ing problem having 18 lines will require a top margin of_____lines.
11. If 8½ x 11″ paper is used, a single-spaced centering problem having 18 lines will require a top margin of_____lines.
12. Using 43 as the centering point, indicate the correct point at which each of the following lines will begin if it is to be centered horizontally:
a. For a line having 48 letters and spaces, set the left marginal stop at_____.
b. For a line having 29 letters and spaces, set the left marginal stop at_____.
c. For a line having 12 letters and spaces, set the left marginal stop at_____.

BUDGET VI

DIRECTIONS: Type one line of the drills and one sentence five times each. Use a different word drill and sentence in each practice period. Set the marginal stops for a seventy-space line. Use single spacing. Double-space between the five-line groups. In each case in which you type a drill and a sentence several times, center your copy vertically.

Drills on Left- and Right-Hand Controlled Words

Spaces 69

are kin act joy bad him ace ill cab pin gas ply fed you bet oil awe ↓

fear mill garb lump face limp fast hill cast moon fact link ever poll

were pool raft mink barb look zest upon rate pomp wave lion grew null

exert lymph award grade puppy gazed based knoll exact serve jolly

breeze revere unholy vacate uphill exceed pinion extras minion assess

Sentence Practice

	STROKES FOR EACH SENTENCE
The sum of 9 and 3 and 6 and 4 and 8 and 5 and 7 and 2 and 6 is 50.	68
It is not good enough to do good; one must do it in a good way.	64
Every day should be spent by us as if it were to be our last day.	66
The sum of wisdom is that time which is devoted to work is never lost.	71
No man can climb out beyond the limitations of his own character.	66

Corrective Drill Paragraphs

In each corrective drill paragraph, all letters of the alphabet are used. One letter, however, is given special emphasis. Careful practice of these corrective drill paragraphs will tend to reduce the number of errors you will make in exercises and timed tests. This practice will strengthen the control of all letters and will build mastery of the reach to the letter singled out for special emphasis.

Type the corrective drill paragraph carefully; try to equalize the power behind all strokes. This is not a task to be done—it is an opportunity to be seized. Focus your attention upon correcting inaccurate letter strokes. Study your manipulative habits and improve them. Hold your eyes on the copy, quicken the carriage return, make effective use of the tabular key, develop a sure and swift control of the shift keys, and type with smoothness—keep the carriage moving continuously.

DIRECTIONS: Set the marginal stops for a seventy-space line. Adjust the tabular stop for a five-space indentation. Use single spacing. Type one corrective drill paragraph in each practice period. Alternate the paragraphs in the various practice periods. Center the paragraph vertically on a half sheet of paper. Do this each time you type a corrective drill paragraph.

a key   Accuracy means absolute correctness. The artist portrays accuracy in line and angle. The singer must have accuracy in tone quality and in interpretation. Business, too, demands accuracy—exactness. It says that workers must realize that work inaccurately done is only half done, and half-done work is never adjudged acceptable. Develop accuracy, therefore; for if you have not accuracy, your speed is but as tinkling cymbal and sounding brass and gains you no lasting success.

b key   Books are my joy and my hobby—books on business, biology, botany, biography; books with beautiful bindings—blue books, black books, brown books. For most of us there are excellent books for every mood—books for blustery days, books for lazy days, books for bright and balmy days, and books for bedtime, too. I like to browse in a quiet library, away from the babble and bother of business. I like to borrow books, lend books, and buy books. Yes, books are my joy and my hobby.

Some of the Simonize from your last shipment has been returned to us with the complaint that it does not give that hard, dry finish that you claim is "equal to a new car." (P) We are satisfied with the Kleener; we are not pleased with the Simonize. Some adjustment, therefore, will have to be made. (P) Would you like us to send to you a few cans from the box of Simonize so that you can see how hard and dry it is? Very truly yours WESTERN AUTO SUPPLY CO. (Dictated by P. B. Phillips) Sales Manager *(428–82)*

Optional Exercise 36

Mr. W. W. Ross 2640 Alamo Place Fort Worth, Texas Dear Mr. Ross: If any WESTERN GIANT fails to give the service you expect, we will repair it without charge to you, or we will replace it with a new tire, charging only for the proportionate service it has given. (P) In the past year we have had few claims to adjust. What better proof of high quality and value can be offered? We realize, though, that a defective tire may leave our factory in spite of all our checks and tests. (P) Do you want us to repair your old tire, or do you feel that we owe you a new tire? Very truly yours WESTERN AUTO SUPPLY CO. (Dictated by P. B. Phillips) Sales Manager *(510–98)*

INSTRUCTIONAL BLOCK V
PROBLEMS IN PERSONAL TYPING

The problems of this instructional block are similar to those you will likely encounter when you type your personal work. Study the forms carefully in order that you may know how to set up your own material. Bring to class and submit to your teacher for approval and suggestions, personal material which you need to have typed. Make effective use of the typing power you have developed. Plan your work carefully before attempting to type it.

Drills for Typing Power

DIRECTIONS: From the drills given on this and the following page, each day choose the ones which provide the drill material which you think will help you to eliminate your weakness in technique. Set the marginal stops for a seventy-space line. Unless you are otherwise instructed, type the drill for five minutes. Type each line twice. Double-space after the second typing of each line. Practice for improvement.

Three-Letter Word Drill *(Length of line, 67 spaces.)*

```
hay air egg lay aid aim ate mad net leg tea cap nap bag pen bet pig
pin gas fix sat dog sit hog sad top raw nor sew mud owe art joy rug
wet oil cry die dry fly ice lie son pie sum ton sun per God the for
has may but due not had was one see you all ask and may can did his
```

Four-Letter Word Drill *(Length of line, 69 spaces.)*

```
gray hate cake dark mark team laid main lead milk lake mill dead camp
deep bear pain beat pair fail park feed pick fell gift pray flat pass
ours silk slip gets sake east desk seat step safe shop fast ball draw
boat coat grow load slow snow soul coal dare loan hall mere hurt luck
plus thus cook foot food lose moon wash none wear noon quit yard ring
song join died inch pipe ride type wide wise mile rush aunt cent gold
rent wild band move bond rule firm crop term drop corn vote from this
```

Five-Minute Timed Writing Practice

All letters of the alphabet are used in each paragraph of timed writing material.

DIRECTIONS: Set the marginal stops for a seventy-space line. Adjust the tabular stop for an indentation of five spaces. Use double spacing. Use a full sheet of paper for this and each following timed writing practice.

	STROKES
What type of man is best equipped for success? I have searched the	72
classics of success, and I have yet to find one place which says that achieve-	152
ment is reserved for the favored few. In order that the man shall count, he	230
must make quite sure that the power in him, the soul's spark plug, is kept	306
perfectly conditioned. Each of us must evolve a personal fixedness. We	381
cannot go roaming mentally, any more than we can go roaming bodily, and	453
not lose much that is prized. Change may mean growth, but it may mean	525
danger, too. Stagnation is the end of standing still, and confusion the end	603
of constant change.	622

Syllable intensity, 1.30

Exercise 47

DIRECTIONS: Set the marginal stops for a forty-space line. Adjust the tabular stops so that you can quickly and accurately indent for all lines not beginning at the left margin. Type Style Letter No. 6 exactly as it is given in the illustration on page 82. According to the placement chart given on page 59, you will have eight line spaces between the date and the inside address.

NOTE: The word *Company* in the signature may be abbreviated in order to secure balance in the closing lines.

Exercise 48

DIRECTIONS: Forty-space line; five-space paragraph indentation; eight single spaces between the date and the inside address; single-spaced indented form; open punctuation. Use the current date for all letters for which the dates are not given.

Marpor Construction Company 270 Western Avenue Denver, Colorado Attention of Mr. H. M. Donaldson Gentlemen: Your folder on recent installations of Marpor interests us. *(P) If you will have your representative call at our office next week, we shall be glad to show him our plans and specifications for an apartment house we may build soon. You can then submit estimates on our Marpor needs. Very truly yours R. G. WALTERS & COMPANY **(Dictated by E. G. Brown) Chief Engineer *(289–49)*

* When this sign (P) is used, begin a new paragraph.
** Do not type this information in parentheses. It is given so that you can get the correct reference initials.

Exercise 49

DIRECTIONS: Forty-space line; five-space paragraph indentation; eight single spaces between the date and the inside address; single-spaced indented form; open punctuation.

This letter is sent from the office of the sales manager of the Marpor Construction Company to the Arizona representative at Phoenix. Since the company signature is omitted from the letter, the official title is typed four single spaces below the complimentary close. Although the letter is two lines longer than the two preceding letters, the same placement on the page can be used because of the omission of the company signature and the attention line. The correct form for the closing lines of this letter is shown below. Your initials will be typed in place of XXX shown in the illustration.

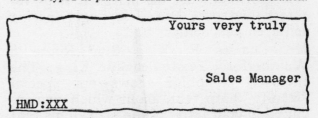

```
                        Yours very truly



                        Sales Manager
HMD:XXX
```

Mr. Arthur J. Morris 3965 Main Street Phoenix, Arizona Dear Mr. Morris: Can you go to Tucson next week for a conference with Mr. E. G. Brown, Chief Engineer of R. G. Walters & Company? A large building project will be started by this company soon. Mr. Brown will go over plans and specifications with you and will tell you how soon we are to submit estimates on their Marpor needs. (P) When you have studied the plans for this Tucson project, please write me. Yours very truly (Dictated by H. M. Donaldson) Sales Manager *(406–72)*

BUDGET V
Review Practice

DIRECTIONS: Set the marginal stops for a sixty-space line. Center the drill vertically. Triple-space between the heading and the drill. Use double spacing. Type the drill twice.

Are the Trigg & Hall $1,000 4¾% bonds (Series B) due in 1947?

boys card done each fill goes hope just kept line make post

seen some time turn view want whom wish work else knew lost

This bank said that this note must have been paid last week.

Five-Minute Timed Writing Practice

DIRECTIONS: Set the marginal stops for a seventy-space line. Set the tabular stop for an indentation of five spaces. Use double spacing.

	STROKES
Not all major battles are fought with gun or sabre or poison gas. The real	79
battleground is in our own consciousness. It is there that for most of us the real	164
battles of life are fought. We can thumb the pages of our history textbooks and	246
find listed there the battlegrounds made famous by the men who have died for a	325
"cause." Let us turn our gaze inward to see the battleground where daily we	405
fight for our "cause." Books will never record these battles; our nearest friends	491
may not know of them. The war goes on without fanfare of trumpet or bugle.	568
Many enemies are to be subdued—doubt, fear, envy, and a host of others of the	648
same kind; the queer urge to lie or to cheat, to do less than our best, to be less	731
than our best. Real courage and stamina are called for. You require no sabre	812
or gun or poison gas. Gird yourself with truth; right is might!	879

Syllable intensity, 1.27

Exercise 35

DIRECTIONS: Set the marginal stops for a forty-five-space line. Use single spacing and open punctuation.

Mr. Charles R. King Star Route 6 Weatherford, Texas Dear Mr. King: The enclosed pamphlet shows our special "lean-to" auto tent, about which you inquired in your letter of the fifth. This tent is just the right size to be used with your car. (P) If you use the tent with a car, you will not need poles. Light, pointed tent poles can be furnished, however, at a very low cost. (P) You can come into our store and walk out with the tent, or, if you prefer, we can deliver the tent to you without delay. Very truly yours WESTERN AUTO SUPPLY CO. (Dictated by P. B. Phillips) Sales Manager Enclosure *(440–83)*

Optional Exercise 35

Messrs. Jessup & Zaner 568-571 Main Street Dallas, Texas Gentlemen: In our

letter of the tenth we quoted you a special price of $8.95 a pair for our BOSCH SHOCK ABSORBERS. We are sure that you cannot get these shock absorbers elsewhere at so low a cost. Is there any further information you would like to have before placing your order? (P) Most cars are now drilled so that BOSCH ABSORBERS can be installed and adjusted very easily. Once installed, "Satisfaction will increase as mileage mounts." (P) We can make immediate shipment upon the receipt of your order. Very truly yours WESTERN AUTO SUPPLY CO. (Dictated by P. B. Phillips) Sales Manager *(514–86)*

Exercise 36

DIRECTIONS: Set the marginal stops for a forty-five-space line. Use single spacing and open punctuation.

Mr. Charles T. Renfro Manager, The Simonize Co. Chicago, Illinois Dear Sir:

MARPOR CONSTRUCTION COMPANY
MARBLE and PORCELAIN

270 Western Avenue

DENVER, COLORADO

May 13, 193-

First Tabular Stop | Second Tabular Stop

R. G. Walters & Company
481 Villa Serena Place
Tucson, Arizona

Attention of Mr. E. G. Brown

Gentlemen:

The attached two-page folder shows
how Marpor has been used in the building
of homes, apartment houses, and hotels.
Since the cost is so low and the quality
so satisfactory, a real vogue for Marpor
has developed.

Why not let us submit estimates for
your next building? We shall be glad to
do this without cost to you.

Yours very truly

MARPOR CONSTRUCTION CO.

H. M. Donaldson
Sales Manager

HMD:CG

Enclosure

Third Tabular Stop at 35 | Fourth Tabular Stop at 40 | Fifth Tabular Stop at 45

(Strokes, 329; Words, 68)

Style Letter No. 6—Single-spaced Indented Form Showing the
Placement of the Attention Line

DONALD T. DOWDEN

1268 North Central Avenue *Radio Shop*
Telephone: AVEnue 7800

FAIRMONT, WEST VIRGINIA.

November 12, 193-

Zenith Radio Corporation
3620 Iron Street
        Chicago, Illinois

Gentlemen:

Please ship to me at once one of your
radios, Model 39, chassis "J," operating
on 110 volts, 60 cycles. I have an inquiry
for this model of radio and have been asked
to have it ready to show the last of next
week.

If you cannot make immediate shipment
of this order, please telegraph me so that
I can arrange for a later showing.

Yours very truly

Donald T. Dowden

DTD:EJS

NOTE: *The correct placement of the reference initials when the company signature and the official title are not used is six to eight spaces below the complimentary close.*

(Strokes, 340; Words, 65)

Style Letter No. 4—Single-spaced Form Showing Placement of
Reference Initials When Company Signature and Official Title
Are Not Used

Exercise 50

DIRECTIONS: Fifty-space line; five-space paragraph indentation; eight single spaces between the date and the inside address; single-spaced indented form; open punctuation.

R. G. Walters & Company 481 Villa Serena Place Tucson, Arizona Attention of Mr. E. G. Brown Gentlemen: As you requested in your recent letter, our Phoenix representative, Mr. Arthur J. Morris, will call at your office next week. When he sends us details of your plans for your new apartment building, we shall submit estimates of your Marpor needs. (P) Marpor combines the best qualities of marble, glass, and porcelain. It will add durability and beauty to the walls of your apartment building. Yours very truly MARPOR CONSTRUCTION COMPANY (Dictated by H. M. Donaldson) Sales Manager *(404–64)*

Exercise 51

DIRECTIONS: Fifty-space line; five-space paragraph indentation; eight single spaces between the date and the inside address; single-spaced indented form; open punctuation. See the illustration with Exercise 49, page 81, for the correct placement of the closing lines.

Mr. Arthur J. Morris 3965 Main Street Phoenix, Arizona Dear Mr. Morris: While in Tucson next week, try to learn the local preference for color combinations for bathrooms, kitchens, etc. If you need to have a man make a house-to-house canvass, confine the check to the plain colors and color combinations we use in making Marpor. (P) The Tucson territory is an undeveloped field for us. If we can interest Mr. Brown in Marpor, we should get bigger orders later. Yours very truly (Dictated by H. M. Donaldson) Sales Manager *(402–67)*

Optional Exercise 52

DIRECTIONS: Fifty-space line; five-space paragraph indentation; eight single spaces between the date and the inside address; single-spaced indented form; open punctuation.

tion. Style Letter No. 4, page 67, shows the correct set-up for this letter.

If the dictator's name is typed, it is not necessary, although it is permissible, to include his initials in the reference line. The stenographer's initials should be typed in the position for reference initials.

Since neither a company signature nor an official title is used with this letter, the use of eight single spaces between the date and the inside address will give the correct placement of the letter.

Mr. H. M. Donaldson Marpor Construction Co. Denver, Colorado My dear Mr. Donaldson: I spent yesterday in Tucson at the office of R. G. Walters & Company. The plans for their new apartment house were studied carefully. You will receive a detailed report about these plans by the end of the week. (P) Mr. Brown has about decided to use Onyxwall. I demonstrated Marpor, showing samples in white, ivory, blue, jade, dark green, and black. I fear, though, that he was not convinced that we have the better product. (P) Shall I follow this matter up, or do you want to handle all further correspondence with Mr. Brown? Yours truly (Arthur J. Morris) *(549–93)*

Optional Exercise 53

DIRECTIONS: Fifty-space line; five-space paragraph indentation; eight single spaces between the date and the inside address; single-spaced indented form; open punctuation.

R. G. Walters & Company 481 Villa Serena Place, Tucson, Arizona Attention of Mr. E. G. Brown Gentlemen: Mr. Morris is preparing a report on which we can base our estimates of your Marpor needs. These estimates will reach you in a few days. (P) Have you thought of using Marpor for top slabs of work tables, radiator grilles, and ventilating hoods? The wide choice of sizes and colors makes it possible for us to meet individual preference. (P) If you wish more information before we submit estimates, we shall be glad to have you write us. Yours very truly MARPOR CONSTRUCTION COMPANY (Dictated by H. M. Donaldson) Sales Manager *(427–74)*

BUDGET IV

Review Practice

DIRECTIONS: Set the marginal stops for a sixty-space line. Center the drill vertically. Triple-space between the heading and the drill. Use double spacing. Type the drill twice.

1 2 12 3 9 39 4 8 48 5 0 50 6 7 67 2 ½ 2½ 2 ¼ 2¼ 5 ¾ 5¾ 12

The sum of 38 and 49 and 27 and 56 and 13 and 30 is 213.

They went near that same road when they left here last week.

June told them that they took that trip from here last year.

Five-Minute Timed Writing Practice

DIRECTIONS: Set the marginal stops for a seventy-space line. Set the tabular stop for an indentation of five spaces. Use double spacing.

STROKES

One need not have in mind at all times the exact nature of the prize which will be the reward of effort well directed or of tasks well performed. It is really the work alone which is important. All of our attention and all of our effort should be given to doing that work to the best of our ability. If we give to the world the best that is in us, no matter what our work may be, the chance of reward ceases to be a chance and becomes a surety. No man ever put his entire soul into his work, just for love of the work itself and solely for that work's sake, without winning a prize at the close of the contest, a prize bigger and better, oftentimes, than he ever anticipated. Such prizes are quite within the reach of all of us.—Adapted from "The Winner."

77
163
243
326
406
484
565
643
724
776

Syllable intensity, 1.30

Exercise 33

DIRECTIONS: Set the marginal stops for a forty-five-space line. Type Style Letter No. 4 exactly as it is given on page 67.

Optional Exercise 33

Mrs. Maxine V. Judd, Principal Lamont Academy for Girls Fairmont, West Virginia Dear Madam: I do not handle the Majestic Radio, about which you inquired in your letter of the tenth. I have other excellent radios, however, which will give you fine service. (P) For use in the general club room of your school, I suggest one of the models of the Zenith Electric DeLuxe. Descriptions of the different models are enclosed. (P) If you wish, I shall be glad to place a radio at your disposal for a week's trial. Yours very truly (Dictated by Donald T. Dowden) Enclosure *(427–75)*

Exercise 34

DIRECTIONS: Set the marginal stops for a forty-five-space line. Use single spacing and open punctuation.

The Grigsby-Grunow Company 4540 Armitage Avenue Chicago, Illinois Gentlemen: Quite often I am asked the price of the Majestic Radio. As I handle the Atwater Kent and the Zenith models only, I am unable to give the information requested. (P) If you do not expect to have a salesroom in this city, perhaps arrangements can be made for me to add the Majestic to my regular stock. (P) Let me hear from you. Yours very truly (Dictated by Donald T. Dowden) *(339–63)*

Optional Exercise 34

Miss Anna Jean Hughes 505 Duff Avenue Clarksburg, W. Va. My dear Miss Hughes: The enclosed circular, illustrating the Zenith Radio, is sent to you in response to your letter of the sixth. (P) Model 34 is particularly attractive, I think. The cabinet is of walnut veneer with a dull finish, shaded with a figured overlay. A magnetic speaker gives the justly famed Zenith tone quality. (P) The price of Model 34 is $230. Yours truly (Dictated by Donald T. Dowden) Enclosure *(351–58)*

Trait Analysis

A study of the causes of failure indicates that more workers fail because of lack of desirable traits than because of lack of skill. If one is to be a stenographer, typing skill is needed; so is skill in taking and transcribing dictation. But even with these skills many stenographers fail to achieve outstanding success in their work. Why? The difficulty frequently is caused by a lack of the personal traits which assure success.

One study of secretarial duties and traits was made by Charters and Whitley. A part of the study deals with personality as a factor in the success of a secretary. The following quotation will help you to understand how the data for this study were gathered:

A number of employers were interviewed in order to find the secretarial qualities in which employers are especially interested, the things which secretaries do which please employers or particularly irritate them, the reasons for discharge, the qualities in which employers would like to improve their present secretaries, and so on.[1]

In order to define what the traits mean, some of the suggestive trait-actions listed by the employers interviewed are used here. These trait-actions serve to focus attention in the classroom upon the actions which best express the desired traits.

Trait Desired—Accuracy

(Ranked first by 86 per cent of the employers interviewed)

Suggestive Trait-Actions

The secretary
1. Does not make mistakes in typing.
2. Does not make mistakes in computing.
3. Spells and pronounces persons' names correctly.
4. Pays attention to details.
5. Files material under the proper headings.
6. Does not make mistakes in keeping records.
7. Gets the exact information requested.
8. Does not lose papers.
9. Does not make mistakes in transcribing dictation.
10. Does not guess when information is desired.
11. Sees that every letter is perfect before it goes out.
12. Checks all work.
13. Does not send out a letter unsigned.
14. Does not make mistakes in proof reading.
15. Checks names, dates, and figures when copying written material.
16. Does not let letters go out unstamped.
17. Never places the wrong address on a package.[2]

These are some of the trait-actions which caused employers to rank accuracy as the first requirement for an outstandingly successful secretary. How would you rank in terms of these trait-actions? You must build them into your daily work habits. Accuracy in typing, important though it is, is not enough; you must be accurate in work habits, too.

[1] W. W. Charters and Isadore B. Whitley, *Summary of Report on Analysis of Secretarial Duties and Traits,* Service Bulletin No. 1, New York: National Junior Personnel Service, Inc., 1924.

[2] *Ibid.,* pp. 48 and 49.

Carbon Copies

In most business offices, a carbon copy of each outgoing letter must be made. This carbon copy is made by placing the sheet of carbon paper, with the glossy side down, on top of a plain sheet of paper. The letterhead sheet is then placed on top of the carbon paper, and all sheets are inserted in the typewriter so that the dull back of the carbon sheet is toward the typist. When paper of ordinary thickness is used, three carbon copies may be made very successfully. If more copies are required, thin sheets of paper should be used. When a good grade of carbon paper and thin writing paper are used, eight or more copies may be made at the same time.

In your school work, you will not need to make carbon copies of all letters, but you must learn how to use carbon paper and how to make it give the most effective service.

Handle the carbon sheets with care. Unsightly streaks or smeared places on carbon copies are inexcusable. No matter how much work must be completed, the stenographer cannot afford to grow careless about the quality of work done. Since copies of letters are kept in the office files, they become, in a way, the stenographer's credentials.

Make a carbon copy of every letter in this budget. This work will give you sufficient practice in the use of carbon paper to enable you to use it effectively when you need to do so.

HARDY & HAMILTON

INCORPORATED

Investment Securities

Borland Building

ST. LOUIS, MISSOURI

December 6, 193-

Mr. Joseph D. Ellsworth
    President, Ellsworth & West
    East St. Louis, Illinois

Dear Sir:

This letter is just a reminder that
the payment of your account is overdue.
We know how easily such things are overlooked and, therefore, take this means
of bringing the matter to your attention.

We know you will realize that prompt
collection of our accounts is required if
we are to meet our own bills on time.

We shall expect a check from you by
return mail.

Yours truly

HARDY & HAMILTON

J. F. Hardy

J. F. Hardy

JFH:PSL

(*Strokes*, 372; *Words*, 67)

Style Letter No. 3—Single-spaced Form Showing Placement of
Typed Signature in Official Title Position

Addressing the Envelope

The envelope address should be practically the same as the address given in the letter. Certain exceptions should be noted. Three-line addresses for envelopes should be typed with double spacing even though the letter is single spaced. This practice insures greater accuracy in the handling of mail by the postal workers. When four or more lines are used for the envelope address, single-space the address. Always use at least three lines for an envelope address. If no street address is given, type the city and the state on separate lines. The city and state names should be separated by a comma when typed on the same line. Never use *City* in the place of the correct name of the city.

Special Lines

The attention phrase may be typed on the line immediately following the company name, or it may be placed in the lower left corner of the envelope.

In Care of, or the special symbol *c/o*, should be typed in either of the positions indicated for the attention phrase. If space permits, it is better to spell out *In Care of* instead of using the symbol *c/o*. Never use the sign %.

Insert the envelope into the typewriter so that the left edge will be against the paper guide. If you are using typewriters other than the Royal, the Underwood, or the Woodstock, move the right paper clamp over the right edge of the envelope so that the envelope will be held firmly in place. If you are using the Royal, the Woodstock, or the Underwood typewriter, the envelope, or card, holder should be used.

The first line of the address should be typed approximately two inches (four triple spaces) from the top of the envelope and approximately two and one-half inches (twenty-five thumb spaces) from the left edge of the envelope. These measurements will usually give the correct placement of an address of average length when the ordinary 3⅝ x 6½" business envelope is used.

When using a large envelope, 4⅛ x 9½", type the first line of the address two and one-half inches (five triple spaces) from the top of the envelope and four inches (forty thumb spaces) from the left edge of the envelope.

These definite instructions for the placement of the address should be followed carefully until you have trained your eyes to judge the correct placement of the address. Once you have trained yourself to estimate the correct placement of the address, you will not need to count or measure the spaces but can twirl the envelope to the correct position without loss of time. Study this problem of correctly typing the address on the envelope. You will be repaid in the time saved and in the added ease you develop in completing your work.

Illustration No. 43, Envelope Address Styles

(1) Single-spaced, block-form, four-line address. Note the method of emphasizing the city and the state. **(2)** Single-spaced, indented, four-line address. This form is commonly used with indented letters when the address is written in four lines. Note the method of emphasizing the city and the state. (3) Double-spaced, indented, three-line address, showing one placement of the attention expression. (4) Single-spaced, block-form, four-line address, showing one placement of the attention expression. Note the extra space before the last line. This extra space makes mail-sorting easier and more accurate. (5) Double-spaced, indented, three-line address. This form is commonly used with indented letters when the address is written in three lines.

HARDY & HAMILTON

INCORPORATED

Investment Securities

Borland Building

ST. LOUIS, MISSOURI

September 7, 193-

Mr. J. B. Zelliott
Box 458
    Dexter, Mo.

Dear Sir:

    Our records show that you still owe
us $3.62. We shall be glad to have you
check your records to see if the enclosed
statement is correct.

    This request is made at this time in
order that the records for last month's
business may be closed as soon as possible.

       Yours very truly

       HARDY & HAMILTON

Earl G. Hays

       Earl G. Hays
       Manager

EGH:PSL

Enclosure

NOTE: *When the typed signature is used, the dictator's initials may be
omitted from the reference notation.*

(Strokes, 268; Words, 50)

Style Letter No. 2—Single-spaced Form Showing Placement of
Typed Signature with Official Title

Folding and Inserting Letters in Envelopes

Folding for the Usual Business Envelope: Fold the lower end of the letterhead upward to within a half inch of the top edge of the paper (see Illustration No. 44, Step 2); fold from right to left, making the fold about one-third the width of the sheet (Step 3); fold from left to right, making the fold slightly less than a third of the width of the sheet and leaving a half-inch margin in order that the letter may be opened easily (Step 4).

In a second method of folding letters, the last fold can be extended beyond the edge of the preceding fold. Some think that this extended fold makes it easier to open the letter than when the method shown in the illustration is used. Personal preference or office custom should determine which method should be used in folding the letters for outgoing mail.

Folding for the Large Envelope: Only two **folds** are required for the large or legal-size envelope. Fold the lower end of the letterhead upward about one-third the length of the paper (Step 2-A); fold the top edge of the paper down to within one-quarter of an inch of the lower fold (Step 3-A). Here, also, it is possible to extend the last fold beyond the edge of the first fold, and thus to bring the top of the paper down so that it extends about one-quarter of an inch over the first fold. When this method of folding is used, it is better to make both folds upward, allowing about one-quarter of an inch to extend beyond the last fold.

Insertion of the Letter into the Envelope: Insert the letter so that it will be in its normal reading position when it is removed from the envelope.

Business letters must be neatly folded and accurately inserted into the envelopes. Carefully study the illustration and check the accuracy of your folding and insertion of letters.

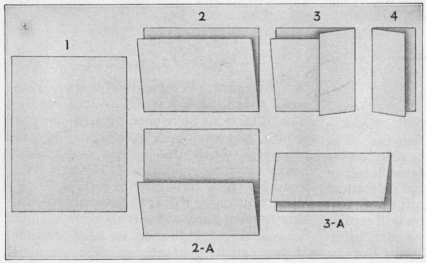 

Illustration No. 44, Folding and Inserting a Letter into an Envelope

DIRECTIONS: Type one line of the drills and one sentence five times each. Use a different word drill and sentence in each practice period. Set the marginal stops for a seventy-space line. Use single spacing. Double-space between the five-line groups.

Drills on Five-Letter Words *(Length of line, 65 spaces)*

```
black place doubt yours known board comes their lines state world
worth found cause great plans guess check bring blank teach serve
thing makes least claim store which clear those grade young where
wrote quote price start quite piece notes might gives trust wrong
could sales draft terms years sweet plant whole think speak parts
```

Sentence Practice

	STROKES FOR EACH SENTENCE
Most things that are well done are done with very great exactness.	67
The sum of 5 and 6 and 2 and 9 and 3 and 7 and 4 and 8 and 7 is 51.	68
The valuable man in business is the man who can and will cooperate.	68
Perform every task at hand as though your very future depended upon it.	72
Do more than you are paid to do. Some day you will collect in full.	70

Five-Minute Timed Writing Practice

DIRECTIONS: Set the marginal stops for a seventy-space line. Set the tabular stop for an indentation of five spaces. Use double spacing.

STROKES

All the world loves a winner. Such being the case, it may be well to give a	80
little thought to the matter and try to uncover something which will help teach	160
us just what it is to be a winner. To win means to succeed in an effort or to excel	246
in a contest; it means the attainment of a desirable end or the acquirement of	325
something by long effort and struggle. That which is achieved, the reward for	405
our effort or struggle, is called a prize. There is no work or exertion of any kind	491
without some definite end in view. That end, in a general way and for lack of a	573
better term, can be called a prize. Whatever may be the reward that comes to us	655
as the result of our endeavor, that is our prize.—Adapted from "The Winner."	737

Syllable intensity, 1.29

Exercise 31

DIRECTIONS: Set the marginal stops for a forty-space line. Use single spacing. Type Style Letter No. 2 exactly as it is given in the illustration on page 64.

In many offices, the name of the dictator is typed one single space above the official title. This is for the purpose of showing an absolutely legible name and thus insuring a correctly directed return letter.

Optional Exercise 31

Mr. William K. Jasper 2659 Holman Street Jefferson City, Mo. Dear Sir: The St. Louis Credit Bureau will be able to give the information requested in your letter of the first. We cannot give direct references as we clear all accounts through the Credit Bureau. (P) We hope that you will realize it is impossible for us to give such information except through the Credit Bureau. Yours very truly HARDY & HAMILTON Earl G. Hays Manager *(316–53)*

Exercise 32

DIRECTIONS: Set the marginal stops for a forty-space line. Use single spacing. Type Style Letter No. 3 exactly as it is given in the illustration on page 65.

Optional Exercise 32

Mr. Arthur L. Winstead Manager, Winstead & Hill St. Louis, Missouri Dear Sir: Our collections have been poor for the past month, yet our own bills must be paid promptly when due. Next week some heavy demands will be made upon us. Will you help us by paying your bill now? (P) We are sure you will realize we are making this request for payment of your account because we are in immediate need of funds. If you can help us at this time, we shall appreciate it. Yours very truly HARDY & HAMILTON J. F. Hardy *(391–74)*

Optional Five-Minute Timed Writing Practice

DIRECTIONS: Set the marginal stops for a seventy-space line. Set the tabular stop for an indentation of five spaces. Use double spacing.

STROKES

The world was tense that day. Some said it could not be done and named	75
other men and women who had attempted and failed. Others said that luck	149
was with those two, and while the radio flashed news of a raging storm at	223
sea, every one knew that more than luck would be necessary for the success	298
of the flight across the ocean. It may have been a splendid mixture of luck	376
and of skill and the wise choice of a time for the flight. Personally, I believe	460
it was hard work and careful planning rather than blind fortune which made	535
it possible for Costes and his partner to realize their ambition. We called it	617
a great conquest when they spanned the ocean. It was indeed; but back of	692
the conquest lay months of carefully planned effort in order that the out-	767
come, the ultimate result, should be glorious achievement and not disastrous	844
defeat. Just so it must be with us if we want our visions to come true. We	923
must put our faith in "work," not in "luck"; we must "plan," not "guess."	1004

Syllable intensity, 1.30

Corrective Drill Paragraphs

DIRECTIONS: Set the marginal stops for a seventy-space line. Adjust the tabular stop for a five-space indentation. Use single spacing. Type one corrective drill paragraph in each practice period. Alternate the paragraphs in the various practice periods.

c
key   Concentration calls into command certain calm factors which clear and classify complex problems. Concentration is cultivation of concern for just one course or problem. To be able to concentrate on a certain course calls into command forces necessary to shut out all contrary calls. Concentration and reasoning are closely related and have much in common. It is amazing how quickly concentration comes when we learn to think clearly and concisely and with control.

d
key   The hard, dull cold of deadly December winds has softened to the mild breezes of the succeeding season. Every tender blade unfolding is a welcome herald of more delightful days. The widespread verdure of meadows, fields, and woods affords unequalled gladness and joy. Affected by such surroundings, the mind can indeed be disengaged from dark, dreary shadows and find food for meditation in an exquisitely beautiful world dedicated to the children of a divine Creator.

Five-Minute Timed Writing Practice

DIRECTIONS: Set the marginal stops for a seventy-space line. Adjust the tabular stop for an indentation of five spaces. Use double spacing.

	STROKES
I know a merchant who is an expert in values. He buys his stock of	71
goods on the basis of worth. He knows the quality of cloth needed, just the	149
sizes and the styles most suited to the tastes of his customers, and the range	228
of prices within which he can buy in order to sell to the best advantage. He	307
knows cloth and style and price; even more than these, though, he knows	379
the importance of a service which will bring him satisfied customers. It is	457
his practical use of a fine social sense, as much as his merchandising genius,	536
which accounts for his great success.	573

Syllable intensity, 1.30

Exercise 54

DIRECTIONS: Set the marginal stops for a fifty-space line. Type Style Letter No. 7 exactly as it is given in the illustration on page 88. Leave six single spaces between the date and the inside address.

For each of the letters in this budget make a carbon copy and address an envelope. Use the style of envelope address that best fits the style of letter.

Exercise 55

DIRECTIONS: Fifty-space line; block form of letter; six single spaces between the date and the inside address; single spacing; open punctuation. Type the dictator's name one space above the official title.

Mr. John O. Bradley Deshler-Wallick Hotel Columbus, Ohio Dear Mr. Bradley: For several months we have not received any orders from the Harding Motor Company, of Zanesville. We used to ship it quite regularly. The manager of the company is Mr. Charles H. McConnell. We have just written him a letter trying to make this an active account again. (P) While you are in the Zanesville district next week, plan to call on Mr. McConnell. We should have at least one good agency in Zanesville handling our tires. If the Harding Company is not interested in putting in Treadwear again, perhaps you can get some other up-to-date dealer there to do so. (P) After you see Mr.

Exercise 29

DIRECTIONS: Set the marginal stops for a forty-space line. Set the tabular stops for the indentations. Control the tabular key by touch. Use double spacing and open punctuation.

Mr. Kenneth L. Glazer Farmers Bank Building Quincy, Illinois Dear Mr. Glazer: Our Chicago Office will send to you confirmation of the purchase of a $1,000 Texas Utilities 5% bond due June 15, 1954. (P) This opportunity of serving you is much appreciated by this office. Yours very truly HALL INVESTMENT COMPANY (Dictated by Walter Lee Cook) District Manager *(198–33)*

Exercise 30

DIRECTIONS: Set the marginal stops for a forty-space line. Use double spacing and open punctuation.

Mr. Norton J. Owens 583 Lincoln Street Springfield, Ill. Dear Sir: A number of well-secured bonds can be bought at this time at amazingly low prices. Now is the time to add these excellent bonds to your account. (P) We can help you take advantage of the present investment values if you wish to consider more investments just now. Yours very truly HALL INVESTMENT COMPANY (Dictated by Walter Lee Cook) District Manager *(266–47)*

Optional Exercise 29

Mr. Paul J. Wilhoyte 1572 College Street Galesburg, Illinois Dear Sir: Knowledge is the foundation of successful investing. This is generally recognized. All too frequently, though, investors do not know where to turn for their information. (P) If you have any questions concerning the bond market, write us. We have some excellent values which we can recommend. Yours very truly HALL INVESTMENT COMPANY (Dictated by Walter Lee Cook) District Manager *(297–45)*

Optional Exercise 30

Mrs. Elizabeth M. Claxton 4850 Ridge Avenue Bloomington, Illinois Dear Madam: Our advisory facilities have long been placed at the disposal of women investors. (P) We have just published a booklet of interest to you. This booklet, "Problems of the Woman Investor," will be mailed on request to you or to any of your friends. Yours very truly HALL INVESTMENT COMPANY (Dictated by Walter Lee Cook) District Manager *(253–43)*

BUDGET III

Review Practice

DIRECTIONS: Set the marginal stops for a sixty-space line. Center the drill vertically. Triple-space between the heading and the first line of the drill. Use double spacing. Type the drill twice.

NOTE: Review the summary of spacing instructions, page 44, for the correct placement of a quotation mark and another mark of punctuation when both follow the same word. Note, also, that in the body of a sentence the interrogation and exclamation points are followed by one space.

5 8 58 2 9 29 1 0 10 3 6 36 4 7 47 1 4 8 148 3 5 0 350 350

Water begins to freeze at 32° Fahrenheit or at 0° centigrade.

He said, "Are you through?" Did he say, "You are through"?

"Who will win the prize?" asked the judge as the race began.

The judge said, "The prize winner!" and led the boy forward.

TREADWEAR TIRE COMPANY
QUALITY TIRES and TUBES
• AUTOMOTIVE BUILDING •

CLEVELAND, OHIO

March 23, 193-

Mr. Charles H. McConnell
Manager, Harding Motor Co.
108 Stockton Street
Zanesville, Ohio

Dear Mr. McConnell:

You were formerly a customer of ours, but for some
reason you have not ordered Treadwear tires during
the past six months. This we regret, for you were
a good customer, and we need you as much as we are
sure you need our tires.

In a thousand miles, tires flex at least 1,500,000
times. Our gum-dipping process increases the flex-
ing life of tires 58 per cent. This means service
to tire users.

You sold the last shipment of Treadwear tires in a
short time. Why not put in another supply of these
tires that move quickly? This will mean money to
you and to us.

Yours very truly

TREADWEAR TIRE COMPANY

J. B. Harman

J. B. Harman
Sales Manager

ESL

(Strokes, 579; Words, 106)

Style Letter No. 7—Block Form Showing the Dictator's Name
Typed One Space above the Official Title

Optional Exercise 27

When typing an optional exercise, use the directions given for the preceding exercise of the same lesson. In each letter for which the date is not given, use the current date.

Mr. Charles J. Thompson 624 Longworth Street Albany, New York Dear Sir: Our stock of Quality Suits will go on special sale next Friday. A private showing of all suits for charge customers only will be held on Thursday. *(P) These suits are of exceptional value. You will have no difficulty in making your selection on Thursday. Yours very truly THE ROY ZIEGLER COMPANY **(Dictated by J. W. Lewis) Sales Manager *(265–44)*

---

* When this sign is used, begin a new paragraph.
** Do not type this information in parentheses. It is given so that you can get the correct reference initials.

Exercise 28

DIRECTIONS: Set the marginal stops for a forty-space line. Set the tabular stops as you did for Exercise 27. Use double spacing and open punctuation.

Mrs. Jack L. Quinn 2470 Brandon Road Troy, New York Dear Madam: We hope that you will make frequent use of the charge account you opened at our store on the sixth. *(P) We are sure that the service we now can give you will enable you to buy to better advantage at our store. Yours very truly THE ROY ZIEGLER COMPANY **(Dictated by J. W. Lewis) Sales Manager *(210–42)*

Optional Exercise 28

Mrs. James K. Preston 4681 Riverview Road Albany, New York Dear Madam: Please come in next week so that we can make an adjustment in regard to the furniture which you state was received in bad condition. We are quite willing to make an adjustment which will be satisfactory to you and fair to us. Yours very truly THE ROY ZIEGLER COMPANY (Dictated by C. O. Marshall) Claim Adjuster *(230–43)*

BUDGET II
Review Practice

DIRECTIONS: Set the marginal stops for a sixty-space line. Center the drill vertically. Triple-space between the heading and the first line of the drill. Use double spacing. Type the drill twice.

3 9 5 395 4 7 2 472 1 6 0 160 4 9 ½ 49½ 5 1 ¼ 51¼ 2 7 ¾ 27¾

The sum of $590 + $372 − $38 = $924. What is 14 + 50 ÷ 2?

are men who cut few his get him job yet law new our run saw

just with zest sane must same this each from life kill fear

harvest normal giving mostly expect insane asylum poison

Five-Minute Timed Writing Practice

DIRECTIONS: Set the marginal stops for a seventy-space line. Set the tabular stop for an indentation of five spaces. Use double spacing.

	STROKES
One who would slash his flesh with a knife until the blood began to run,	75
would be shut up in an insane asylum; yet we cut our mental selves with the	151
edged thought-tools of fear, prejudice, anger, revenge, and imagine we are	226
quite sane and normal. Each thought is a seed from which develops a mental	303
plant just the same as itself. If there is venom in the seed thought-plant,	381
there will be venom in the fruit; this venom will poison life and will kill our	461
zest for happiness and for success. If we sell ourselves to a selfish life, a life	546
of taking and of never giving, we must expect our harvest to be mostly thistles	626
and thorns.—Adapted.	648

Syllable intensity, 1.27

McConnell, send us a complete report, please. Yours very truly TREADWEAR TIRE COMPANY J. B. Harman Sales Manager *(663–111)*

Exercise 56

DIRECTIONS: Fifty-space line; block form of letter; six single spaces between the date and the inside address; single spacing; open punctuation. Type the dictator's name one space above the official title.

Mr. Charles H. McConnell Manager, Harding Motor Co. 108 Stockton Street Zanesville, Ohio Dear Mr. McConnell: Mr. Bradley, our representative in your territory, telephoned this morning that you are not satisfied with our last shipment of Treadwear tires. (P) You know, Mr. McConnell, we guarantee each tire we sell. Our tires are made with two extra cord plies under the tread. These extra plies are so placed that you get 56 per cent greater protection against punctures and blow-outs than from most tires. This is a part of our guaranty. (P) Please send us a complete report of the complaints you have had on our tires. If you have had trouble with Treadwear, we want to know what is wrong. Yours very truly TREADWEAR TIRE COMPANY J. B. Harman Sales Manager *(595–102)*

Exercise 57

DIRECTIONS: Set the marginal stops for a fifty-space line. Type Style Letter No. 8 exactly as it is given in the illustration on page 90. Leave six single spaces between the date and the inside address.

Exercise 58

DIRECTIONS: Fifty-space line; block form, same as that of Style Letter No. 7; six single spaces between the date and the inside address; single spacing; open punctuation. Type the dictator's name one space above the official title.

Mr. Charles H. McConnell Manager, Harding Motor Co. 108 Stockton Street Zanesville, Ohio Dear Mr. McConnell: As soon as we can make a test of the tire you are returning to us, we shall let you know what seems to be the cause of the trouble you have had with our Treadwear tires. This test will be completed within a day or two after the laboratory receives the tire from you. (P) Our records show that we shipped 12 tires for the Ford, Chevrolet, Whippet, or Plymouth car. These tires were billed to you at $12.32 a pair. (P) Please let us know the number of tires which have been returned to you as unsatisfactory, the amount of rebate you gave your customers, etc. With this information at hand, we are certain we can arrange a satisfactory adjustment of this difficulty. Yours very truly TREADWEAR TIRE COMPANY J. B. Harman Sales Manager *(675–123)*

Optional Exercise 59

DIRECTIONS: Fifty-space line; block form without company signature, same as form of Style Letter No. 8; six single lines between the date and the inside address; single spacing; open punctuation.

Treadwear Tire Company Automotive Building Cleveland, Ohio Attention Mr. J. B. Harman Gentlemen: As requested in your recent letter, we are pleased to give you the details regarding the last Treadwear tires we bought from you. (P) Eight of the tires are unsatisfactory. We have replaced three of them with new tires of another kind. This leaves five tires still in use. The complaint has been made by the users of these tires that the tread is worn so smooth the tire does not have even normal non-skid protection. (P) If you will make a satisfactory adjustment for these defective tires, we shall be glad to consider using Treadwear tires again. Yours very truly, (Dictated by Charles H. McConnell) Manager *(556–96)*

Optional Exercise 60

DIRECTIONS: Fifty-space line; block form, same as that of Style Letter No. 7; six single spaces between the date and the inside address; single spacing; open punctuation. Type the dictator's name one space above the official title.

Mr. Charles H. McConnell Manager, Harding Motor Co. 108 Stockton Street Zanesville, Ohio Dear Mr. McConnell: Our laboratory test of the defective

The ROY ZIEGLER COMPANY

ESTABLISHED 1893

WHOLESALE AND RETAIL

ALBANY, NEW YORK

September 28, 193-

First Tabular Stop

Second Tabular Stop

Fourth Tabular
Stop at 40

Mr. John E. Weston

1384 Baxter Avenue

Utica, New York

Dear Sir:

We do not have in stock the plaque

you ordered in your letter of the tenth.

We shall be glad to order this for you if

you do not need it immediately.

We can have the plaque here within

two weeks. May we order it for you?

Yours very truly

THE ROY ZIEGLER COMPANY

J. W. Lewis

Sales Manager

Robert Howard

JWL:RRM

Third Tabular
Stop at 35

Fourth Tabular
Stop at 40

Fifth Tabular
Stop at 45

Adjustment of Tabular Stops: Left margin plus indentation of 5 = position for first
tabular stop. Left margin plus indentation of 10 = position for second tabular stop. These
two tabular adjustments take care of the second and third lines of the inside address. Set
the third tabular stop at 35 for the complimentary close. Set the fourth tabular stop at
40 for the company signature and the date line. Set the fifth tabular stop at 45 for the
official title. As illustrated here, the letter was typed with a centering point of 40.

(Strokes, 223; Words, 47)

Style Letter No. 1—Double-spaced Form

HARDING MOTOR COMPANY
108 STOCKTON STREET ZANESVILLE, OHIO

March 26, 193–

Treadwear Tire Company
Automotive Building
Cleveland, Ohio

Attention Mr. J. B. Harman

Gentlemen:

We had so many complaints from our customers about
your Treadwear tires not wearing well, it seemed
advisable to put in a stock of some other kind of
tire. This is the reason we have not ordered any
of your tires for several months.

We are returning to you by express a tire which a
customer asked us to replace. This tire was used
for approximately 5,000 miles. You will see that
the tread is worn smooth. Even the pyramid-shaped
blocks of rubber on the side wall are worn through.
Five thousand miles do not represent enough use to
cause the wear which this tire shows.

We can return to you two or three other used tires
from this same shipment, if you wish us to do so.

Yours very truly,

Charles H. McConnell

Manager

CHMcC:MRB

*Note the correct form of the reference initials when the dictator's name belongs
to the Mc group of names.*

(Strokes, 687; Words, 128)

***Style Letter No. 8*—Block Form with Attention Phrase**

Letter-Placement Table

Double-Spaced Letters

Number of lines in the body of letter	Spaces between date line and inside address
Fewer than 6	8 single spaces
6, 7	7 " "
8	6 " "
9, 10	5 " "

NOTE: It is generally better to single-space a letter having ten or more lines in the body of the letter.

Single-Spaced Letters

Number of lines in the body of letter	Spaces between date line and inside address
5, 6	10 single spaces
7- 10	8 " "
11, 12	7 " "
13- 15	6 " "
16- 18	5 " "
19, 20	4 " "

BUDGET I

Unless otherwise directed, use full sheets for the exercises of this instructional block. The review practice may be typed on half sheets.

Review Practice

DIRECTIONS: Set the marginal stops for a sixty-space line. Center the drill vertically. Triple-space between the heading, *Review Practice,* and the first line of the drill. Use double spacing. Type the drill twice.

```
4f$f 3d#d 9l(l 8k'k 2s"s 0;); 5f%f 7j&j 6j_j -;*; ½;¼; /;¾;

rfvf p;/; edcd ujmj wsxs ik,k qaza ol.l tfbf yjnj gfaf hj;j

We answered your letters of April 6, 10, and 12 on April 17.

and sow big how pay not why get one the can let out for but

queer doubt plant wheat thing comes while years think exact
```

Five-Minute Timed Writing Practice

DIRECTIONS: Set the marginal stops for a seventy-space line. Set the tabular stop for an indentation of five spaces. Use double spacing.

THE BELL: The ringing of the bell is a warning that the carriage will lock when you type six or seven more spaces. If you are typing a word of one syllable when the bell rings, complete the word; then start a new line. If you are typing a word of more than one syllable when the bell rings, complete the syllable, strike the hyphen once, throw the carriage, and complete the word on the next line. The dash is made with two hyphens, without space before or after.

	STROKES
Is it not a queer fact that while men know with no doubt that what they	74
sow or plant in the soil will come back to them in exact kind, that it is not	152
possible to sow corn and get a crop of wheat, they entirely forget this law	228
when it comes to mental sowing? On just what principle can we expect a	302
crop of happiness and of success when for years we have been sowing seed	375
thoughts of exactly the opposite kind? How can we expect to achieve big	450
things when we let lazy habits bind us? As we sow, so we reap; as we think,	529
so we achieve. The outcome is certain.—Adapted.	580

Syllable intensity, 1.22

Exercise 27

DIRECTIONS: Set the marginal stops for a forty-space line. Adjust the tabular stops so that you can quickly and accurately indent for all lines not beginning at the left margin. Use double spacing. Type Style Letter No. 1 exactly as it is given in the illustration. According to the placement chart, you will have seven line spaces between the date line and the inside address.

Treadwear you returned to us shows that the liquid rubber failed to cover all the fiber. This permitted an unusual amount of friction and heat, causing the cord body to deteriorate. This does not altogether explain, however, the worn condition of the tire. (P) A new tire can be easily ruined through the use of an old tube. If a motorist wants to get the best mileage from a tire, it is advisable to use a new tube. Doubtless your customers used old tubes in these tires. Did you check this with them? (P) We are willing to replace the tires which were not satisfactory, making a proportionate charge for the mileage which the user got on the old Treadwear. Will this be satisfactory to you? Yours very truly TREADWEAR TIRE COMPANY J. B. Harman Sales Manager *(742–130)*

Ten-Minute Timed Writing Practice

DIRECTIONS: Set the marginal stops for a seventy-space line. Adjust the tabular stop for an indentation of five spaces. Use double spacing.

Seeking

STROKES

When we seek, we find. The frozen areas of the North and the South   73
Poles were sought, found, and charted. Those who went on the quests which   150
ended in giving to the world new knowledge about these great unknown   219
places did heroic deeds. Only a few men may explore the South Pole region;   298
others must venture on less spectacular quests. It may be that we shall not   376
always discover just the exact opportunity for which we seek, but we may   449
be certain that every real search has a sure reward. If we stick to our quest,   530
we can usually find that for which we search; then we can go in and possess   606
it. The tragedy is that so often that for which we seek is not worthy of the   685
time or the effort we give to our quest. *(726)*   726

All of us have quests. We seek no frozen regions yet unexplored; we do   801
not defy death with a casual gesture. Our search is adjusted to our capacity   880
to discover. Some of us seek "the moon," but we should not know what to   955
do with it if we were to find it. Some of us seek money, but we would not   1031
know how to employ it if we could obtain it. We would not then possess   1104
money; money would possess us. Some of us seek fame, and bargain our   1176
birthright of honor for the insecurity of achievement which is founded on   1250
fraud. "Seek and ye shall find," but the finder must have the capacity to   1327
possess or he will be possessed by that which he finds. *(657)*   1383

I remember a boy who sought honor grades while he was in school, but   1454
he sought them through dishonorable methods. He got his grades, yet he   1527
lost himself. Since then, his business experience has been a continual seek-   1606
ing for a new job. He continues to try to "get by"; he does not seem to   1682
realize that life is passing him by. He is on the quest, however, and he   1757
pushes his search with a zeal which presents certain reward. He is moving   1833
toward the fulfillment of his quest; he will find that for which he seeks. It   1913
is tragic that his search is pitched on such a low level, that his goal is not   1992
a more worthy one. *(628)*   2011

Seek and you will find. Seek to improve your abilities, and you will de-   2088
velop in proportion to the zeal with which you labor toward your objective.   2164
That which you concentrate upon with all your heart and soul and con-   2235
sciousness, you can have. Know what you want; then go after it. Just to   2311
realize that you can have good is not sufficient; you must express intelli-   2387
gence that is equal to the task of taking it. If you want typing power, you   2465
can have it. If you want happiness, it can be yours. If you want success,   2543
you can achieve it. If you want to be and to do the best of which you are   2619
capable, that, too, may be yours. *(641)*   2652

Syllable intensity, 1.30

official title will indicate the space for the pen-written signature. This is a practice generally used. The dictator's name is frequently typed even when an official title is used.

Example: THE MORRISON COMPANY

E. R. Webster

E. R. Webster
Office Manager

Reference Initials

A business letter should show the initials or the name of the dictator and the initials of the stenographer, typed flush with the left margin, two spaces below the official title. Type the dictator's initials first; separate them from the stenographer's initials by a colon or some other mark of separation. The reference initials are typed without the use of periods. Study the following illustrations:

JCB:MOS   JCB   JCBoyle/mos
                 MOS

Enclosures

If an enclosure is mentioned in the letter, type the word *Enclosure* at the left margin of the letter, one double space below the reference initials.

When the letters have been signed by the dictator and are being folded and made ready for the mail, the enclosure reference will provide a check which will prevent the failure to include the enclosure called for in the letter.

Style Letters

The style or letter form to be used will be determined by the length of the letter or the custom of the office in which you work. The various letter forms will be presented in this text; you will be held responsible for knowing how to set up letters in these different forms. Study each illustration as it is presented; know the details of the form illustrated.

Four illustrations of style letters are to be studied and used in this instructional block. These are standard forms, the single-spaced and double-spaced letters with uniform indentations. Modifications of these accepted letter styles will be illustrated, discussed, and used in later sections of the text. Master the details of the forms now illustrated.

The exercises to be typed call for the use of the information given below:

Style Letters Nos. 1 and 2: These illustrations show the *indented form* of the double-spaced and the single-spaced letter. The length of the letter will determine the spacing to be used. In general, letters having fewer than sixty words in the body of the letter should be spaced double. This is not an inflexible rule. An unusual number of lines in the address or in the closing lines must be taken into consideration when determining the spacing to be used and the placement of the letter on the page.

In the indented form, the second and third lines of the inside address are indented five spaces beyond the beginning of the preceding line. The first line of each paragraph also must be indented five spaces.

Placement of the Letter

Letters are the personal representatives of the writer. You would not care to have a poorly groomed person represent you; neither should you be satisfied to have inaccurately typed or poorly arranged letters represent your work. The appearance of the letter is one of the first things noted by the reader. The accurate typing and arrangement of the letter are your responsibility.

The total number of strokes and the total number of words in the body of the letter are given for each letter in this text. Determine the number of lines required for the body of the letter by dividing the total number of strokes by the length of the line used. An unusual number of paragraphs may increase the number of lines by one or two because several of the paragraphs may end with very short lines. Other adaptations of the placement table must be made for special letters, such as those including tabulated material.

Unless the marginal stops are adjusted so that approximately half of the line will be typed to the left and half to the right of the center of the paper, the horizontal centering of the letter will be imperfect. If you are using a known centering point, such as 40, 42, 43, or some other point, you must check the placement of the paper guide to make certain that the center of the paper, when inserted, will be at the centering point used. If you are using a backing sheet with a line indicating the center of the paper, placing half of the words of the line on each side of the center of the paper is comparatively simple. Whatever method you use, know how to use it with mathematical precision.

Use the placement table given on the following page for the letters in this instructional block. This table assumes the use of a two-inch letterhead and of the usual number of lines for the inside address and the closing lines.

BUDGET VIII
Trait Training

Traits do not spring into being in the twinkling of an eye; they are the outcome of daily living and thinking. The business man says that if workers will develop certain personal traits along with skill, their success in business will be assured. Reading about what the business man wants will not guarantee the development of these qualities. You must develop these qualities through your daily work.

Trait Desired
Responsibleness
(Ranked second by 82 per cent of the employers interviewed)

Suggestive Trait-Actions
The secretary
1. Takes details off the employer's shoulders.
2. Does not have to be told everything that must be done.
3. Sees that the employer has at hand everything in the way of detail that he needs in the course of a big job.
4. Does not have to be reminded about routine duties, but sees that they are done on time.
5. Does not give alibis when things go wrong.
6. Takes on duties without being told to do so.
7. Sees that a transaction which has been started is finished.
8. Keeps the employer in touch with the office work.
9. Is aggressive when the occasion demands aggressiveness.

DIRECTIONS: Type one line of the drills and one sentence five times each. Use a different word drill and sentence in each practice period. Set the marginal stops for a seventy-space line. Use single spacing. Double-space between the five-line groups.

Drills on Six-Letter Words   *(Length of line, 69 spaces)*

```
chance bought signed please health friend change months states things
street placed thanks strong church though spring prompt charge course
cannot anyway before inform become within forget indeed myself forego
surely giving hardly during nearly trying lovely having kindly saying
excuse fellow except decide answer letter reason matter unable others
```

Sentence Practice

	STROKES FOR EACH SENTENCE
Excellence is never granted to man but as the reward of labor.	63
Put your faith in honest work and let others take the chance.	62
The first step toward a position in leadership is preparation.	63
The sum of 3 and 9 and 5 and 8 and 2 and 6 and 4 and 7 and 6 is 50.	68
No one is too poor to help enrich the lives of others whom he meets.	69

Corrective Drill Paragraphs

Each person should be challenged to play perfectly the role he has been given in life. To some extent we must all take a leading role in life's drama, whether we enjoy doing so or not. We must, then, beware of the efforts to *e* key deter our progress; we must guard against the call of pleasure and the lure of easy achieving. Though we begin quite zealously, some one else may become the winner if we do not hold ourselves to our best performance at all times.

For the first few seconds of the new work, it is found fairly effective to fix in mind the full benefit which will follow just from flicking the keys *f* lightly with the fingers. For some, a few finger gymnastics will free the key muscles of stiffness and thus afford a far quicker key-stroking than that obtained from tense muscles. Relaxation is necessary for the full development of typing skill. This fact must be fully realized if real skill is to be developed.

vidual without using *Mr.* or whatever other personal title is correct. The following are abbreviated forms of personal titles used with names:

Mr.	for a man
Messrs.	for two or more men
Mrs.	for a married woman
Dr.	for a doctor

Messrs. precedes firm names composed of the names of two or more persons. A period follows all abbreviated forms of titles.

The period is not used with the following titles as they are not abbreviated forms of titles:

Miss	for an unmarried woman
Misses	for two or more unmarried women
Mesdames	for two or more married women

Spell out such titles as *Professor, President, Captain, General, Colonel, Reverend,* etc.

The *official title* in an address should be placed at the beginning of the second line, followed by a comma and a space. This title indicates the official position in relation to the company named in the second line. If the second line is very long, however, the official title may be typed on the first line, with the personal name.

(1)

Mr. Willard Chester Harman
Treasurer, Harman Oil Company
5689 Baxter Avenue
Oklahoma City, Oklahoma

(2)

Mr. T. C. Spence, Manager
Queen City Sand and Gravel Company
541 Third Street
Cincinnati, Ohio

When used as names of streets, numbers less than one hundred should be spelled out. Do not place the number sign, #, or the abbreviation, *No.,* before a street number. Spell *Street* and *Avenue* in full unless abbreviations are required in order to secure balance in the address.

Salutation

The correct forms of salutations for business letters are illustrated below.

For a man:	Dear Sir:
	My dear Sir:
	My dear Mr. Summers:
	My dear Professor Young:
	Dear Mr. Hall:
	Dear Dr. Long:
For a woman:	Dear Madam:
	My dear Madam:
	My dear Miss Harrington:
	My dear Mrs. Brown:
For a firm of men:	Gentlemen:
For a firm of women:	Mesdames:
	or
	Ladies:

When preceded by the word *My, dear* should not be capitalized in the salutation. The salutation is typed flush with the left margin. In the business letter, the colon is the mark of punctuation used with the salutation. Two line spaces separate the salutation from the last line of the address and from the first line of the opening paragraph.

Body of the Letter

Letters may be spaced single or double. The length of the letter will usually determine the spacing to be used within the paragraph. There must always be two spaces between the paragraphs of the letter. This does not call for any extra spacing with the double-spaced form. With the single-spaced form, operate the line-space and carriage-return lever once extra for the correct spacing.

Complimentary Close

The complimentary close of a letter is the *Yours truly,* or whatever courteous ending the writer may wish to use. Only the first word of the complimentary close is capitalized. In general, business letters use the following forms:

Yours truly,
Very truly yours,
Yours very truly,

The use of the comma after the complimentary close is optional when the open punctuation form has been used in the heading and the address.

Signatures

The firm name should be typed in all capital letters two spaces below the complimentary close. A short firm name may be indented five spaces beyond the complimentary close; long firm names should begin to the left so as not to extend beyond the right margin of the letter. No punctuation mark is required at the end of the firm name unless an abbreviation is needed.

The dictator's official title should be typed four spaces (two double spaces) below the firm name. This gives sufficient space for the pen-written signature which should be a part of the closing lines of each letter. No punctuation mark is required after the official title.

Example: SMITHFIELD & TURNER

F. M. Turner
President

If an official title is not used, typing the dictator's name in the position usually given to the

Five-Minute Timed Writing Practice

DIRECTIONS: Set the marginal stops for a seventy-space line. Adjust the tabular stop for an indentation of five spaces. Use double spacing.

STROKES

Too many of us are just guessing today, and guessing wrong. Too	68
many of us expect the wheel of fortune to come full circle and to bring rich	145
chances for which we are only half prepared. Queer, is it not? Yet it goes	225
on from day to day and from year to year. It continues in spite of the waste	304
in human effort, the cost in unhappiness, and the loss in worth-while pro-	379
duction. What we need is to get the facts and face them squarely without	454
evasion. We need to base our preparation on facts and not on hazy guessing.	532
When the wheel of school life is come full circle and the first position is	609
taken, there will then be fewer misfits than at present.	665

Syllable intensity, 1.30

Modifications of the Block Form

Style Letter No. 9 shows one modification of the block form. In this form the lines of the inside address and the paragraphs are blocked, but the closing lines of the letter are indented to 35 (the beginning of the complimentary close) and are blocked in that position.

Style Letter No. 10 shows another modification of the block form. In this form the inside address is blocked, but the paragraphs are indented. The closing lines are blocked at the point at which the complimentary close is typed when the indented form is used.

Exercise 61

DIRECTIONS: Fifty-space line; modified block form; six single spaces between the date and the inside address; single spacing; open punctuation. Type the dictator's name one single space above the official title. Observe that this exercise is the same as Style Letter No. 9. It should be arranged in exactly the same form.

The Office Equipment Co. 286-290 Sixth Street Flint, Michigan Gentlemen: Please send us a catalogue of your office supplies. We are particularly interested in comparing prices you quote on desks, chairs, filing cabinets, etc., with prices other manufacturers quote on the same equipment. (P) We usually buy office equipment from Hall & Jordan, of Indianapolis. Since they do not carry in stock any of your office equipment, we are writing to you direct even though we understand that you usually sell through agencies only. If you wish us to send our inquiry through a sales agency, let us know to whom the letter should be addressed. (P) Please let us have this information promptly. Yours very truly Francis B. Harrington Director of Purchases *(618–102)*

Studebaker Publishing Company
HIGH SCHOOL TEXTS

MUNCIE, INDIANA
September 7, 193-

The Office Equipment Co.
286-290 Sixth Street
Flint, Michigan

Gentlemen:

Please send us a catalogue of your office supplies. We are particularly interested in comparing prices you quote on desks, chairs, filing cabinets, etc., with prices other manufacturers quote on the same equipment.

We usually buy office equipment from Hall & Jordan, of Indianapolis. Since they do not carry in stock any of your office equipment, we are writing to you direct even though we understand that you usually sell through agencies only. If you wish us to send our inquiry through a sales agency, let us know to whom the letter should be addressed.

Please let us have this information promptly.

Yours very truly

Francis B. Harrington
Francis B. Harrington
Director of Purchases

Style Letter No. 9—Modification of the Block Form with Closing Lines Indented to the Position for the Complimentary Close and Blocked in That Position

Exercise 62

DIRECTIONS: Fifty-space line; modified block form; six single spaces between the date and the inside address; single spacing; open punctuation. Type the official title in the inside address on a line by itself; type the dictator's name and his official title on one line. Observe that this exercise is

INTRODUCTION TO THE BUSINESS LETTER

If you have intelligently followed directions and thoughtfully practiced all preceding lessons, you have the foundation skill in typing on which greater typing power can be built. Emphasis upon improved rate and accuracy must be continued. You must hold yourself to the development of your maximum skill; less than your best is not acceptable. Typing power means something more than mere speed and accuracy of typing, though; it means the intelligent use of speed and accuracy in the typing of business and personal papers.

The Business Letter

A letter is written for the purpose of conveying a message to the reader. It must be accurate as to facts, clear, concise, and complete in its content, and must give unmistakable evidence of a courteous attitude toward the reader. The content of the letter is the dictator's responsibility; the typist must assume responsibility for the correct punctuation, spelling, syllabication, capitalization, balance, and arrangement of the letter.

Forms of Punctuation

Two forms of punctuation are used, the close and the open. The close punctuation form places the regular punctuation mark at the end of each line of the heading and the address of a business letter. The open punctuation form drops end punctuation except the period after abbreviations. In both forms, abbreviations must be followed by the period, and the name of the city and that of the state must always be separated by the comma. In the close form of punctuation, the comma is used at the end of each line of the address except the last, at the end of which the period is used.

The use of the close or the open form of punctuation is a matter of personal preference or office custom. The open form is preferred by most correspondents. Do not attempt to link up a definite form of punctuation with a particular style of letter. Either the close or the open form of punctuation may be used with any style of letter.

Parts of a Business Letter

Letterhead

Most offices use letterheads for correspondence. The standard page is 8½ x 11". The company name, together with the company address, is usually given at the top of the page. Other information may be included in the letterhead, such as the telephone number, a cable address, or the names of the executive officers.

Date Line

The date line is usually placed in relation to the city and the state printed on the letterhead. Type the date on a separate line two spaces below the city and the state. The date line may be centered under the city and the state, indented, begun under the first letter of the city, or placed so that it will end at approximately the right margin of the letter. If the letterhead is unusual in its arrangement, the date line may be placed in relation to the body of the letter.

Never abbreviate the month in the date line. May, June, and July should not be abbreviated under any circumstances. In the body of the letter, the other months may be abbreviated, although abbreviations are avoided by careful writers.

When the month, day, and year are given in one line, indicate the day of the month by figures only and separate it from the year by a comma. Do not use *d, st,* or *th* after the number that indicates the day of the month, unless the number precedes the month.

The following forms of date lines may be used with letterheads:

(Customary date line)	March 18, 193—
(Infrequently used form)	8th of February 1 9 3 —
(Special form)	June Eleventh Nineteen Thirty-three

Address

Use the correct title before the name of the person being addressed. This rule applies to the inside address as well as to the address on the envelope. Never address a letter to an indi-

the same as Style Letter No. 10. It should be arranged in exactly the same form.

A long official title in the inside address may be correctly placed on a separate line in the manner shown in this illustration. The street address was omitted from the inside address in the letter because to have given the street address would have increased the inside address to five lines. So many lines in the inside address should be avoided if possible. The street number and name should, however, be typed on the envelope in the manner shown in Illustration No. 43 on page 85.

Mr. Francis B. Harrington Director of Purchases Studebaker Publishing Co. Muncie, Indiana Dear Sir: We are sending you today our catalog No. 56. On pages 10-35 you will find described the office equipment about which you inquired in your recent letter. (P) Formerly our office equipment was handled by R. H. Milton & Son, of Indianapolis. At the death of Mr. Milton, Senior, the business was closed out. We have not yet completed arrangements for another sales agency in Indianapolis. (P) Since we have no sales agency in Muncie or in Indianapolis, you may order direct from the factory whatever equipment you need. (P) We shall give your inquiries prompt attention. Very truly yours THE OFFICE EQUIPMENT COMPANY E. R. Locke, Sales Manager Catalog No. 56 Mailed *(583–94)*

Exercise 63

DIRECTIONS: Fifty-space line; modified block form, same as that of Style Letter No. 10; six single spaces between the date and the inside address; single spacing; open punctuation. Type the official title in the inside address on a line by itself; type the dictator's name and his official title on the same line.

Mr. Francis B. Harrington Director of Purchases Studebaker Publishing Co. Muncie, Indiana Dear Sir: A copy of our catalog No. 56 was mailed to you yesterday. If it does not reach you promptly, let us know, please. (P) Unusual combinations are possible in sectional steel filing cabinets. For instance, on page 35 Illustration No. 08131 shows a combination of three letter-size drawers, one

three-drawer legal blank section, and a two-drawer 3 x 5 card index section. This makes a compact filing cabinet for an office. (P) There are several other desirable combinations possible in our filing equipment. We are eager to help you select the most suitable office fixtures. If you need other information, write us. Very truly yours THE OFFICE EQUIPMENT COMPANY E. R. Locke, Sales Manager *(627–100)*

THE OFFICE EQUIPMENT COMPANY
Office Equipment and Supplies

FLINT, MICHIGAN
September 9, 193—

Mr. Francis B. Harrington
Director of Purchases
Studebaker Publishing Co.
Muncie, Indiana

Dear Sir:

We are sending you today our catalog No. 56. On pages 10-35 you will find described the office equipment about which you inquired in your recent letter.

Formerly our office equipment was handled by R. H. Milton & Son, of Indianapolis. At the death of Mr. Milton, Senior, the business was closed out. We have not yet completed arrangements for another sales agency in Indianapolis.

Since we have no sales agency in Muncie or in Indianapolis, you may order direct from the factory whatever equipment you need.

We shall give your inquiries prompt attention.

Very truly yours

THE OFFICE EQUIPMENT COMPANY

E. R. Locke

E. R. Locke, Sales Manager

JC

Catalog No. 56 Mailed

Style Letter No. 10—Modification of the Block Form with Indented Paragraphs and Closing Lines Indented to the Position for the Complimentary Close and Blocked in That Position

Exercise 64

DIRECTIONS: Fifty-space line; modified block form, same as that of Style Letter No. 9, with attention phrase placed in same position as in Style Letter No. 8, page 90; six single spaces between the date and the inside address; single spacing; open punctuation. Type the dictator's name one line above the official title.

The Office Equipment Co. 286-290 Sixth Street Flint, Michigan Attention Mr. E. R. Locke Gentlemen: Your catalogue No. 56 came this morning. (P) The filing

Material to be written should be examined to see that the pages are in proper order. Failure to do this will not be considered in the result.

Headings and titles are not to be written.

Do not follow copy line for line as printed. (See Rule No. 2.) If bold face type or italics appear in the printed matter, the words should be written as though they were printed in ordinary type.

A pencil mark may be used to show the contestant that he is nearing the end of the sheet, but it must be made in a way that will not interfere with the proper correction of the work. An error should be checked by a complete circle around the word in which it occurs.

Write on one side of paper only, unless a sufficient supply has not been provided.

Every contestant must stop the instant time is called regardless of whether a word is finished or not.

1. *Line Spacing.* Work must be double spaced—"two notches." Every line wrongly spaced is penalized one error in addition to all other errors in the same line.
2. *Length of Line.* Except at end of a paragraph, any line having fewer than 61 or more than 76 characters and spaces is penalized one error in addition to all other errors in the same line.
3. *Length of Page.* With paper 8½" by 13", each page, except the last, must have at least 35 lines of writing; with paper 8½" by 11", each page, except the last, must have at least 29 lines of writing. One error is charged for a short page—not one error for each line that the page is short.
4. *Paragraphing.* Paragraphs must be indented five spaces, and only five. An error in paragraphing is penalized in addition to all other errors in the same line.
5. *Spaces and Punctuation Points.* A space and a punctuation point are treated as parts of the preceding word; but if they are incorrectly made, inserted, omitted, or in any manner changed from the printed copy, an error must be charged unless the preceding word has already been penalized.
6. *Spacing after Punctuation.* If punctuation is followed by a quotation mark, the spacing follows the rule laid down for the punctuation point.

    After a period used to denote abbreviation, one space is required, unless the abbreviation ends a sentence. At the end of a sentence, the final mark of punctuation is followed by two spaces.
7. *The Dash.* A dash must be written with two hyphens, without spacing before or after. If a dash is necessary at the beginning of a line, there should be no space between it and the following word.
8. *Cut Characters.* Any word written so close to top, bottom, or side of sheet, that a portion of any letter is cut off, must be penalized.
9. *Words Wrongly Divided.* A word wrongly divided at the end of a line must be penalized. A word hyphenated at the end of a line in the printed copy may or may not need the hyphen if it occurs medially in the contestant's work. For instance: "Devilfish" might be hyphenated at the end of a printed line, but if it appears medially, the contestant's rendering is not wrong if it conforms to any standard dictionary.

10. *Faulty Shifting.* If only parts of the proper character appear, an error is charged. If the complete character is discernible, no error is charged.
11. *Lightly Struck Letters.* If the outline of any character is discernible, there is no error.
12. *Transposition. Letters* transposed in any word constitute an error. *Words* transposed are penalized one error for the transposition; additional penalties are imposed for errors in the transposed words.
13. *Rewritten Matter.* In rewritten matter every error must be penalized, whether in first or second writing, and one additional error must be charged for rewriting.
14. *Words Omitted.* (See Rule No. 23.)
15. *Words Inserted.* (See Rule No. 23.)
16. *Crowding.* No word shall occupy fewer than its proper number of spaces.
17. *Piling.* If any portion of the body of one character overlaps any portion of the *body* of another character, or extends into the space between words to the extent that it would overlap any portion of the *body* of a character were there a character in that space, an error must be charged.
18. *Left-Hand Margin.* Characters beginning lines, except in paragraphs, must all be struck at the same point of the scale. If one is printed to the left or right of that point, an error must be charged.
19. *Erasing.* The use of an eraser is not allowed.
20. *Errors in Printed Copy.* Errors found in the printed copy may be corrected or written as they are in copy, but in no case shall an error be charged against such words unless they are omitted.
21. *Last Word.* An error made in the last word written, whether completed or not, must be charged.
22. *One Error to a Word.* But one error shall be penalized in any one word.
23. *General Rule.* Every word omitted, inserted, misspelled, or in any manner changed from the printed copy (save in the case of *transposition* and *rewritten matter*) must be penalized.
24. *Penalty.* For every error, *ten words* must be taken from the *gross number of words*.
25. *Gross Words.* The gross number of strokes shall be reckoned from the *printed copy* of matter used, and shall be *divided by five,* the result being the number of gross words from which all deductions for errors shall be made. Strokes in rewritten matter are not to be counted in the gross. When a typist ends his test with an unfinished word, he shall be given credit for each character written.

The straight copy material in this text has been stroked so that each machine manipulation is counted as one stroke. For instance, each letter and each space is counted as a stroke; similarly, each carriage return, shifting for a capital, etc., is counted as an extra stroke. In getting the gross strokes written, therefore, take the figures given for the last completed line and add the additional strokes needed, counting one for each letter and space and one extra for each shifting, etc.

cabinet we want is similar to No. 03865, shown on page 34 of your catalogue. Is the price given on the supplementary sheet, $42.75, f.o.b. your factory? Also in what colors can the cabinet be furnished? (P) We shall be needing vertical guides, too. Please quote us a price on 9½ x 11¾″ letter-size guides in 100 lots. (P) Although our office needs are not large just at this time, we shall be needing tables and other office equipment from time to time. When you again open an agency in Indianapolis, please let us know. Yours very truly Francis B. Harrington Director of Purchases *(588–102)*

Exercise 65

DIRECTIONS: Fifty-space line; modified block form, same as that of Style Letter No. 10; six single spaces between the date and the inside address; single spacing; open punctuation. Type the official title in the inside address on a line by itself; type the dictator's name and his official title on the same line.

Mr. Francis B. Harrington Director of Purchases Studebaker Publishing Co. Muncie, Indiana Dear Sir: Yes, the price of our filing cabinet No. 03865 is $42.75, f.o.b. our factory. This cabinet can be furnished in olive green or oak finish. The shipping weight of the cabinet is 215 pounds. (P) We supply letter-size vertical guides in heavy Manila, with or without the eyeleted locking-rod tab at the bottom. The price of these blank guides is $1.70 a hundred. When a thousand or more of the guides of any one size are ordered, a reduction of $2.50 is allowed from the price quoted on the basis of lots of 100. (P) We can ship the cabinet and the guides to you as soon as your order is received. Very truly yours THE OFFICE EQUIPMENT COMPANY E. R. Locke, Sales Manager *(609–110)*

Optional Exercise 66

DIRECTIONS: Fifty-space line; modified block form, same as that of Style Letter No. 9, with attention phrase placed in same position as in Style Letter No. 8, page 90; six single spaces between the date and the inside address; single spacing; open punctuation.

Type the dictator's name one line above the official title.

The Office Equipment Co. 286-290 Sixth Street Flint, Michigan Attention Mr. E. R. Locke Gentlemen: Please ship us at once filing cabinet No. 03865 and 100 letter-size vertical guides. Bill us for this shipment at the prices quoted in your latest letter. (P) If you have not already looked up our credit rating in Dun or Bradstreet, please do so. If additional information is needed, you may write to our local bank, the Second National Bank. Mr. J. C. Havelock will be glad to answer any request for information concerning our financial standing. (P) We found your prices on quartered oak office desks considerably higher than the quotations which were given us by other manufacturers. Yours very truly Francis B. Harrington Director of Purchases *(599–98)*

Optional Exercise 67

DIRECTIONS: Fifty-space line; modified block form, same as that of Style Letter No. 10; six single spaces between the date and the inside address; single spacing; open punctuation. Type the official title in the inside address on a line by itself; type the dictator's name and his official title on one line.

Mr. Francis B. Harrington Director of Purchases Studebaker Publishing Co. Muncie, Indiana Dear Sir: We thank you for your order for filing cabinet No. 03865 and 100 letter-size vertical guides. You should get this shipment early next week. (P) Are you certain that you compared the quality, as well as the prices, of the desks we sell with the same quality and prices of desks sold by other leading manufacturers? We have long given best quality at the lowest cost. (P) On page 31 of our catalog, we show a picture of a desk 32″ wide, 60″ long, and 30″ high. This desk is made from quarter-sawed white oak and can be furnished in light golden oak, mahogany, walnut, or fumed oak finish. We know of no other manufacturer who sells the same quality of desk at the price we quote—$64.20, f.o.b. factory. Very truly yours THE OFFICE EQUIPMENT COMPANY E. R. Locke, Sales Manager *(721–128)*

n drill

nun can run sun fun gun hand sunk bunk junk rung null next hunt
nineteen nutrient naturalness nocturnal nonsense nutrition nunnery
nightingale notwithstanding Newfoundland nonattendance nonresident

o drill

bold room look long cold wool fool hold loan pool sold told wool
obsolete outlook orthodox opinion o'clock October out-of-doors
opposition officious offshoot opponent overcome observe overlook

p drill

pack pass plus pull pity plan pick play post soap paid poor past
pamphlet paragraph participant proposition philosophy prosperity
proportion phonograph perpetual partnership perhaps pauper proper

q drill

quick quiet quite quits queen quote queer quart quantity qualities
quintessence quotations quartermaster qualification questionnaire
require acquire inquire inquest quizzical quest question quickness

r drill

rage form fear from free four farm refer regal river rigor fire
raffle regard refine reflex refuge reform refuse rifler reveal
robber repose remark relief retrain refresh revere regular reprove

s drill

samples satisfy sarcasm serious season special strange slipshod
speechless sterilize storehouse strenuousness submissive surpass
seasickness self-seeking self-possession short-sighted son-in-law

t drill

tuft lift waft lost fast fact most both tube twig loft next fist
theft fight stiff thigh thief tight tufty twist stab twixt thought
taste flight thieves thought titbit tonight Tibet though twelfth

u drill

until under sunder unjust adjust adjure conjure injure jury humbug
humor humorous umbrella unsound unconscious unqualified jujutsu
unscrupulous unpunctual jujuism judge unsullied unnatural unsuited

v drill

very ever give five gave have love favor adverse reverse average
vagrant valvular vanity furtive fervor fugitive avarice avenge
cover clever fervid vapor forgave forgive fugitive never quiver

w drill

wash wish swim swam swat Swiss swift sword swear swift swell swoon
window swallow wayward willow withdraw watchword worker wayworn
wealth when sown wreck snows waste wrath waltz waxen waxwork west

x drill

fix six lax mix six wax box tax six mix sixth exceed extra excess
exactly examine excited exercise expense express mixtures example
experience axiomatic auxiliary deoxidize exasperate oxygen oxidize

y drill

yield yearn hurry yearly mainly canopy saying lovely apply July
happy ready reply Friday kindly really policy nearly Yaqui yoke
payment inquiry ready January company entirely Thursday everybody

z drill

zinc hazy zone lazy zeal maze size quiz daze blaze zephyr zenith
realize zigzag wizard glazed penalize recognize appetize amazed
benzene benzoate blizzard buzzard externalize generalize magnetize

[54]

BUDGET IX
Trait Training

Are you accurate in what you do, as well as in how you do it? Will you assume responsibility for doing a piece of work even though you are not told to do it? Business men say they want workers who are accurate and who have developed the trait of responsibleness. They say that they must have workers who are also dependable. Note some of the trait-actions of a dependable person, which are listed below; then try to build these desirable trait-actions into your daily life.

Trait Desired
Dependability
(Ranked third by 75 per cent of the employers interviewed)

Suggestive Trait-Actions

The secretary

1. Is punctual.
2. Gets work out on time.
3. Is regular in attendance at work.
4. Works as well when the employer is not there as when he is.
5. Works consistently, not well one day and inaccurately or erratically the next.
6. Never leaves the employer in an emergency without planning for the emergency.
7. Does not forget routine duties that have to be done at certain times.
8. Sees that something which the employer has asked to be laid on his desk by the next morning is there at that time.
9. Is right there when needed.

DIRECTIONS: Type one line of the drills and one sentence five times each. Use a different word drill and sentence in each practice period. Set the marginal stops for a seventy-space line. Use single spacing. Double-space between the five-line groups.

Word Drills Emphasizing Special Letter-Sequences

```
must mull much mump mugs murk brig brag bred numb null cede cent
break bring broad brass brush river check thumb every never brake
swing sword swell swish swore swear sweep swift sweet swain swarm
willing reading calling sending writing morning waiting holding
up-to-date two-by-four well-to-do two-thirds son-in-law up-town
```

Sentence Practice

	STROKES FOR EACH SENTENCE
Carry on every enterprise as if all depended on the success of it.	67
The sum of 4 and 8 and 7 and 29 and 16 and 40 and 58 and 31 is 193.	68
We must conquer our weaknesses or they will certainly conquer us.	66
Cultivation is as necessary to the mind as food is to the body.	64
Your orders #49 and #53, dated May 20 and 26, amount to $237.85.	69

Corrective Drill Paragraphs

g key   A good man is a great blessing to any community. Generally, goodness goes out of its way to give genuine happiness and joy to all mankind—good and bad alike. Great goodness is a God-given gift, for God is absolute goodness. Going quietly along in one's own way, doing the most good one can do, is the best expression of goodness one can give. The truly good realize this and bless all with whom they come in contact.

h key   The health of the stenographer has much to do with achievement in his or her chosen work. The stenographer needs bodily strength and poise to withstand the exhausting demands of such a position. Haphazard habits of living may heavily handicap, just as a thoughtfully regulated existence may help one along the path to success. Good health is based quite largely upon a balanced diet, helpful and refreshing exercise, and eight hours of sleep each night.

Corrective Drills

a drill
Alabama abatable almanac actual acclaim awkward alfalfa attainable
Appalachian acquaintance approximate analyzable approach Australia
available asphyxiation authoritative appearance animated amortize

b drill
fob rob fib rib tab tub big bar bug beg buy bag fob rob rub tub fob
bride brail blaze break bribe buggy burst birch beaux bring barbs
barbarous bribery brambles bugaboo barbecue barber barbarity break

c drill
checks decade expect checker decree except decency scarce chance
December circumspect clerical collect commerce conscience conduct
conducive consequence connect confidence decadence candid descend

d drill
deeds died drudge deaden demand descend devoted discord divided
dwindled dedicated demented depended decadent discredit dependent
deductions displeased deserved disdained disagreed disadvantage

e drill
ever dead edge deed cede made read else deck need seed been head
exclude esteemed essence element envelope exceed entreat exchequer
eagerness eloquence external even-handed earache enfeebled eyelet

f drill
fifth fault first filed farce flare fixed forms force fable favor
fanciful forefinger fireproof fiftieth far-off frightful fortify
four-footed forefather fateful forgetful football forfeit fitful

g drill
great fight guard doing thing large group gives grown green gorge
greasing grasping thoughts grating glancing fighting geography gone
grade grateful grudging gorgeous gurgling exaggerating aggregating

h drill
high hurt hand they hope them hate have help inch hush harm hash
hardly highly hunch thanks hyphen health handle heart rhythm height
hairbrush hothouse household half-hearted hemisphere hemorrhage

i drill
kink kind king link sink rink sick wick stick thick point owing
Indiana idiotic illicitly irritability impartiality imagination
impracticability idiomatic individuality illustrious inconspicuous

j drill
June just join July joke jobs jump joys jar junk judge joint juicy
January journal jeopardize judgment justify jealous adjust injure
Judith judicial judicious jugular jugulate junior jurisprudence

k drill
kick kept Kirk lack lake kink kill pink keep rink link rake sink
wink knock think drink thank kodak kinsfolk knickknack knock-kneed

l drill
loll live lull loan like load list roll told look lost cold fold
label local would lilac could lodge legal labor libel loyal royal
lastingly legible legalize loyalty literal lifelessly likely liable

m drill
mum rum hum sum gum him bum may map mud aim ham sum hum gum him sum
made jump bump hump much make dump some limp lump must most pump
maximum mummify murmur mature martyrdom mesmerism matchmaker mystic

Five-Minute Timed Writing Practice

DIRECTIONS: Set the marginal stops for a seventy-space line. Adjust the tabular stop for an indentation of five spaces. Use double spacing.

	STROKES
Business men say that there are too many young workers who show	65
some skill but display little intelligence in the use of that skill. They are	145
like bolts without threads. A producer could make such bolts and let some	222
one else put the threads on them, but that would be a wasteful and expen-	296
sive process. To be utilized, bolts must be complete; they must be equipped	374
with threads. Beginning workers are often like bolts with no threads—they	451
are workers who type but do not think, who adopt but never create, who	522
stick to their jobs but seldom grow in their work. If you would become a	592
leader, start now to use your eyes to see and your ears to hear. Only in	667
this way can you develop yourself to your fullest capacity.	727

Syllable intensity, 1.30

In this budget of letters, the manager of The Bell Telephone Company of Pennsylvania answers inquiries and complaints from customers in the Pittsburgh district. This budget is not a record of transactions completed; it is a cross section of a day's work in the busy office of the manager of a large company. The letters cannot be filed because follow-up reports or investigations must be made. The original letters and the carbon copies of the answers are kept in the manager's desk in a special folder marked "Follow Up." The manager goes through the letters in this folder each day to see if any of the correspondence can be finally disposed of.

The letter style used in the office of the manager of The Bell Telephone Company of Pennsylvania is the modified block form of letter with certain changes which the manager approves. Note particularly the placement of the date to balance the printing on the left of the letterhead, the ten-space indentation for paragraphs, and the alignment of the official title of the dictator with the right margin. The reference notation shows the initials and the name of the dictator as well as the initials of the stenographer. Since the date is placed so that it balances part of the letterhead, the period is omitted after the date even though close punctuation is used in the inside address.

Exercise 68

DIRECTIONS: Fifty-space line; modified block form; six single spaces between the date and the inside address; single spacing; close punctuation. Type the dictator's name in the position for the reference initials. Observe that this exercise is the same as Style Letter No. 11. It should be arranged in exactly the same form. Make two carbon copies of the letter.

Mr. Kenneth L. MacArthur, 2979 Brighton Road, Bellevue, Pennsylvania. Dear Mr. MacArthur: We appreciate the request for telephone service contained in your recent letter. (P) Before we can say definitely that we can furnish the service at your new place of business, it will be nec-

essary for us to investigate all the facilities available. Our Bellevue lines are used practically full time. (P) The survey of available facilities will be completed in a day or two. If any class of service is available, we shall immediately send you an application card. (P) We certainly wish for you all success in your new business venture. Yours very truly, (Dictated by F. M. Johnson) Manager Copy to Mr. Wexford, Service Engineer *(542–89)*

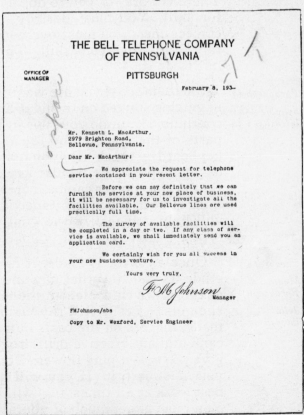

Style Letter No. 11—Modification of the Block Form with Special Variations

Paragraph 10
Syllable intensity, 1.27

I walked into a typewriting classroom the other day, and the teacher was, as she expressed it, in the midst of "laying them out." I looked around the floor to see how many had already been "laid out," but they were very much alive—too much so, for I felt that those pupils were getting a keen sense of joy out of seeing the teacher all wrought up. What was the matter? You can guess without much trouble. The teacher had been trying quite without success to get the pupils to check their own errors. I must admit that the papers I saw seemed to have been marked by pupils who had little zeal for accurate work. *(630)*

1273
1344
1411
1479
1551
1620
1688
1757
1821
1840

Paragraph 11
Syllable intensity, 1.28

That was not good sportsmanship, neither was it good business on the part of those students. They thought they could "get by" without marking all of their own errors. They believed the teacher would be too busy or too tired to check their work. They just did not stop to realize that they were acquiring a habit of work which would cripple them when they got into business. Had I mentioned that fact to them, they would have answered that in business they would not expect to get by, thus forgetting that habits fasten themselves on us through the repetition of thought and of act. Each day we spin the web of our lives, good or evil, never to be undone. *(672)*

1907
1978
2049
2120
2192
2258
2321
2391
2460
2512

Paragraph 12
Syllable intensity, 1.29

Are you making your nervous system your ally or your enemy? In typing, for example, have you acquired habits which will give you automatic and correct responses? Have you guarded against growing into the habits of typing that will be a disadvantage to you? If you have not, the challenge is yours and you dare not fail to meet it. There is work for you to do. This work calls for zeal just as it calls for skill. You must destroy all wrong habits of work and set up correct ones; you must overcome the cause of your low production rate to improve your skill. This is your work to do. You must not fail to do it. *(634)*

2580
2646
2713
2785
2856
2930
2996
3061
3131
3146

Paragraph 13
Syllable intensity, 1.30

Check to see if you are wasting time in returning the carriage and in getting started on the next line. Do you keep the carriage moving continuously, or do you type in jerks and spurts? Do you operate the parts of the machine by touch just as you control the keys of the keyboard by touch? Do you hold your eyes on the copy, for instance, as you depress the tabular key or the back-space key? You will find that typing power can be increased by getting rid of the waste motions quite as much as by speeding up the stroking. Each little gain will help you realize the goal you have set for yourself—a usable typing power. *(639)*

3215
3286
3358
3424
3495
3566
3633
3704
3771
3785

Paragraph 14
(Measurement Paragraph)
Syllable intensity, 1.25

Once an error is made, it is valuable. I said that to a group of students just the other day and a big chap mumbled, "Gee, he tells us errors are valuable, but the teacher flunks us for them each chance she gets." Yes, I still say errors are valuable once they have been made, for it is on the basis of a thoughtful study of errors that you can build a corrective drill program which will raise your skill and give you real typing power. Your teacher cannot give you this skill; you must earn it. If you will quit trying to "get by" and do your best work at all times, this will be one way by which you can earn it. You must exact much of yourself. The prize of typing power cannot be bestowed; it must be achieved. *(737)*

3854
3924
3995
4067
4137
4206
4277
4347
4418
4485
4522

NOTE: All letters of the alphabet are used in each paragraph of the exercises given in this instructional block.

Exercise 69

DIRECTIONS: Type a copy of the incoming letter from Mr. MacArthur. This copy will be sent to Mr. Wexford, the service engineer, together with a carbon copy of the manager's answer to this letter. Use a forty-space line and the modified block style of letter with five-space paragraph indentations and indented closing lines. Begin the street number and name ten spaces from the top of the sheet so that the date will be in the correct position. Type the word *COPY* approximately an inch from the top of the page to indicate that this is a copy of the original letter.

Since the second arrangement suggested below can be typed almost as quickly as the first, it may be used.

Type (*Signed*) and the signature on a line four spaces below the complimentary close. Note the following illustration:

2979 Brighton Road
Bellevue, Pa.
February 6, 193—

Bell Telephone Company
Seventh Avenue
Pittsburgh, Pa.
Gentlemen:

I should like to have a telephone installed at the address given above as soon as possible. I have started a moving and hauling business and need a telephone immediately.

I want to have a private line if possible. A party line would interfere too much with my business calls.

Please let me know how soon you can put in this telephone for me.

Yours truly,
Kenneth L. MacArthur

Exercise 70

DIRECTIONS: Fifty-space line; block form, same as that of Style Letter No. 7, page 88, with typed signature; six single spaces between the date and the inside address; single spacing; open punctuation.

The Bell Telephone Company Seventh Avenue Pittsburgh, Pennsylvania Gentlemen: We are enclosing a check for your final bill. Please credit this to our account. (P) We want to make application for the use of a telephone for our new offices at Forbes Street and Moorewood Avenue, which we expect to be occupying after the first of next month. A private wire is needed to take care of our incoming and outgoing calls. (P) If it is possible for you to do so, we should like to have our new telephone number the same as the number we now have—Grant 4000. We understand, of course, that the exchange will not be the same, but we hope that we shall be permitted to continue the use of 4000 for our new telephone. Very truly yours PITTSBURGH FINANCE COMPANY A. R. Marshall Enclosure *(639–120)*

Paragraph 5
Syllable intensity, 1.29

Covertly I began to watch Max while he was typing. For the first time I became aware of the almost effortless way in which he worked. While I pounded the keys with ever-increasing fury and vigor, Max typed along with seemingly little concern for speed and with no great effort. He kept the carriage moving; there were no jerks or spasms in his typing; he seemed to be typing at about half the speed I knew he must be making. All at once I seized upon a great truth; I learned the secret of the triumphant typing of Max. The truth was quite plain; he believed in himself and backed up that faith in self with right work habits. No wonder that he led the class! *(685)*

2621 2689 2755 2823 2890 2960 3028 3096 3161 3232 3241

Paragraph 6
Syllable intensity, 1.30

Max sat erect; his whole body expressed alert eagerness, well controlled. His was the position of the sprinter ready to run a race. While typing, he did not move his eyes from the copy; he gave his whole thought to the work he was doing. He wrote with rhythm; there was a smooth, continuous movement of the carriage which told that he knew the secret of speed in typing. Even figures did not slow up his typing speed. He had a quick, forceful stroke; there was equal power behind all of the strokes. He had no fear; he realized that his work habits were accurate. He had confidence in his ability to do his best; he said that all there was to it was to "just write." *(686)*

3310 3379 3446 3510 3572 3640 3711 3775 3843 3918 3927

Paragraph 7
(Measurement Paragraph)
Syllable intensity, 1.25

In that long ago when Max and I were rival typists, I did not quite know the worth of confidence in my own ability. Fear sat at the typewriter with me each day and cheated me out of the fine work that should have been mine. Much of my effort was lost, for I did not work with right habits. Just as I thought, so I wrote—with fear and trembling. It was only when I learned the waste of fear and the value of confidence that I went back to build the foundation of right work habits, the very base of which is confidence. When I had done that, on test days both Max and I wrote perfect papers, oozed satisfaction, and grinned triumphantly. *(660)*

3994 4062 4130 4199 4272 4339 4408 4479 4548 4587

Exercise 26
HABITS

Paragraph 8
(Measurement Paragraph)
Syllable intensity, 1.25

Business men and women have a keen interest in the work which students and teachers are doing in the classrooms of our schools, for they realize that out of these schools will come the men and women who will be the next leaders in business. Leadership is not now confined just to the men; there is quite a large number of women who lead the parade, so to speak, of those who achieve the unique and the worth while in business. There is just as much chance for success now as there has ever been, but the world of business requires more of its workers now than it did before. *(581)*

64 134 201 267 332 398 466 537 581

Paragraph 9
Syllable intensity, 1.26

As I meet these business people, I often ask them to tell me just what I shall say to young men and women who are now training for business. For the most part, I get the same suggestion, in different words, of course, but the same in thought. They say they require workers who can work without constant supervision, who can prove their own work and know that it is right or wrong. They say, too, that they expect students, while yet in school, to learn to work up to capacity, to form the habit of holding themselves to their best production at all times. There is no place in business for the lazy man or woman. *(629)*

651 717 789 856 921 989 1060 1129 1200 1210

Exercise 71

DIRECTIONS: Fifty-space line; modified block form, same as that of Style Letter No. 11, with ten-space paragraph indentations; six single spaces between the date and the inside address; single spacing; close punctuation. Make two carbon copies.

Mr. A. R. Marshall, Pittsburgh Finance Company, Vandergrift Building, Pittsburgh, Pennsylvania. Dear Sir: Thank you for your prompt payment of the final bill for telephone service for Grant 4000. (P) We must investigate the class of service we can furnish at Forbes and Moorewood. When this survey is completed, we shall immediately send to you an application for the best type of service we have available. (P) Telephone number 4000 for the Schenley exchange has been used by the same customer for the past ten years. We are sorry that it will not be possible for us to let you have this number as your new Schenley number. We would be glad to do this for you if it did not mean inconveniencing another customer. Yours very truly (Dictated by F. M. Johnson) Manager Copy to Mr. Wexford, Service Engineer *(618–110)*

Exercise 72

DIRECTIONS: Fifty-space line; modified block form; six single spaces between the date and the inside address; single spacing; open punctuation. Type the dictator's name and his official title on the same line. Observe that this exercise is the same as Style Letter No. 12. It should be arranged in exactly the same form.

The Bell Telephone Company Seventh Avenue Pittsburgh, Pennsylvania Attention Mr. F. M. Johnson Gentlemen: SUBJECT: Copy for Directory Advertisement (P) We want to increase our advertising space in the next issue of your directory. This directory is one of our most effective advertising mediums. (P) In the next issue of the directory, we want to use a half column. According to our contract, a column is 2½ x 10¼". We believe that the copy we enclose is properly spaced for a half column. If you find that changes must be made in our copy, however, submit proof for our approval. (P) Let us remind you that in the last printing of the directory our address was incorrectly listed. Our office is located in the Grant Building and not in the Oliver Building. Yours very truly WRIGHT SIGN AND POSTER COMPANY Jasper L. Wright, President Enclosure *(668–115)*

WRIGHT SIGN AND POSTER COMPANY
GRANT BUILDING

PITTSBURGH, PENNSYLVANIA
February 10, 193—

The Bell Telephone Company
Seventh Avenue
Pittsburgh, Pennsylvania

Attention Mr. F. M. Johnson

Gentlemen:

SUBJECT: Copy for Directory Advertisement

We want to increase our advertising space in the next issue of your directory. This directory is one of our most effective advertising mediums.

In the next issue of the directory, we want to use a half column. According to our contract, a column is 2½ x 10¼". We believe that the copy we enclose is properly spaced for a half column. If you find that changes must be made in our copy, however, submit proof for our approval.

Let us remind you that in the last printing of the directory our address was incorrectly listed. Our office is located in the Grant Building and not in the Oliver Building.

Yours very truly

WRIGHT SIGN AND POSTER COMPANY

Jasper L Wright

Jasper L. Wright, President

RCM

Enclosure

Style Letter No. 12—Modification of the Block Form with Blocked Attention and Subject Lines. Note that the word "Subject" is made prominent by being typed in capitals.

Enclosure for Exercise 72

DIRECTIONS: Center this copy vertically and horizontally on a full sheet of paper. Use double spacing with a triple space between the heading and the following line Type the heading in capitals.

WRIGHT SIGNS

Wright Signs at the Right Prices
Signs for Every Purpose
Silk Screen Displays
Picture Painting
Outdoor Signs
Card Signs
WRIGHT SIGN AND POSTER CO.
Grant Building
Telephone ATlantic 4838

DIRECTIONS: Unless otherwise instructed, use 8½ x 11″ paper for the paragraph practice. Set the marginal stops for a seventy-space line. Adjust the tabular stop for an indentation of five spaces. Have a top margin of one and one-half inches. Use double spacing. Type each paragraph once. Record the number of errors on Part I of your achievement graph. Make a careful analysis of all errors. Record the errors on the error chart and choose the corrective drill which will help to eliminate your faulty technique. Just below the paragraph, type each line of the corrective drill at least twice. Under the direction of your teacher, the second part of the achievement graph will be used for timed writing periods.

NOTE: The paragraphs are not set in typewriter type. Your line of typing, therefore, may not be the same as the printed line. If typing a one-syllable word when the bell rings, complete the syllable and start the succeeding line. If typing a word of more than one syllable when the bell rings, complete the syllable, strike the hyphen, and complete the word on the succeeding line.

Exercise 25
"AS A MAN THINKETH"

STROKES

Paragraph 1
(*Measurement Paragraph*)
Syllable intensity, 1.25

When I was quite young, I learned one of life's great facts; I 69
learned the waste of fear and the value of confidence. It was not that 142
I was a timid boy, but I had what we now would call an inferiority 211
complex. In my own judgment, I never seemed able to do the things 280
I wanted to do with as much ease or assurance as others whom I 345
knew. It always seemed to me that I had the desire to do big things 416
but the ability to do only small things. It was in a typing contest, 487
when Max and I were friendly rivals, that I realized the truth that 558
"as a man thinketh," so does he type. (598) 598

Paragraph 2
Syllable intensity, 1.26

I knew that my I. Q. was as high as that of Max Block; I knew 667
that my fingers were as flexible and that my wits were just as nimble 737
as his; yet Max could type with speed and accuracy which were 800
far better than mine. Max was fat; he had large, stubby fingers. 867
His skill must have been in spite of his fingers and not because of 936
them. He had a placid look which did not indicate rare intelligence. 1007
Still, day after day, he oozed happiness, wrote perfect papers, and 1076
grinned proudly. It was that grin which got me. Now I know that 1145
he was being merely good-natured about it all; then I thought that 1213
he was being superior. (638) 1236

Paragraph 3
Syllable intensity, 1.27

(To make the dash, strike the hyphen twice.)

I asked, "Just what qualities of mind or muscle do I need to excel 1308
in typing?" Our teacher said, "Set up the association between the 1380
controlling finger and the key to be controlled; then the process is 1449
merely one of right practice." I did not like that word "merely"; 1520
it seemed too casual for the hard work I did. With me it was not 1588
a case of "merely"—not at all. "The fingers will move to the right 1661
keys when the impulse to type comes with force." That was not true 1731
with me. My fingers would not go in the beaten paths. They made 1799
motions, but even I realized that the motions were quite futile. (629) 1865

Paragraph 4
Syllable intensity, 1.28

On test days I would grit my teeth, hunch my shoulders, wind my 1932
feet around the chair legs, and vow to write the complacent look 1997
from the face of Max Block. But I didn't. The harder I worked, 2069
the worse I typed. With fingers cold down to the very tips, with 2137
perspiration trickling from my forehead, and almost cross-eyed from 2205
glancing from copy to typewriter and back again, I pounded frantically. 2271
It all seemed quite simple, and certainly must be, for Max 2342
was a simple youth, and he led the class. The thing amazed me. 2407
There must be more to it than merely punching a key. My teacher 2474
said that the mental patterns must be definite. Max said you just 2542
had to write. (691) 2556

Optional Exercise 73

DIRECTIONS: Fifty-space line; modified block form, same as that of Style Letter No. 11, with ten-space paragraph indentations; six single spaces between the date and the inside address; single spacing; close punctuation. Since the company name is long, type the official title in the inside address on the first line and separate it from the personal name by a comma. Unless the printed letterhead indicates the position of the subject line, the subject should be typed one double space below the salutation. In the indented style of letter, the subject line may be centered or begun at the paragraph point. A correct placement of the subject line is shown in the following illustration.

Mr. Jasper L. Wright, President,
Wright Sign and Poster Company,
Grant Building,
Pittsburgh, Pennsylvania.

Dear Sir:

      SUBJECT: Directory Advertisement

      Thank you for the copy for your directory advertisement. We are glad to increase your space to a half column.

Illustration No. 45, Placement of the Subject Line at the Paragraph Point

Mr. Jasper L. Wright, President, Wright Sign and Poster Company, Grant Building, Pittsburgh, Pennsylvania. Dear Sir: SUBJECT: Directory Advertisement Thank you for the copy for your directory advertisement. We are glad to increase your space to a half column. (P) The second line of the copy you sent will not exactly fit the space. The column is 2½″ wide. Unless the line is set in small type, we shall have to crowd the copy somewhat to get it on one line. Would you agree to have the line read as follows?

Wright Signs—Right Prices

With this change, the line will look well and can be set in the same type as the other lines in the copy. (P) If you have some other suggestion which we can use in setting up this advertisement, write us. Yours very truly, (Dictated by F. M. Johnson) Manager *(647–118)*

Optional Exercise 74

DIRECTIONS: Fifty-space line; single-spaced indented form, same as that of Style Letter No. 6, page 82, with five-space paragraph indentations; six single spaces between the date and the inside address; open punctuation.

In re means in the matter of or concerning. It takes the place and the position of *Subject*. Some dictators use *re* without *in*. The most careful writers now avoid the use of either *in re* or *re*. The word *Subject* is preferred.

The *in re,* or subject, heading is typed one double space below the salutation and before the first line in the body of the letter. In this illustration, the line is centered. The correct placement of the line beginning *In Re* is shown in the following illustration.

The Bell Telephone Company
  Seventh Avenue
    Pittsburgh, Pennsylvania

Gentlemen:

      In Re Advertising Space

    Two weeks ago we notified you to discontinue our advertisement in your directory, yet today we received a request for the payment for space in the next issue of your directory.

Illustration No. 46, One Placement of the *In Re* Heading

The Bell Telephone Company Seventh Avenue Pittsburgh, Pennsylvania Gentlemen: In Re Advertising Space Two weeks ago we notified you to discontinue our advertisement in your directory, yet today we received a request for the payment for space in the next issue of your directory. (P) Probably the sending of a statement to us was a clerical error. Since you were notified that we do not want to take space in the next printing of your directory, we shall disregard the request. (P) We find that it is necessary for us to reduce our appropriation for advertising. The use of copy which is not changed from month to month does not seem to be justified under present conditions, but we may want to take space at some later time. Very truly yours PITT ELECTRICAL COMPANY Ralph J. Faulkner *(657–117)*

Computing Your Net Rate

All writing should be graded according to the International Contest Rules, extracts from which will be found on page 55. Each exercise is stroked; this will make it easy for you to get the total number of strokes written. (The number of strokes and the syllable intensity for each paragraph of the exercise are given so that the work on the different paragraphs may be compared more easily. Do not type the figures at the end of the line or at the end of the paragraph.) First, get the gross number of strokes written. In the International Contest Rules, five strokes are counted to a word; therefore, divide the gross number of strokes by five. This will give you the gross words written. As the penalty for your errors, deduct ten words for each error made; then divide the net number of words by the length of the writing period. This will give your net words a minute.

Your Achievement Record

Your teacher must make a record of exercises completed, tests passed, and general progress made, in order that grades can be given and evidence recorded of work completed. Make your own record of work completed in order that you can note your progress.

On this page you will find an achievement graph which shows one student's progress in this paragraph practice. Record your progress on a similar graph.*

Part I of the achievement graph provides a record of the number of errors made in each paragraph in each of the writings. After you have completed the writing of a paragraph, record in the proper space the number of errors made. There should be a steady growth in typing power, which should be shown in the increased accuracy with which the paragraphs are typed.

Part II of the graph shows the progress made in decreasing errors and in increasing net speed. After completing a test, place a dot in the center of the square which is opposite the number of errors and under the proper date. Also place a dot in the square which is opposite the net speed and under the proper date. Connect the dots representing the number of errors with a broken line as in the illustration, and connect the dots representing the net speed with a solid line. The chart will then show your progress in decreasing errors and in increasing speed.

The work of this section practiced intelligently will raise the level of your skill and give you endurance and control in all your work at the typewriter.

PART I—Errors

PART II—Speed and Error Chart

Illustration No. 42, Achievement Graph

---

* Prepare an achievement graph on blank paper. A speed and error chart is provided in the Workbook accompanying this text. If you do not have the Workbook, prepare this form also on blank paper.

Ten-Minute Timed Writing Practice

DIRECTIONS: Set the marginal stops for a seventy-space line. Adjust the tabular stop for an indentation of five spaces. Use double spacing.

REAL VALUES

STROKES

This is an age and an era when we are quite likely to place too much	71
stress on getting money and when we are prone to give too little thought to	147
the real value of money. All of us are rich in time, rich in abilities rarely	227
used to the fullest extent, and rich in chances to achieve something useful.	304
Such riches are far greater in value than mere money, if we would just rea-	381
lize their true worth. If we will take stock of what we have and what we are	460
and what we want to be, we will find that the things which have true worth	535
are the things which all may have. *(570)*	570

In taking stock of our personal assets, we must rank high in the list of 645
our possessions those qualities which have to do with real values. We should 724
not want to accumulate money just for the sake of money, but we should 795
want to have money for the sound social use which can be made of it. We 869
do not need time in order that we may squander more hours, but we need to 943
use our time more intelligently in order that we may enrich life. We should 1021
not want to extend our abilities in order that we may dazzle our little world 1099
with a vain show of brilliance, but we need greater capacity to do in order 1175
that we may add to the total wealth of the world. *(655)* 1225

Wealth is not made up just of the assets known as stocks and bonds 1294
and cash and real estate. We are beginning to realize that the true wealth 1371
of a man is to be found by taking stock of his ideas and his ideals, of his 1447
habits and his attitudes, of his regard for the fine things in life, and of his 1527
understanding of his relationship to others. If a man excels in these things, 1607
we may be quite sure that he has true wealth. When he makes the shift in 1682
emphasis from money to ideals, he begins to achieve a sense of values. *(528)* 1753

Just why should one weigh this problem of values while still in school? 1828
What has it to do with training for business? Some students waive such 1903
questions as being of no concern to them. Some feel that if the net words 1979
typed in a ten-minute test are enough, a good position is sure. If one excels 2059
in typing, getting a position may not be hard—skill is in demand. Unless 2135
other qualities are developed on a par with skill, the problem will come in 2211
trying to keep the place. Skill is fine, but with it must go many other mental 2292
and social traits if one is to realize lasting success. *(595)* 2348

Judgment, courtesy, and tact are qualities which bring success in all 2420
work. Good sense is as needful as skill when it comes to doing the varied 2496
work which office workers must do. Sound judgment may come with experi- 2570
ence; it may come, too, as a result of intellectual growth gained through the 2648
solving of problems instead of evading them. Regard for others sums up 2721
what is meant when such words as "courtesy" and "tact" are used. Being 2798
thoughtful of others is one of the most useful traits which an office worker 2875
can have. Most men win or fail in business on the basis of traits plus skill. 2955
Do not be content with skill alone. True values are to be found in the traits 3036
which will help you to use your skill. *(727)* 3075

Syllable intensity, 1.30

Syllabication

An incorrectly divided word is as much an error as an incorrectly spelled word. You must develop a "feeling" for correct syllabication. This may be done through observation and through frequent reference to a dictionary. The simple rules which follow will aid you in understanding the basic principles of syllabication:

1. Divide words between syllables only.
2. Never divide words of one syllable.
3. Do not separate a syllable of one letter from the rest of the word. In words having three syllables or more, a one-letter syllable should be typed on the preceding, rather than the succeeding, line.
   Example: sepa-rate
       not sep-arate
4. As a rule, divide a prefix and the letter following it.
5. As a rule, divide between a suffix and the letter preceding it. When a final consonant is doubled before a suffix, the additional consonant goes with the suffix.
   Examples: trip-ping, permit-ted, omis-sion. When the root word ends with a double letter, separate the suffix from the root word.
   Examples: stress-ing, bluff-ing.

Avoid dividing words at the ends of more than two consecutive lines, if it is possible for you to do so. Do not divide a word at the end of a page; carry the entire word to the second page.

Method of Practicing Paragraphs

Unless your teacher gives you other instructions, use 8½ x 11" paper and type each paragraph once. Check the writing carefully and record the errors on the error chart. Determine the errors which are repeated most frequently and select from the corrective drills on pages 53 and 54 the drills which are designed to correct these errors. Type each line of the corrective drill at least twice. After all paragraphs have been typed, retype each paragraph.

Analysis of Errors

The first step in eliminating errors is to discover the tendency to make certain types of errors. You must eliminate the major types of errors before they become habitual. To discover these major types of errors, keep an accurate record of errors made.

A chart showing the errors made by one student of typewriting is shown below.

ERROR CHART

Name of Pupil _Philip Howard_   Class _9:00 - 9:45_   Date _October 29_

	A	B	C	D	E	F	G	H	I	J	K	L	M	N	O	P	Q	R	S	T	U	V	W	X	Y	Z	.	:	"	.	-	?	Space
Paragraph 1				nd				e										t				b											
Paragraph 2											,			sp.							a	n											m
Paragraph 3				ᴧ															z														
Paragraph 4	ᵍ			ᴧ															s														n
Paragraph 5		v	d															t															
Paragraph 6	ᵍ	n					b		sp						d/w	ᵍ																	
Paragraph 7																		ᵍ	f														n
Paragraph 8																		f	n														
Paragraph 9							t		u						p							b											
Paragraph 10																			s														
Paragraph 11																		ᵍ							l								
Paragraph 12													o	sp.					w						sp.								
Paragraph 13														sp.					ᵍ														
Paragraph 14				ᵢ															w/w			b											(

Illustration No. 41, Error Chart

To record each error, enter in the column for the correct letter, on the line for the paragraph being written, the letter inaccurately struck for the correct letter. (The abbreviation *sp.* can be used for *space*.)

In addition to the classification of individual letters inaccurately struck for correct letters, record the other types of errors on the back of the error chart under general headings such as Errors of Transposition and Errors of Omission (letters, words, phrases, or sentences). Also list what are usually known as machine errors. Most of the errors will be classified easily, but when the chart does not seem to provide space for all types of errors, make a special notation on the back of the paper to determine whether the errors recur with sufficient frequency to justify special corrective drills.

TABULATING

The typist is frequently called upon to arrange statistical or other material in columns. This process is called *tabulating*. Probably the most important feature in tabulating is the planning of the work. In doing this, keep in mind that clearness and compactness are the two most essential features. Analyze carefully the facts and the figures to be tabulated before you determine the general headings and the headings of the columns. The width of each column and the general lay-out of the whole must then be determined. All this should first be worked out with pencil and paper.

In tabulated work, you will usually have a main heading and secondary or column headings. The main heading gives a brief statement of what is contained in the entire tabulation; the column headings describe the contents of the columns.

In the arrangement of words or phrases in tabulated form, the left margin of the column should be kept straight. In the tabulation of figures, the right of the column should be kept straight unless decimals are being used, in which case the decimal points must be kept in a vertical column.

Make use of the equipment on your machine to aid you in more rapidly tabulating work. Whether your machine is equipped with decimal tabular keys, a column selector, or any other form of tabulator, be sure you understand the use of this mechanism.

Check List for Tabulation

Six single line spaces make a vertical inch. Ten thumb spaces make a horizontal inch. Paper 8½ x 11", therefore, has 66 writing lines of 85 spaces each. When using paper other than that 8½ x 11", make allowance for the difference in the available lines and spaces. Adjust the paper guide so that the left edge of the paper will be at 0. The center of the paper will then be at 43. (Note: There are 12 thumb spaces to a horizontal inch of elite type. Paper 8½ x 11", therefore, has 66 lines of 102 elite spaces each.)

Tabulation Steps (*Mathematical Placement**)

1. Plan your tabulation with pencil and paper before you attempt to type it.
   a. Decide on a brief but clear main heading.
   b. Determine the number of columns required and, when desirable, give a suitable heading to each.

2. Determine the vertical placement.
   a. In the tabulation exercises in this instructional block, use triple spacing between the main and the secondary headings; use double spacing between the secondary heading and the first line of the tabulation. Count the number of lines required to type the material. Include all extra lines required between the main and the secondary or column headings.
   b. Subtract this number from 66, the number of available lines on the 8½ x 11" paper.
   c. Divide by 2. This result is the number of lines you must space down from the top of the paper before you type the main heading. (Disregard fractions.)

3. Determine the horizontal placement of the columns.
   a. Count the number of spaces which will be used in typing the longest line in each column.
   b. Add the spaces for all the columns and subtract this sum from 85.
   c. Divide the result by *one more than* the number of columns in the tabulation. This number represents the number of spaces to be left in each margin and between the columns. If the number is not evenly divisible, add the remaining spaces to the width of the left and right margins.

4. Set the left marginal and the tabular stops.
   a. Set the left marginal stop at the point corresponding to the number of spaces in the left margin.

   b. Add to this number the number of spaces to be used in typing the longest line of the first column and the number of spaces to be left between the first and second columns. Set the first tabular stop at the point which corresponds to the sum.
   c. To the number representing the tabular stop for the second column, add the number of spaces to be used in typing the longest line in the second column and the number of spaces to be left between the second and third columns. Set the second tabular stop at the point which corresponds to the sum.
   d. Continue in this way until the tabular stops for all columns have been set.

5. Determine the placement of the main heading.
   a. Space down to allow the top margin determined in Step 2.
   b. Center the main heading. (Rules for horizontal centering are given on page 33.)

6. Determine the placement of each column heading.
   a. Find the difference between the number of spaces in the column heading and the number in the longest line in the column.
   b. Divide by 2.
   c. If the column heading is longer than the longest line in the column, back-space the required number of spaces (Step b) from the left margin of the column; if the column heading is shorter than the longest line in the column, indent the required number of spaces from the left margin of the column.

7. Determine the placement of the columns.
   a. Space down to allow the number of spaces desired between the main or secondary heading and the body of the tabulation.
   b. Start the columns at the points at which the left marginal and the tabular stops were set in Step 4.

*In Part III of this text, you will be taught judgment placement of tabulated problems.

Four-Letter Words

(Length of line, 69 spaces.)

back bank been best bill blue book both boys call came card care cars
case cash club cold come cost date days deal dear does done door down
each else eyes face fact fair fall farm fear feel feet felt file fill
find fine fire five form four free from full game gave girl give glad
goes gone good hair half hand hard have head hear held help here high
hold home hope hour June just keep kept kind knew know land last late
left less life like line list live long look loss lost lots love made
mail make mean meet mind mine miss Miss more most much must name near
need news next nice note once page paid part past plan play poor post
rain rate read rest road room said sale same save says seem seen sell
send sent ship show sick side sign size sold some soon sort stay stop
such suit sure take talk tell than that them then they this till time
told took town trip true turn used view wait walk want warm week well
went were what when whom wife will wire wish with word work year your

Phrases—No. 1 (2-3)

(Length of line, 69 spaces.)

by the in our of you we can is not to get we beg if you to put to you
to say we are he can on the of one up the of his do not he had in the
he was of all if the do you at our it has is our we may in its it can
as you in all to the he did of our at all if not of the on our to our
to see in his to ask to his at the is the to pay it was as the on his

No. 2 (3-3)

(Length of line, 63 spaces.)

are not and our for the and are you had for you who are and not
may not and was you may has not and the you did was the are you
you are but the who was why not may our who had was not you see
can you did you who can for him you can and see did not she had

No. 3 (2-4)

(Length of line, 71 spaces.)

of time it will on that is that we take in time as they at that to send
in this we will of this if they we feel at this of that we must by this
to take on this we hope to that we find at last we want to make if this
to sell so much to call on your to give to them in fact we wish to have

BUDGET X
Trait Training

If you were to make a case study of outstandingly successful office workers, you would find that they are accurate and dependable. You would find, too, that they are *intelligent*. What are the earmarks of the kind of intelligence business men want their workers to have? Study the suggestive trait-actions listed below.

Trait Desired
Intelligence

(Ranked third, the same as the trait of dependability, by 75 per cent of the employers interviewed)

Suggestive Trait-Actions

The secretary

1. Learns a new terminology quickly.
2. Can grasp an idea from just a suggestion.
3. Does not have to be told the same things over and over.
4. Can get the gist of a report and summarize it for the employer.
5. Thinks of things to do to improve the office service.
6. Requires a minimum of explanation.
7. Does not make the same mistake again and again.
8. Learns new work quickly.
9. Does not give the dictator a letter which fails to make sense.
10. Does not have to be told to correct obvious mistakes in work.

Most of the trait-actions of an intelligent person suggest the use of mere common sense. The employer rates the ability to prove work, and, hence, to know that it is right or wrong, as a necessary trait of a successful office worker. In terms of these suggestive trait-actions, are you being intelligent in doing your classroom work?

Sentence Practice

DIRECTIONS: Use a different sentence in each practice period. Type the sentence five times. Set the marginal stops for a seventy-space line. Use double spacing.

STROKES FOR
EACH SENTENCE

The sum of 69 and 83 and 47 and 51 and 30 and 29 and 75 and 18 is 402.	71
The O'Day & Company note (due 9/1/38) is for $5,000 at 4½% interest.	75
On December 16, car PRR #245,480 was shipped on your order #579-YX.	75
Underscore titles of books; place in quotations titles of "articles."	80
When typing several carbon copies, use ¼ and ¾ instead of ¼ and ¾.	73

Corrective Drill Paragraphs

DIRECTIONS: Set the marginal stops for a seventy-space line. Adjust the tabular stop for a five-space indentation. Use single spacing. Type one corrective drill paragraph in each practice period. Alternate the paragraphs in the various practice periods.

i key

I believe ideas and ideals are an infinite part of an individual's life. His ideals lift him higher and higher, widening his horizon. Idealism lifts civilization. When idealism appears, then exit ignorance, idleness, and instability—all, incidentally, insidious ills, injuring humanity and killing progress in all times. Idealism, instead, enlightens lives with a quiet simplicity which points to illuminating industry. It is idiomatic that that man lives twice who lives the first life well.

j key

Jelmer's Jap-Rose perfume is just the ideal perfume for you. You buy jewelry that is a luxury; why not buy perfume that is distinctive? We believe in quality, not quantity. We could write you a two-page letter on the value of Jelmer's Jap-Rose perfume, but we just want you to try it for yourself. If you wish a sample jar, check the enclosed blank. Sending in the blank will also entitle you to enter the Jelmer contest. The first prize will be a jade ring; the second prize will be a jet black Japanese jardiniere.

DEVELOPING TYPING POWER

Mastery of the fundamentals of typing, presented in the preceding lessons, must be followed by an insistence upon correct procedures which will give correct results in all work at the typewriter. If you have successfully completed the work of the preceding lessons, you can begin this drive for improved typing power with confidence in your ability to do the work in an intelligent and satisfactory manner. Daily check and analyze the errors made; then practice corrective drills in order to eliminate the faulty keyboard control shown by the analysis of the errors. If improvement is not made through corrective drill practice, it is usually because remedial thinking has not preceded the practice.

Daily Check on Fundamental Habits

1. Keep the carriage moving smoothly and continuously; eliminate the jerks in typing.

2. Hold the eyes on the copy.

3. Throw the carriage swiftly and begin typing the succeeding line immediately.

4. Control the machine parts by touch—the tabular key, the back-space key, the shift keys, the line-space and carriage-return lever, the margin release.

5. Hold yourself to your best production.

6. Demand of yourself daily progress. Enter into competition with yourself.

7. Compare your achievement day by day and week by week.

At the completion of this section devoted to the development of typing power, you should show measurable improvement. If you do not, you will need to check carefully your technique of typing, your sincerity of effort, and your habits of work.

Word and Phrase Drills

In the beginning of your study of typing, you read the copy letter by letter. Through word and phrase drills, you progress from letter recognition to word recognition, a higher order habit in the development of skill in typing. Word recognition calls for seeing the word as a whole; you think the word, not the individual letters of the word.

Each word in the following word drills is a one-syllable word. Words of the same length are arranged in line drills in order to emphasize rhythm. In practicing these drills, see the word, think the word, type the word. This will increase your speed; in no sense does it mean, however, that you are to type beyond your control. Push yourself for greater typing power, but remember that typing power calls for absolute control as well as for maximum speed.

In drill practice you can experiment with the best rate at which you can type with accuracy. In the typing of an exercise or in timed writing, never type at your highest rate. Type well within the margin of your maximum speed in order that you may have a feeling of easy control.

DIRECTIONS: For the daily drill practice, set the marginal stops for a seventy-space line. Use single spacing. Unless otherwise instructed, each day type ten lines, each line twice. Double-space after the second typing of each line.

Two-Letter Words *(Length of line, 71 spaces.)*

am an as at be by do go he if in is it me my no of on or so to up us we

Three-Letter Words *(Length of line, 71 spaces.)*

act add age all and are arm ask bad bed beg big bit box boy but buy can

car cut day did due eat end eye far fat fee few fit for fun fur get got

had has hat her him his hot how its job kid law let lot low man may May

men met new not now off old one our out own pay red run saw say see set

she sir six ten the too try two use war was way who why win yes yet you

Five-Minute Timed Writing Practice

DIRECTIONS: Set the marginal stops for a seventy-space line. Adjust the tabular stop for an indentation of five spaces. Use double spacing.

STROKES

No one needs to be idle at any time. No cycle of depression can rob one 76
of work. There are skills to be made more exact, problems to be solved, and 154
books to be read. More than these, there is self to be conquered. There is no 236
need for one to be idle at any time. Two hours a day of good reading will 312
make life rich. In our libraries there are great books covered with dust be- 391
cause their wisdom is not recognized by modern readers. While we as a 463
nation go on in our economic illiteracy and sink more and more into despair, 540
we feed our lives with cheap thinking and let the subtle forces of decay in 616
character go unchecked. 639

Syllable intensity, 1.30

Exercise 75

DIRECTIONS: Type in one column the list of words at the right, making one carbon copy. Type the exercise once without error.

Use a main heading and a subheading. Triple-space between the main heading and the subheading, and double-space between the subheading and the column. Note that the triple space between the main heading and the subheading requires only two extra lines and that the double space between the subheading and the column requires only one extra line. Use single spacing for the list of words. Type the main heading in capitals. Center the headings and the longest line in the column.

The completed exercise will be similar in arrangement to the printed copy. You should, however, carefully study the problem and the analysis, as this study will aid you in solving similar problems in tabulation.

Analysis of Problem

Vertical Placement

Total lines available 66
Lines required:
By main heading 1
By space between main heading and second-
ary heading 2
By secondary heading 1
By space between secondary heading and
column 1
By column (34 lines single-spaced) 34   39
Lines available for top and bottom margins 27
Lines available for top margin: $27 \div 2 = 13$ (1 over).
Proof: $13 + 39 + 14 = 66$.

Horizontal Placement of Column

Total spaces available 85
Spaces required by longest line of column 14
Total spaces to be used in margins 71
Spaces to be left in each margin: $71 \div 2 = 35$ (1 over).
Left marginal stop, 36.
Proof: Spaces in left margin 36
Spaces in longest line of column ... 14
Spaces in right margin 35
Total spaces 85

Horizontal Placement of Headings

Spaces required:
By main heading (to be centered) 10
By secondary heading (to be centered) 15

WORD STUDY

Spelling Demons

accommodation
acquaintance
beginning
benefit
choose
committee
dependent
efficiency
equipped
extension
financial
government
hoping
immediately
laboratory
manufacture
necessary
noticeable
occasionally
occurred
omitted
possessive
referring
secretary
successful
superintendent
swimming
therefore
thorough
undoubtedly
until
victorious
villain
welfare

Exercise 24

DIRECTIONS: Set the marginal stops for a sixty-space line. Use an indentation of five spaces. Type the exercise, centered vertically, once to a page. Triple-space after typing the heading. Use double spacing for the paragraph. Type the exercise twice.

STROKES

```
     That study educates which gives to you the power to do      57
things, the power to think things, and the power to feel things, 122
whether that study is a part of a quiet school day or a part    183
of an amazing and perplexing office routine.  You must have     244
the power to do things, for that is your way of taking up your   307
share of the world's work; you must have the power to think      368
things, for only in that way can you grow; you must have the     429
power to feel things, for feeling is life itself.  All learn-   492
ing must be tested in terms of these three abilities and not    553
in terms of just one of them.  Develop now the ability to       612
do, to think, and to feel.                                      638
```

Syllable intensity, 1.25

Optional Exercise 24

Measurement paragraph

STROKES

```
     All people love to win.  It is a fine feeling to be on      58
top, to be first in whatever we try to do.  Often the prize     119
is not worth the effort, but still we want to win.  Perhaps     180
this desire to win, fostered in all who enter competition, is   242
the best prize of all.  In games, only one can be best; there   305
is only one first prize.  In life, each one can win; there is   368
a place for each of us and a work for us to do.  The next time  432
you question this, just look around you and see the wonderful   494
things that remain to be done.  The winner must achieve his     555
victory; it cannot be bestowed on him.  If you will develop     616
superior ability in the doing of one thing, you, too, can be    677
a winner.                                                       686
```

Syllable intensity, 1.25

The Care of the Typewriter

The typewriter is an expensive machine. It gives good service when it is properly cared for. If you want your typewriter to aid and not to hinder you in the development of typing power, see that it is well taken care of.

Dust and dirt, when allowed to collect on the mechanism of the typewriter, will cause difficulty. The carriage rods should be kept free from gummed matter. Rub the rods with an oiled cloth, but *do not attempt to oil the typewriter except under the direction of your teacher*. An excess of oil is likely to be as injurious as too little oil. Use an oiled cloth to clean the dust from the surface and from the mechanism of the typewriter. *Dust your typewriter daily*.

Dirty type produces unacceptable work. To clean the type, brush it carefully with a stiff brush. Use a forward and backward motion; do not brush the type from left to right. If certain letters are clogged, such as *e, o, a*, use a sharp splinter to dislodge the caked dirt. Benzene should be used cautiously, if at all. If it is used, place a blotter under all the type bars so that the excess fluid will be absorbed. There are special preparations for cleaning the type. If these are available, your teacher will instruct you in their use.

You have the responsibility of keeping your typewriter free from dust and dirt. Dust it each day. When it is not in use, keep it covered. Excellent care of your typewriter will be a good investment.

[45]

Exercise 76

DIRECTIONS: With pencil, number the words on the carbon copy made in Exercise 75. Type the word study in Exercise 75, but divide the list into two columns. Type the odd-numbered words in the left-hand column and the even-numbered words in the right-hand column. Omit the numbers from the typed copy.

Use the main heading and the subheading. Triple-space between the main heading and the subheading, and double-space between the subheading and the columns. Use double spacing for the columns. Study the Check List for Tabulation carefully and compare your figures with those given in the following analysis of this problem.

Type the exercise once without error.

Analysis of Problem

Vertical Placement

Total lines available		66
Lines required:		
By main heading		1
By space between main and secondary headings		2
By secondary heading		1
By space between secondary heading and columns		1
By columns (17 lines double-spaced)	33	38
Lines available for top and bottom margins		28

Lines available for top margin: $28 \div 2 = 14$.
Proof: $14 + 38 + 14 = 66$.

Horizontal Placement of Columns

Total spaces available		85
Spaces required:		
By longest line of first column		13
By longest line of second column	14	27
Total spaces to be used in margins and between columns		58

Spaces to be left in each margin and between columns: $58 \div 3 = 19$ (1 over).
Left marginal stop, 20.
Tabular stop for second column,
  $20 + 13 + 19 = 52$.

Proof: Spaces in left margin	20
Spaces in longest line of first column	13
Spaces between columns	19
Spaces in longest line of second column	14
Spaces in right margin	19
Total spaces	85

Horizontal Placement of Headings

Spaces required:	
By main heading (to be centered)	10
By secondary heading (to be centered)	15

Exercise 77

DIRECTIONS: Type the words of this exercise in a single column, centered as to top, side, and bottom margins. Use single spacing. Make one carbon. Carefully follow the tabulation check list in working out this problem.

After typing the words in a single column, rearrange and type them in two double-spaced columns. Use the same working plan as you did for Exercise 76.

top mar. for double space 15   *top mar. 14 single space = 8*

A STUDY OF WORDS

Expressions Written as One Word = 16

typewritten afternoon anything southwest steamship northeast

afterward percentage already moreover today tomorrow cannot

yourself everybody inasmuch somewhat itself whatever sometimes

notebook schoolhouse classroom twofold bookstore dressmaker

schoolboy workingman grandfather postscript overpaid oneself

[105]

LESSON 24

Attitudes to be Developed

Self-appraisal: Challenge yourself daily to do the best work of which you are capable.

Receptive mood for new work: Be willing, even eager, to attack new problems. Your attitude toward each new problem influences your success.

Recognition of the worth of the work being done: The drills and the exercises are organized so as to provide the skill development needed for continuous improvement; they should command your best effort. This is the daily challenge.

The habit of making careful analyses: Analyze all errors to discover the weaknesses in technique causing them; analyze your habits of work and improve them; analyze each typing problem before attempting to type it.

Accuracy and neatness: Cultivate the desire for accuracy and for neatness in your work. These attitudes will pay rich dividends.

Summary of Spacing Instructions

1. Space once after the comma and the semicolon; space once after the period when it is used with an abbreviation. Space once, also, after the exclamation point and the interrogation point when they are used *in the body of a sentence,* not at the end of a sentence.
2. All punctuation marks used at the end of sentences are followed by two spaces.
3. Space twice after the colon.
4. The dash is made by striking the hyphen twice, without spacing before or after.
5. At the end of a quotation, a period or a comma should precede the quotation mark.
6. A semicolon or a colon should follow the quotation mark.
7. *a.* In a quotation, a question or an exclamation mark should stand first if it applies to the quotation, not to the sentence containing the quotation.
   b. The quotation mark should stand first if the question or the exclamation mark applies to the sentence containing the quotation, not to the quotation.
8. A quotation within a quotation is enclosed in single quotation marks. Double quotation marks are placed with relation to other punctuation marks as follows:

   ```
   He said, "The title of the article is 'The Inner Urge.'"
   He said, "Is the title of the article 'The Inner Urge'?"
   ```

9. When a quotation consists of several paragraphs, a quotation mark should be placed at the beginning of each paragraph and at the end of the quotation.
10. When referring to articles and books, it is customary to place in quotations the titles of articles and to underscore or type in all capitals the titles of books. In writing the name of a newspaper or of a periodical, the *The* limiting the noun of the title should not be capitalized or italicized, even if it is part of the title.

Review Practice 24

DIRECTIONS: Set the marginal stops for a sixty-space line. Center the drill vertically. Triple-space after typing the heading. Type each line twice with single spacing. Double-space after the second typing of each line.

```
I have not read "Conquest"; I have, however, read "The Goads."

He said, "Is this good work?"  Did he say, "This is good work"?

Mr. Jackson wrote, "I have not yet read 'The Inner Urge.'"

I have the book Jalna, but not the article, "Our Chief."

In his report, his U's were like V's and his 2's like Z's.
```

[44]

Exercise 78

DIRECTIONS: Type the words of this exercise in a single column, centered as to top, side, and bottom margins. Use single spacing. Double-space before and after each of the two subheadings. Make one carbon copy. Carefully follow the tabulation check list in working out this problem.

A STUDY OF WORDS

Hyphenated Expressions

```
half-hearted ninety-three one-half law-abiding out-and-out first-class
three-fourths bird's-eye co-author ready-made horse-power man-of-war
up-to-date gilt-edged heel-and-toe take-off high-grade feeble-minded
self-reliance left-hand
```

Expressions Written as Separate Words

```
bills of lading  inasmuch as  notary public  one's self  post office
drug store  post card  all right  San Francisco  per annum  per diem
no one  per cent  parcel post  any other  en route
```

Exercise 79

DIRECTIONS: Type each group of words in Exercise 78 in two columns. Use double spacing. Carefully follow the same working plan as that used in Exercise 76.

Exercise 80

DIRECTIONS: Make one carbon copy. Type this exercise in two columns. Type the abbreviations in one column and the words in another column, opposite the abbreviations. Center the columns as to top, side, and bottom margins. Triple space between the heading and the columns. Use single spacing for the columns. Carefully follow the tabulation check list in working out this problem.

After typing the abbreviations and words in two columns, rearrange and type them in four columns. Use double spacing. Use the same working plan as that you used in Exercise 76.

ABBREVIATIONS

acct.	account	assoc.	associate
asst.	assistant	atty.	attorney
A.M.	Master of Arts	avdp.	avoirdupois
bal.	balance	bbl.	barrel
B.A.	Bachelor of Arts	B/L	bill of lading
B/S	bill of sale	Bldg.	Building
Blvd.	Boulevard	C.O.D.	collect on delivery
c/o	in care of	c/c	carbon copy
Cr.	credit	cwt.	hundredweight
Dr.	debtor or Doctor	f.o.b.	free on board
ft.	foot or feet	gal.	gallon or gallons
h-p.	horse-power	in.	inch or inches
Jr.	Junior	kw.	kilowatt
Ltd.	Limited	M.D.	Doctor of Medicine
memo.	memorandum	mfg.	manufacturing
Mgr.	Manager	P.S.	postscript
SE.	southeast	S.S.	Steamship
SW.	southwest	treas.	treasurer
vs.	versus (against)	viz.	namely
vol.	volume	wt.	weight

LESSON 23
Characters Not on the Keyboard, Manipulation Drill

Multiplication sign: x $4 \times 16 = 64$
Use the small *x* with, or without, space before and after. Either form is correct. This sign is also used for *by* as in *6 x 2*.

Minus sign: — $28 - 5 = 23$
Strike the hyphen; space before and after.

Caret: ⌐/   they think/is
Type an underscore under the last letter of the word before the caret; then strike the fractional mark (the diagonal).

Review Practice 23

DIRECTIONS: Set the marginal stops for a sixty-space line. Center the drill vertically. Triple-space after typing the heading. Type each line twice with single spacing. Double-space after the second typing of each line.

The sum of $51.38 and $73.46 and $14.15 is $138.99.

This is the problem: 12 x 13 ÷ 3 + 109 — 59 = 102.

li oo iv ly st op es oe ro ip oa tr ce ni os ic mo pa ge ys

live poor stop only goes road trip nice most page says week

He lives best who lives for others most; a sure reward is his!

Exercise 23

DIRECTIONS: Set the marginal stops for a sixty-space line. Use an indentation of five spaces. Type the exercise, centered vertically, once to a page. Triple-space after typing the heading. Use double spacing for the paragraph. Type the exercise twice.

	STROKES
Many great things have been done in the past few years.	58
Lindbergh flew over the ocean, Byrd charted the South Pole	121
regions, Eckener circled the globe in the Graf Zeppelin. These	188
are events to quicken the thoughts of everyone. All of these	251
feats required high courage mixed with fine judgment; they	310
called for trained men and strong machines. Each man made use	374
of the great power of the machines of today; yet the man and	435
not the machine is now acclaimed by the world. We still yell	498
ourselves hoarse for the man. The man counts when he can com-	562
mand a machine and control himself.	597

Syllable intensity, 1.27

Optional Exercise 23

	STROKES
As a nation, we think and talk in large terms. We have	59
too much cash, too many goods, too much raw material, and too	121
much service. Surplus usually means loss to some one, for it	184
is more than enough for the needs of a people; too much of any-	248
thing quite naturally means waste. With all of our surplus	309
resources, there is one resource of which we have less than	369
our fair share: we have a surplus of man power but not enough	433
soul power. Thus are we poor, indeed! When we realize that	498
we can develop our soul power to its maximum just as we have	559
developed our man power, then shall we be rich, indeed.	614

Syllable intensity, 1.28

[43]

BUDGET XI
Sentence Practice

DIRECTIONS: Use a different sentence in each practice period. Type the sentence five times. Set the marginal stops for a seventy-space line. Use double spacing.

STROKES FOR
EACH SENTENCE

The sum of 59 and 64 and 38 and 20 and 72 and 18 and 46 and 97 is 414.	71
The asterisk (*) is frequently used to indicate a footnote reference.	71
The special symbols ¢ and @ are not frequently used in ordinary work.	71
What is the sum of 219, 364, 582, 736, 607, 925, 180, 347, and 1,587?	71
We enclose a check for $496.37 in payment of your bill #580 of May 12.	74

Corrective Drill Paragraphs

DIRECTIONS: Set the marginal stops for a seventy-space line. Adjust the tabular stop for a five-space indentation. Use single spacing. Type one corrective drill paragraph in each practice period. Alternate the paragraphs in the various practice periods.

k key Knowledge is knowing. A keen desire for knowledge kindles a kindred zest in others. Just to have knowledge of many things and books, marks one as being progressive and keeps one quite well informed on things that are existing around him. "If a man knows not and knows not that he knows not, he is a fool—avoid him. If a man knows not and knows that he knows not, he is ignorant—teach him. If a man knows and knows not that he knows, he is asleep—awake him. If a man knows and knows that he knows, he is a leader—follow him."

l key The psychology of laughter is peculiar. Is it physical or emotional in nature? All have heard the expression, "I nearly died laughing." Ripley tells us that this expression was evolved from overzealous Orientals who delighted in literally tickling their victims to death. Certainly we have seen people slip quickly on a banana peeling. How the public laughs, even though the fall may prove fatal! Since we unjustly laugh in high glee at such an episode, laughter must be physical rather than emotional in nature.

Five-Minute Timed Writing Practice

DIRECTIONS: Set the marginal stops for a seventy-space line. Adjust the tabular stop for an indentation of five spaces. Use double spacing.

STROKES

The trend in business seems to be toward more and bigger mergers. The	74
call of business seems to be for more varied intelligence and less specialized	153
skill. Business seems to seek men and women who can bring to the work	225
some ripeness of thought and of judgment and the power to cope with busi-	299
ness complexity. Now, as in the past, there is a need for some workers who	376
will be content to stay in the low level positions. Now, as in the past, there	457
is need for some stenographers and bookkeepers. Business needs this help,	533
but the business need is not equal to the number being trained for such work.	611
Now, and even more so in the business world of tomorrow, the need for clear	688
thinkers must be met by those who wish to build lasting success.	751

Syllable intensity, 1.30

Exercise 81

DIRECTIONS: Type the following report in the tabulated form shown. Center the tabulation as to top, side, and bottom margins. Use triple spacing between the main heading and the first secondary heading, double spacing after the secondary headings, and single spacing in the body of the exercise. The period, followed by a space, is frequently used as a leader between widely spaced columns.

LESSON 22
Characters Not on the Keyboard, Manipulation Drill

Division sign: ÷ Strike the colon, back-space, and strike the hyphen.

Equal sign: = Strike the hyphen, back-space, turn the cylinder forward slightly (or depress the shift key slightly), and strike the hyphen again.

Algebraic terms: $(x + y)^3$ When there are several terms, type the letters and symbols first and fill in the exponents later. To place the exponent, turn the cylinder back (toward you) slightly.

Review Practice 22

DIRECTIONS: Set the marginal stops for a sixty-space line. Center the drill vertically. Triple-space after typing the heading. Type each line twice with single spacing. Double-space after the second typing of each line.

The sum of 58 and 360 ÷ 2 + 94 ÷ 3 + 107 = 208.

ir su ti am le sa id il fo rm vi el ur ma rt pl ti wh kn ca

some mail form left then view else talk went four said part

made file plan time what wire knew such near down fire hope

call days fact half must sale used wife same came deal fair

Exercise 22

DIRECTIONS: Set the marginal stops for a sixty-space line. Use an indentation of five spaces. Type the exercise, centered vertically, once to a page. Triple-space after typing the heading. Use double spacing for the paragraph. Type the exercise twice.

	STROKES
There are greater things possible for each of us than we	59
have yet realized, but we do not seem to know how to possess	120
them. We can widen the scope of our usefulness and enlarge	181
the range of our influence, yet we fill our days with little	242
duties. There is exquisite music, but we do not know how to	304
enjoy it; there are lovely things to see each day, but our	363
eyes are blind. This is all wrong. We should rise in the	424
power that is ours and resist the thought which would limit	484
our achievement to the trivial or the unenduring!	535

Syllable intensity, 1.28

Optional Exercise 22

	STROKES
All of us have problems to solve. This we can do just	58
where we are. Some have solved their problems in a fiery	117
furnace of the public gaze; some, in a lion's den of opposi-	179
tion; some, in a wilderness of loneliness. Problems are on	240
every hand. Some come as a result of the failures of the	299
past; some are new opportunities of the present. We should	360
forget past failures and make plans for "from now on." We	422
should expect much of ourselves, just as we should give much	483
to others. The question is not, "How much will I get?" but,	550
rather, "How much can I give?"	585

Syllable intensity, 1.30

UNIVERSAL STEEL COMPANY
Record of Iron Ore Shipment, 1932

Month	Tons
January	6,262
February	6,508
March	1,991
April	8,691
May	6,337
June	8,476
July	4,810
August	4,088
September	8,454
October	3,079
November	3,068
December	4,170

Exercise 82

DIRECTIONS: Type the following report. Use double spacing with triple spacing between the main heading and the column headings.

NUMBER OF EMPLOYEES
and
AMOUNT OF ANNUAL PAY ROLL

Year	Employees	Pay Roll
1926	48,877	$79,317,972
1927	42,801	72,855,061
1928	41,509	73,761,145
1929	49,985	88,303,365
1930	43,827	81,921,432
1931	31,276	55,980,470
1932	25,385	40,217,386

Exercise 83

DIRECTIONS: Fifty-space line; modified block form with closing lines indented to the position for the complimentary close and blocked in that position; eight single spaces between the date and the inside address; single spacing; open punctuation. Tabulate the report given in the letter, leaving a double space before and after the tabulation. All indented quoted matter of this kind should be single spaced. Observe that the letter in this exercise is the same as Style Letter No. 13 on page 109. This letter should be arranged in exactly the same form.

Determine the horizontal placement of the quoted matter in the following manner: Subtract the total number of spaces in the longest lines of both columns from the number of spaces in the letter line. Divide the difference by one more than the number of columns to be tabulated. The result represents the number of spaces to be left in the left and right indentations and between the two columns.

Horizontal Placement of Quoted Matter

Total spaces in the letter line 50
Spaces required:
  By longest line of first column 9
  By longest line of second column 5 14
Total spaces to be used for left and right indentations and between the two columns 36
Spaces to be indented on the left and the right, and to be left between the two columns: $36 \div 3 = 12$.

LESSON 21
Characters Not on the Keyboard, Manipulation Drill

Degree symbol: 12° To place the degree symbol, turn the left cylinder knob (No. 30) back (toward you) slightly; hold it with the left hand; strike the small *o*; then return the cylinder to the line position.

Chemistry symbols: H_2SO_4 Type the capitals, leaving space for the exponents; then back-space to the position for the first exponent, turn the cylinder slightly forward (away from you), and type the exponent.

Plus sign: + Lock the shift key, turn the left cylinder knob back (toward you) approximately half the line space, strike the underscore, and return the cylinder to its line position. Back-space, and strike the apostrophe. The apostrophe should meet the upper side of the underscore. Back-space, turn the left cylinder knob forward (away from you) approximately half the line space, and strike the apostrophe.

Review Practice 21

DIRECTIONS: Set the marginal stops for a sixty-space line. Center the drill vertically. Triple-space after typing the heading. Use single spacing. Type each line twice with single spacing. Double-space after the second typing of each line.

Water begins to freeze at 32° Fahrenheit or at 0° centigrade.

The sum of 74 + 16 + 83 is 173. Fine! That is correct.

ot wn ru ow cu ay wi of me an to ye ba en fi ey it ad in wa

add lot age own ago war low run got cut day win are say off

met any see too yes bad yet end few hot far fit its eye ten

Exercise 21

DIRECTIONS: Set the marginal stops for a sixty-space line. Use an indentation of five spaces. Type the exercise, centered vertically, once to a page. Triple-space after typing the heading. Use double spacing for the paragraph. Type the exercise twice.

STROKES

Goals may be worthy or otherwise; they may be difficult	58
to attain, or just within reach. To set up a scholastic goal	121
for yourself means that you have decided what you want your	181
daily school experience to give you. Your goal should set a	243
high standard for daily work and thought; it should lead you	304
to live upon the highest level of which you are capable. If	366
your goal has not been set, set it quickly; then hold your	425
gaze on it until you reach it. Win out; don't lose out!	485

Syllable intensity, 1.27

Optional Exercise 21

STROKES

One of the greatest wastes in the world is in the lives	58
that are not made meaningful because of lack of right motiva-	120
tion. A piece of work is eagerly begun but just as quickly	181
laid by; the worker does not stick to it until it is finished.	244
Whose fault is it? Can we fix the blame? Many fail in busi-	311
ness because of wrong habits set up while in school. It is	372
hard to get students to realize this fact. In business, the	434
worker must be self-motivated; in school, the student too	492
often looks to the teacher for guidance. Thus failure comes!	556

Syllable intensity, 1.29

Left marginal stop, 18.

Tabular stop for first column: $18 + 12 = 30$.

Tabular stop for second column: $30 + 9 + 12 = 51$.

Proof: Spaces in left indentation 12

Spaces in longest line of first column   9

Spaces between two columns 12

Spaces in longest line of second

column 5

Spaces in right indentation 12

Total spaces in letter line 50

Mr. Thomas Price The Justice Service Bureau 26 Walnut Street Philadelphia, Pa. Dear Sir: In reply to your recent inquiry in regard to the number of employees enrolled at our Carlton Plant, I submit the following report for the four months ending on September 30, 193–:

June	1,043
July	1,267
August	1,298
September	1,375

We shall be glad to be of any further service you may desire. Yours truly CARLTON MANUFACTURING COMPANY R. F. Bartlett *(310–53)*

Style Letter No. 13—Modified Block Form of Letter Containing Tabulated Report

Exercise 84

DIRECTIONS: Arrange the following report in two columns, using *Book* and *Author* as column headings. Double-space. Do not type the punctuation marks between the various names.

BOOKS OF INTEREST TO A STUDENT

Education of a Princess, Marie, Grand Duchess of Russia; Cyrano de Bergerac, Edmond Rostand; Ropers Row, Warwick Deeping; The Return of the Native, Thomas Hardy; Of Human Bondage, W. Somerset Maugham; Sorrel and Son, Warwick Deeping; Jalna, Mazo de la Roche; The Good Earth, Pearl S. Buck; East Wind, West Wind, Pearl S. Buck; Eroica, S. Chotzinoff

Exercise 85

DIRECTIONS: Fifty-space line; modified block form with five-space paragraph indentations; eight single spaces between the date and the inside address; single spacing; open punctuation.

Mr. J. H. Fields Purchasing Agent, Hopwood Mills Reading, Pennsylvania Dear Sir: We enclose our formal quotation, covering prices on three sizes of cases, which you requested in your letter of the twelfth. (P) In submitting this quotation, we wish to call your attention to the fact that, on account of fixed machine set-up costs, prices of corrugated boxes vary inversely according to the quantities to be run. We have quoted prices on lots of 75 and 50. Should you find it possible to increase your order to 75 of each size, the quoted prices will apply. Very truly yours D. A. HARPER BOX COMPANY (Dictated by D. A. Harper) President Enclosure *(481–84)*

LESSON 20
Characters Not on the Keyboard, Manipulation Drill

Exclamation point: ! The exclamation point is made by the use of two regular keyboard characters, the apostrophe (') and the period (.). Shift with the left hand, hold the space bar down with the left thumb, and strike the apostrophe (') and then the period (.) *before releasing either the space bar or the shift key.* Space twice after the exclamation point.

NOTE: Most typewriters complete the space movement when the space bar is released, not when it is depressed. If your typewriter makes the movement when you depress the space bar, strike the period, back-space, and then strike the apostrophe.

Review Practice 20

DIRECTIONS: Set the marginal stops for a sixty-space line. Center the drill vertically. Triple-space after typing the heading. Type each line twice with single spacing. Double-space after the second typing of each line.

(Shift drill)
May, Larry, Paul, and Harry will go to Maryland in January.

You must think! You must act! Then you will be a real man!

On Order #347, dated May 9, car #296,581 has been shipped.

act now but all who fun ask beg boy one has can why let man

kept give each once play size next want wish told both case

Exercise 20

DIRECTIONS: Set the marginal stops for a sixty-space line. Use an indentation of five spaces. Type the exercise, centered vertically, once to a page. Triple-space after typing the heading. Use double spacing for the paragraph. Type the exercise twice.

STROKES

    If I were in school once more, I think that I should know   63
how to make better use of the abilities I have. I should not   127
care about measuring my achievement against that of my fellow   189
students; I should try to measure my achievement by my capacity. 255
I might not excel in quantity of work--I would excel in my zeal   321
and in my joy in my work. What others have done I, too, can   384
do! More, what others have not done I may yet do if I work   449
to my full strength!   471

Syllable intensity, 1.26

Optional Exercise 20

STROKES

    You and I have written the story of our lives up to now.   60
The records are so written that all who wish may read. They   123
are to be found in our habits of work and our attitudes of   182
mind. We cannot escape the results of our days of half-hearted 247
effort, nor can we quickly put aside the outcomes of careless   309
living. These defeats, though, need not rob us of the final   371
joy of achieving. We can use past experience as a guide for   433
the future. An hour of wise thinking is worth far more than   495
a dozen hours of gloomy muddling!   530

Syllable intensity, 1.28

[40]

DIRECTIONS: Triple-space between QUOTATION SHEET and To Hopwood Mills; double-space throughout the remainder of the exercise. Center the exercise vertically and horizontally.

To prevent the insertion of figures, do not space between the dollar sign ($) and the following figure.

QUOTATION SHEET

To Hopwood Mills

Size	Quantity	Price per M
16x10x18	75	$78.00
ditto	50	96.00
16x10x24	75	92.00
ditto	50	109.00
16x10x30	75	105.00
ditto	50	122.00

D. A. HARPER BOX COMPANY

Current date

BUDGET XII
Sentence Practice

DIRECTIONS: Use a different sentence in each practice period. Type the sentence five times. Set the marginal stops for a seventy-space line. Use double spacing.

STROKES FOR EACH SENTENCE

The sum of 76 and 28 and 39 and 63 and 40 and 95 and 57 and 81 is 479. — 71

The Loew's 6% $1,000 bond (Series B) will be due on February 25, 1940. — 80

Do you type the asterisk (*) and the diagonal (/) without hesitating? — 74

The order from Barr & Co. reads: "Ship 18¼ dozen #37-A @ 95¢ each." — 80

"To thine own self be true" is a quotation from Shakespeare's Hamlet. — 84

Corrective Drill Paragraphs

DIRECTIONS: Set the marginal stops for a seventy-space line. Adjust the tabular stop for a five-space indentation. Use single spacing. Type one corrective drill paragraph in each practice period. Alternate the paragraphs in the various practice periods.

m key   Many improvements have been made in this year's model of Mammoth motors. More miles on much less gasoline makes the demand for them very great. Smooth power makes it quite easy to move through traffic zones. Mammoth motors have just about three times as much power as most common kinds of cars. Many mechanics remark that motors must now meet more exacting demands and that Mammoth motors meet all the demands of the most exacting driver.

n key   Never neglect to do anything that will insure a happy conclusion for whatever you undertake. First, summarize the entire situation. Second, find or acquire the skills and the instruments you need. Third, enter the work with the determination to finish it. Fourth, and last, try to make the work as interesting and entertaining as you can. Be willing to expend the necessary time and energy in following every source of information bearing on your problem. You will find a just satisfaction in work done to the best of your ability.

LESSON 19

Technique Guide: Inspect the completed page to determine your weak controls. Light and dark letters dotting the page are evidence of unequal stroking power. Consciously strive to equalize the power behind all strokes. Direct the blow to the center of the key; release the key quickly. The letters *q*, *a*, *z*, *x*, and *s* for the left hand, and the letters *p*, *l*, and *o* for the right hand, will need frequent drill in the development of the same easy yet definite control that you use with other keys.

Accuracy must be stressed at all times—accuracy in spelling, in punctuation, and in arrangement. Twenty words or more can be written by the skillful typist in the time it takes to make a single erasure. Be accurate in your work. Erasing is not permitted.

Review Practice 19

DIRECTIONS: Set the marginal stops for a sixty-space line. Center the drill vertically. Triple-space after typing the heading. Type each line twice with single spacing. Double-space after the second typing of each line.

NOTE: After typing the last line of this drill, remove the paper, reinsert, gauge, and type over the line. This reviews the manipulation drill given on page 34.

12 121 38 384 59 590 16 165 71 710, #9 #3; 3/4 or $\frac{3}{4}$, 1/4 or $\frac{1}{4}$

Are the Scott & Ward $1,000, 5½% bonds (Series B) due in 1956?

Use of special symbols: * for footnotes; ¢ and @ in invoices.

quit sold next quiz sale zeal next quit zone next lose quiz

It is well to think well; it is divine to act well.--Mann

Exercise 19

DIRECTIONS: Set the marginal stops for a sixty-space line. Use an indentation of five spaces. Type the exercise, centered vertically, once to a page. Triple-space after typing the heading. Use double spacing for the paragraph. Type the exercise twice.

PLACING OF QUOTATION MARKS: A period or a comma should precede the quotation mark. A semicolon or a colon should follow the quotation mark.

	STROKES
The young worker must "begin on the lowest rung of the	58
ladder of success"; he must start "from the ground and work	120
up." Working up is better than sliding down; it may not give	184
quick success, but it will bring lasting success. It is well	247
to realize that our position in life is what we make it; as	307
soon as we learn our life-lessons on one level, we take the	367
next step upward on our journey. Thus progress comes.	422

Syllable intensity, 1.25

Optional Exercise 19

	STROKES
There are tricks in all trades, people say, but the best	59
trick of all is the trick of working to capacity, of making	119
small capital pay large dividends. This we do through the	179
zeal with which we work, as much as through our native ability.	243
It is said that we are born with our full quota of what the	304
world calls "native ability"; this we cannot greatly increase.	369
We can, though, excel in the use of this ability. More and	431
more we will be judged in terms of what we do with what we	490
have.	495

Syllable intensity, 1.27

Five-Minute Timed Writing Practice

DIRECTIONS: Set the marginal stops for a seventy-space line. Adjust the tabular stop for an indentation of five spaces. Use double spacing.

STROKES

Just as the marble has within it a statue, as the acorn has within it the	76
strength of the oak, so every man has within him the power to do big things	152
if he is willing to discipline himself in the accomplishment of a worth-while	230
piece of work. No man can be greater than he longs to be. No man can	303
give what he has not acquired. No man can express what he has not real-	377
ized. It is in the thinking that one achieves greatness. It is in the choosing	460
between the right and the wrong, between the low and the high, between	531
the good and the best, that one gives the measure of his own stability.	603
There is something wrong with a nature that would rather live in the base-	679
ment than on the rooftop. There is something wrong with a person who pre-	755
fers the dampness to the sunshine. There is something wrong, too, with the	832
unemployed who prefers idleness to the effective use of his time.	897

Syllable intensity, 1.30

Exercise 86

DIRECTIONS: Fifty-space line; modified block form with closing lines indented to the position for the complimentary close and blocked in that position; seven single spaces between the date and the inside address; single spacing; open punctuation. Tabulate the report given in the letter according to the directions for Exercise 83. Observe that the letter in this exercise is the same as that illustrated at the right. This letter should be arranged in exactly the same form.

Mrs. H. C. Patterson 708 Highland Avenue Pittsburgh, Pa. Dear Mrs. Patterson: We have received the lace cloth and scarf that you returned, but we regret we are unable to furnish another scarf in the particular length you desire. The scarfs nearest in size to the one desired are:

18 x 36	. . . . . .	$4.50
18 x 45	. . . . . .	5.75
18 x 72	. . . . . .	8.65

If you are interested in any of these, we shall be very glad to hear from you. A telephone call from you giving the size of scarf which you can use is all that is necessary. Delivery will be made without delay. Very truly yours, McCreery and Company (Dictated by Nora B. Kane) Personal Service Shopper *(505–91)*

Style Letter No. 14—Modified Block Form of Letter Containing Tabulated Report with Leaders

The company signature is typed in small letters because of the use of the small *c* in *McCreery.*

Exercise 87

DIRECTIONS: Type the following report in the form shown. In determining the placement, follow the steps given in the Check List for Tabulation, page 102. Use double spacing.

NOTE: Per cent should be written as two words without the period. The symbol % is used with figures in tabulated material.

LESSON 18

Technique Guide: Typing practice which is self-motivated is productive of better results than practice which is imposed by classroom procedure. You must learn to be your most severe critic; hold yourself to your best work at all times. Nothing less than the work of your best effort should be acceptable to you. Appraise yourself daily; appraise the sincerity of your effort as well as the worth of your production.

Review Practice 18

DIRECTIONS: Set the marginal stops for a sixty-space line. Center the drill vertically. Triple-space after typing the heading. Type each line twice with single spacing. Double-space after the second typing of each line.

NOTE: The second line of the following drill gives practice on the accurate and quick stroking of the space bar.

```
31 40 26 58 67 92 10 19 #3 $4 5% 6½ 4¼ 9¾ 6¼% 5/8 2/3 $4.50

r z u / v q m p t x y . b w n o g a h ; e s i l c d , k f j
```

(Shift drill.)
```
April Spend Spent Speak Apply April Speak Apply Spent April

Joe saw old Mr. May pay him the fee due him for the law job.

That club will keep your cash from this date till next June.
```

Exercise 18

DIRECTIONS: Set the marginal stops for a sixty-space line. Use an indentation of five spaces. Type the exercise, centered vertically, once to a page. Triple-space after typing the heading. Use double spacing for the paragraph. Type the exercise twice.

STROKES

```
    Most of us are cheaters.  We fill our days with a lot of      60

small tasks and put off the big ones.  A big task faces us;      121

"Just let it go until tomorrow," we say.  At the last minute,    187

then, we rush it through, with a sigh of relief when it is       246

done--even though it is done not quite so well as we had         303

expected to do it.  Yes, we cheat ourselves by not utilizing     365

to the fullest every hour of every day.                          404
```
Syllable intensity, 1.24

Optional Exercise 18

STROKES

```
    It is well to realize that nothing worth while is ever       57
had for nothing.  We pay for everything we get.  For skill,      119
we pay with our effort and with our sincerity.  For failure,    181
we pay with our unhappiness and with our sense of futility.     241
We can always be quite certain that the price we pay will be    303
in exact ratio to the worth of that which we get.  Nature is    365
just; we get what we pay for--no more, and no less.             416
```
Syllable intensity, 1.26

[38]

THOMPSON STEEL COMPANY

Per Cent of Steel Produced to Rated Capacity

	1931	1930	1929
First Quarter	75.3%	79.8%	79.6%
Second Quarter	63.2%	75.6%	82.5%
Third Quarter	56.7%	69.3%	82.3%
Fourth Quarter	57.3%	69.5%	83.7%

Exercise 88

DIRECTIONS: Type the following report in tabulated form in four columns. Use double spacing. Do not type the punctuation mark between the year and the amount, or the amount and the year.

INVENTORIES
Fiscal Years of 1923 to 1932

1923, $68,971,104; 1924, $80,863,048; 1925, $73,143,213; 1926, $79,242,098;
1927, $72,545,951; 1928, $61,473,416; 1929, $56,585,346; 1930, $66,376,402; 1931,
$49,096,162; 1932, $44,180,682

Exercise 89

DIRECTIONS: Type the following in the tabulated form shown. Use double spacing.

AREA AND POPULATION OF CONTINENTS

Continent	Square Miles	Population
North America	9,355,000	164,715,000
South America	7,464,900	78,955,000
Europe	3,668,000	476,822,000
Asia	16,785,400	1,048,413,000
Australia	2,974,540	6,168,000
Africa	11,660,000	134,097,000
Antarctic	5,000,000	Not given

Exercise 90

DIRECTIONS: Type the following report in three columns. Use double spacing. Type Reports on Vocational Conferences of 1932 as the main heading, Peabody High School, Pittsburgh, Pennsylvania, as the secondary heading, and Subject, Speaker, and Reporter as the column headings.

Architecture, Mr. Edward B. Lee, Victoria Kachioris; Art, Mr. Robert Kennedy, Helen Dancison; Aviation, Mr. Karl E. Voelter, Ellen Monaghan; Banking, Mr. W. W. Richards, Bella Fox; Ccmptometer, Miss Catharine Deer, Ruth O'Malley; Electrical Engineering, Mr. William R. Work, Margaret Moore; General Art, Miss Mayna Eastmen, Dorothy Crooks; Home Economics, Miss Irene McDermott, Alice Rosner; Insurance, Mr. John R. Stevenson, Florence McClurg; Investments, Mr. Henry B. Bassett, Ellen Monaghan; Medicine, Dr. B. Z. Cashman, Alice Rosner; Music, Mr. Charles N. Boyd; Helen Fritz; Nursing, Miss Gertrude Sutherland, Regina Klinvex; Printing, Mr. Chalmers Siviter, Martha Fuller; Social Service, Miss Helen Hart, Irene Freinstein; Stage as a Career, Mr. Elmer Kenyon, Minnie Reichman; Teacher Training, Mr. Herbert L. Spencer, Yetta Bronstein

LESSON 17

Technique Guide: Curve the fingers and lift the hands from the keyboard; then lower the hands until the fingers barely establish contact with their home keys. Improved stroking will come as a result of holding the fingers above the keys instead of letting them rest on the keys.

All awkwardness of stroking must be overcome through the improved control of each finger. Develop a quick, decisive, well-controlled snatch stroke. Direct the finger to the center of the key. When the stroke has been given, release the key immediately.

Review Practice 17

DIRECTIONS: Set the marginal stops for a sixty-space line. Center the drill vertically. Triple-space after typing the heading. Type each line twice with single spacing. Double-space after the second typing of each line.

```
4f$f 0;); 2s"s 6j_j 5f%f 91(l 3d#d 7j&j 8k'k 2s"s -;*; /;¾;

it is, to be; if it is to be; he is to go; is he to go in it?

Lax six wax box was mix six fix put map sip lap cap dip cup

Size open look gaze quit haze love come zone zinc size quit

Jim did not try the new red car the men had out for his use.
```

Exercise 17

DIRECTIONS: Set the marginal stops for a sixty-space line. Use an indentation of five spaces. Type the exercise, centered vertically, once to a page. Triple-space after typing the heading. Use double spacing for the paragraph. Type the exercise twice.

STROKES

```
     "Behold, now is the accepted time," was the cry of a man     61

writing long years ago.  It was true then; it is just as true    124

now.  This is the day for you to do things--not next week or      186

next year.  Nothing will paralyze effort and retard success      247

quite so much as the habit of putting things off until a later   310

time.  Do now that which needs to be done and do it the very     372

best you can.                                                    385
```

Syllable intensity, 1.23

Optional Exercise 17

STROKES

```
     Few of us work to capacity even for one hour out of each     59
day.  On every hand the lament is heard that there isn't time    123
enough in which to do all the things that must be done.  We      184
skim a little here, trim a little there, evade, pretend, bluff,  248
just muddle through--this seems to be the temper of the times.   311
A great hurry has seized us.  We have an excess of motion but    375
not quite enough sense of direction.                            411
```

Syllable intensity, 1.25

[37]

THE DEVELOPMENT OF SPEED

Speed without accuracy has only a limited value in the business world. All effort directed toward attaining greater speed must be secondary to the fundamental requirement of accuracy. Accuracy is the result of correct technique in machine manipulation and in finger control. More than that, accuracy in typewriting is the result of accurately *seeing* letter sequences, definitely *thinking* words, and correctly *directing* every finger movement.

Establish a rhythmic control; develop the habit of writing continuously. As you write, try to increase the rhythm with which you type, the speed with which you return the carriage and start the next line of writing, and the ease with which you recognize words. Let your eyes grasp the entire word. In this way you will become prepared for the next step in the development of speed.

At the beginning of this word reaction, try to control only the short words as single-word stimuli. Gradually extend the process to longer words, and then begin the grouping of words into phrases.

In all this straight-copy practice, constantly try to improve your writing habits, to reduce to a minimum the awkwardness of hand movements, and to set up standards of correct writing to which you must strictly adhere at all times. Enter into competition with yourself. Today determine to do better work than you did yesterday. Make a definite check on all your habits of machine control, and learn your weak points and how to overcome them. Realize the power of hard work, intelligently planned and carefully completed. Keep faith in yourself in all you do; live up to the best that is within you, and success will be yours.

Phrase Drills

In drill practice you may experiment with the best rate of speed at which you can type with accuracy. You may push yourself for greater typing power. In the typing of an exercise or timed writing material, never type at your highest rate. Type well within the margin of your maximum speed in order that you may have a feeling of easy control.

DIRECTIONS: Set the marginal stops for a seventy-two-space line. Single-space. In each practice period use ten lines of the drills. Type each line twice. Double-space after the second typing of each line.

No. 1 (2-4)   *(Length of line, 71 spaces)*

```
at once to find in such to come he will of such to this of them to tell
of what to keep to look he does in your to work on hand to know as much
```

No. 2 (2-5)   *(Length of line, 71 spaces)*

```
in these he could at first of these in order we could by which to think
we shall if there we trust it would to place he would in reply in their
in which we would to which to write to bring of which to serve in favor
to learn at least to those no doubt to their to speak of their on which
```

No. 3 (3-4)   *(Length of line, 71 spaces)*

```
and that you will the time for that and will you want and have who have
you know and make you have few days you wish ten days may have has been
```

No. 4 (4-3)   *(Length of line, 71 spaces)*

```
with the have the will you that the have you will not from the this may
than the with its when the from our over the with our that are they had
upon the give you into the send you does not that you upon his they can
```

LESSON 16
Manipulation Drill

In this drill you are to fill in letters which have been omitted from a sentence. Use the same machine parts as those used in the preceding manipulation drill.

1. Insert a sheet of paper and type the following sentence exactly as given:

    There is no pri e too dear to pay for perfec ion.

2. Remove the paper. Reinsert it, accurately gauge the line horizontally and vertically, and fill in the letter *c* omitted from *price* and the letter *t* omitted from *perfection*.

Practice this drill several times. Repeat it in each of the next three lessons.

Review Practice 16

DIRECTIONS: Set the marginal stops for a sixty-space line. Center the drill vertically. Triple-space after typing the heading, *Review Practice 16*. Type each line twice with single spacing. Double-space after the second typing of each line.

NOTE: The first line of the following drill is a simple reach stroking drill.

gf hj qa p; za /; xs .l ws ol bf nj "s (l #d); $f _j &j 'k *;

1 8 3 183 4 2 9 429 1 5 6 156 7 0 1 701 3 6 9 369 5 8 0 580

re ho at or me nd he ou er th yo ha wi ve an is em ur te mu ar

How may our man get the red hat and the fur you had for her?

That will help them very much with this late fall farm work.

Exercise 16

DIRECTIONS: Set the marginal stops for a sixty-space line. Use an indentation of five spaces. Type the exercise, centered vertically, once to a page. Triple-space after typing the heading, *Exercise 16*. Use double spacing for the paragraph. Type the exercise twice.

STROKES

I know two young men who began their business life with — 58

what appeared to be equal chances for success. For a time it — 121

was a puzzle to me as to why one should move ahead and the — 180

other make no apparent progress. I then learned that one just — 244

made motions, while the other got rid of excess motions. One — 307

knew his goal and held to the work which led to that goal. — 365

Syllable intensity, 1.22

Optional Exercise 16

STROKES

All of us have the inner urge which can lift us out of — 57
life's routine. Too often we kill this urge, let the hands — 119
lie idle, while the mind grows dull. Just as the coral polyp — 182
builds on its dead self, so with success; each advance step — 242
quickens the vision and extends the scope of service. It is — 304
the zealous effort that succeeds; the urge to do educates. — 362

Syllable intensity, 1.25

No. 5 (4-4)

from this that this your name that they when they with that have made
with your this will last year with this will have more than from them
have been that will very glad they were very much they will this must

No. 6

for it who is can be let us may be let me and is for us and in she is
for these you could and their for their for which the whole you shall
this is will be that it what is must be with us send us that is from
that there from which they would your order five cents your favor

No. 7 (Shift Drill)

I am I can I will I could I shall I think I should I believe
I do I was I had I have I want I know I wish I can't I don't

No. 8

he cannot we regret in making we cannot he should we desire of course
we believe at present to receive as follows to believe to furnish
this morning your letter your account this matter five pounds
you cannot and brother and company you desire your attention

No. 9

this is the, if you can, it will be, at this time, in this case,
there will be, in this way, you will have, you will find, we are not,
we trust that, in this matter, we have not, at the time, as soon as,
it has been, in your letter, will you please, in order that, if it is
we shall be, if you wish, we should like, to have you, kindly let us,

No. 10

on the other hand, call your attention, we shall be pleased to have it
for some time, we should be glad, by return mail, if you do not know,
at the present time, in connection with this, under separate cover,
we shall take pleasure, will you please, on account of, in the future
we are sending you, in this country, we shall have, we wrote you that
we have been, we should be pleased, kindly let us know, as well as,
in addition to your, hear from you, should not be, thank you for,
we shall be glad, I should like to know, at this time, more or less,
we should be pleased, two or three, in the past few days, if you will

Exercise 15

DIRECTIONS: Set the marginal stops for a sixty-space line. Adjust the tabular stop for an indentation of five spaces. Type the exercise once to a sheet. Center the exercise vertically. Type the heading, *Exercise 15*. Triple-space after typing the heading. Use double spacing for the paragraph. Use a half sheet for each typing of each exercise in this Instructional Block. All exercises should be typed twice.

Each letter of the alphabet is used in each exercise of Instructional Block II.

Exercise 15

	STROKES
All of us must work. That is certain. The question is,	61
Just how shall we work? We can serve time at our tasks, doing	127
as little as we can to get by, and lazily drift into life's	188
group of failures; or we can face whatever we have to do with	250
faith that we can excel in doing it, and place ourselves in	310
life's group of winners.	335

Analysis of Vertical Centering

Lines Used				Therefore:	
Heading	1	Available lines	33	Top margin	9
Extra spaces	2	Lines used	14	Lines used	14
Paragraph	11	Top and bottom margins	19	Bottom margin	10
Total lines used	14	19 ÷ 2 = 9½			33

Syllable intensity, 1.21

Optional Exercise 15 *

	STROKES
There are some workers who make drudgery of all they do,	59
just as there are others who make glorious the doing of each	120
task. It is not in the work but in the mind of the worker that	185
these qualities inhere; it is the zeal with which he works and	248
not the kind of work he does that causes him to excel and that	311
lifts him above the level of the commonplace.	356

Syllable intensity, 1.23

* In typing an optional exercise, use the directions given for the preceding exercise.

Exercise 91

DIRECTIONS: Set the marginal stops for a seventy-space line. Adjust the tabular stop for an indentation of five spaces. Use double spacing. Type one paragraph of the following exercise once. After you have finished typing the paragraph, check your errors and choose from the corrective drills on pages 53 and 54 the drill which will help to eliminate your faulty technique. Just below the paragraph, type each line of the corrective drill at least twice. Under the direction of your teacher, the entire exercise will be used for timed writing practice.

NOTE: Each paragraph in the following exercises contains every letter of the alphabet and has a syllable intensity of 1.30.

OTHER FACTORS

Paragraph

STROKES

1   Ray had skill, he knew, yet each new position had lasted for just a few   73
weeks. Business was bad, each employer had said as he expressed regret that   151
Ray's services were no longer needed. The first time this happened, Ray took   233
it as a part of the necessary adjustment he had been told would come to each   310
beginner in business. The second experience caused him to puzzle over the   386
fact that others, who were quite as new to the world of business as he, were   463
kept working. He had skill, he knew, yet for the third time in six months he   542
had been told that business was so bad his services were no longer needed.   617
(617)

2   "I am out of a job again. What's wrong with me?" was his greeting when   695
he came into my office, from which he had so confidently gone six months   768
before. He wanted me to give him the key to the puzzle. I did not have that   848
key, but I thought that I knew where I could get it for him. No additional   928
information could be obtained from him. He had sufficient skill for his work,   1008
we both knew. Neither the leader nor the trailer in school, he had made a   1084
quite satisfactory record. His failure in business, then, was something apart   1164
from grades earned and courses completed. The key must be in the keeping   1239
of the men who had told him that his services were no longer needed. *(691)*   1308

3   The starting point of all preparation for business is to learn what the busi-   1387
ness man wants of the beginner. Is it skill? Does he expect machinelike   1464
precision and very little else? Ray knew he had enough skill for his work,   1542
yet three times he had failed as a beginning worker. In trying to answer the   1621
question as to why he had failed, I knew the starting point was the business   1699
men who had judged him a failure. They held the key which would, I hoped,   1776
unlock for him the door to new opportunities. I realized that the one needful   1856
thing for him was to see himself as these others had been seeing him. *(618)*   1926

4   The first man for whom Ray had worked saw him as a boy who lacked   1994
experience but who would doubtless grow into a capable office man. It was   2070
hard times in that business, which had caused Ray's release. I could not get   2151
the key that Ray needed from this man. The other two men for whom Ray   2225
had worked were more to the point. They saw him as a boy with skill but   2299
without the personal qualities which would make that skill effective. They   2376
spoke of "other factors" which he lacked. They suggested that skill is not   2455
enough for any worker; it is just the minimum equipment all men expect of   2529
all beginners in business. Each man emphasized the fact that to this mini-   2606
mum equipment must be added traits of character which make skill worth   2676
while. Here was the key Ray needed. *(789)*   2715

MAKING HABITS PERMANENT

The way in which habits of typing are initiated is important. Equally important, however, is the organized follow-up practice which will make those habits permanent. Each day of practice should show measurable improvement in typing skill. The way you practice is more important than how much you practice. Be orderly in your practice procedures and thoughtful in your interpretation of printed and oral instructions. Demonstrate improved skill each day.

LESSON 15
Manipulation Drill

You will often find it necessary to remove the paper from the typewriter before you have completed the work. This is a drill on reinserting the paper, accurately gauging the line, and completing the typing of the problem, when the paper has been removed before the completion of the work.

1. Insert a sheet of paper and type the following sentence:

He can who thinks he can.

Before throwing the carriage after typing the sentence, locate the line scale (No. 19). The top of the scale just touches the bottom of the letters. Move the carriage so that one of the white lines of the scale points to the letter *i* in the word *thinks*. Notice that this line points to the exact center of the letter *i*.

NOTE: Since typewriters may vary slightly, study the machine you are operating.

2. Remove the paper from the typewriter. Reinsert the paper. Gauge the line horizontally, and, through the use of the variable line spacer (No. 29), set the line so that the top of the line scale will just touch the bottom of the letters in the line typed.

See the note in the preceding paragraph.

3. Through the use of the paper release, move the paper to the left or right, as necessary, and gauge for the correct letter spacing by centering with the letter *i*.

4. Retype the sentence over the first writing. The second writing should print exactly over the first writing. Strike the keys lightly. If you have gauged the line and the letter spacing correctly, the retyping of the line should not show. Practice this drill several times. You will often need this skill.

Centering the Drill or the Exercise

Before beginning to type the drill or the exercise in each of the following lessons, determine the exact top and bottom margins to be used for the correct placement of the typed material on the page. Centering is thoroughly explained on pages 32 and 33.

The placement of the paper guide is very important in horizontal centering. Each day you should check the placement of the paper guide to see that it is accurate.

Review Practice 15

DIRECTIONS: Set the marginal stops for a sixty-space line. Center the drill vertically. Type the heading, *Review Practice 15*. Triple-space after typing the heading. Type each line of the drill twice with single spacing. Double-space after the second typing of each line. Use half sheets for typing each Review Practice.

```
4f$f  0;);  2s"s  6j_j  3d#d  9l(l  5f%f  8k'k  2s"s  7j&j  5f%f  -;*;

tf p;  za yj  bf /;  qa nj  ws mj  xs uj  ed .l  cd ol  rf ,k  vf ik

if he is to do so or we go by it as no us an of me at up am

She had him buy for her the big red box and the old fur set.

Mary gave them work just when they quit that ship last July.
```

5   What are these "other factors" which all beginning workers must have   2788
to make their skill worth while? It was the lack of these qualities which had   2869
caused Ray to fail. Business men seem to feel that Ray is not alone in his   2948
failure because of the lack of these traits. In finding for Ray the key to his   3030
own puzzling failures, I may give help to some other beginner who needs to   3106
unlock the door to new opportunities. The starting point must be what the   3182
business man wants—and he says that he wants workers who are accurate and   3257
careful. Tact and courtesy, too, must be ingrained traits. These four traits   3338
help one to get along with others. They are just a few of the "other factors"   3420
which make for success, but they offer an excellent beginning for the student   3498
who would train for success in business. *(824)*   3539

6   It is easy to name the traits of character which business men want all   3612
beginning workers to have. The hard part comes in trying to develop these   3688
personal qualities in those who are now preparing for business. Far too often   3768
the teacher talks about these traits, but the students do little to develop   3844
them. They seem to think that these traits will spring "full blown" when   3921
they need them. Many times this belief is the cause of failure, an experience   4001
which may cost far too much for the good it does. Until his services were   4077
no longer needed, Ray did not realize that he had just skill, not the right   4154
traits. This fact, then, was the key to his problem. *(670)*   4209

7   I handed Ray the key to his problem, but I could not solve that problem   4285
for him. I told him what the business men wanted in addition to his fine skill,   4367
but I could not give him those qualities. I hoped that I was sounding the   4445
bugle call to thought and action, for he had to make vigorous effort to save   4522
himself. I know that the demands of business are exacting. Skill is not   4598
enough; the "other factors" determine success or failure just as much as skill.   4680
This is the knowledge, the key, which will solve for Ray and for others the   4758
puzzle of failure in business. *(580)*   4789

Exercise 92

DIRECTIONS: Follow the directions given for Exercise 91, page 115.

OVERCOMING

8   "He that overcometh shall inherit." This is a promise which was made of   77
the things of the spirit, I know, but it applies just as surely to the world of   158
material things. The terms of the pledge are quite clear, and the reward is   236
sure. In order that we may gain the power to do big things, there must be   312
the conquest of many small things. Most of us expect to inherit without   386
effort, but the law does not work in that way. We cannot evade problems;   461
we cannot let inertia take the place of zeal to do. We must overcome if we   538
wish to inherit. *(555)*   555

9   There are many things to be surmounted if the work of each day is to be   629
done in such a way that there will be a sense of satisfaction when it is viewed   709
at the close of day. In typing, just for example, we can make a long list of   788
problems which must be solved if we wish to achieve our best skill. One of   865
the first problems to be faced is that of self-mastery. Control of self must   944
always precede control of machine, of conditions, or of office problems. We   1022
must rule self so that we can produce on an increasing quantity and accuracy   1099
scale. Great typists well know this fact. They realize that self-mastery wins   1181
contests. *(636)*   1191

Vertical Centering. To center vertically, count the lines required to type the drill or the exercise; subtract this number from the number of available writing lines (sixty-six for a full sheet, thirty-three for a half sheet); then divide by two to obtain the width of the top and bottom margins. If the result contains a fraction, let the extra line appear in the bottom margin.

Horizontal Centering. Horizontal centering is based on the longest line in the drill. The problem is to set the margins so that half of the letters and spaces in the line will be on each side of the center of the page. The center of the paper, when inserted, should be at the center of the carriage scale.

Rules for Horizontal Centering

(Understand all rules for centering; choose one to be used in your work.)

1. To center headings or lines, move the carriage so that the carriage-frame pointer is at the center of the paper, back-space once for each two letters or spaces in the line to be centered, and begin writing at the point where the back spacing is completed. Disregard fractions.

2. Count the number of letters and spaces in the line to be centered, divide by two, and subtract from the number representing the center of the paper. This gives the point at which the typing should begin. Disregard fractions.

3. Instead of counting the letters and spaces in the line to be centered, you can determine the spaces by setting the carriage-frame pointer at 0 and spacing through the line striking the space bar once for each letter and space in the line. The total spaces in the line will be indicated on the front scale by the carriage-frame indicator. Divide the total spaces by two and subtract from the number representing the center of the paper.

NOTE: If you are using an Underwood Typewriter, set the carriage-frame pointer at 0 and strike the space bar once for each letter and space in the line to be centered. The figure on the front red scale to which the carriage-frame indicator points will be the point on the white scale at which the carriage-frame indicator should be set for the beginning of the line to be typed.

DIRECTIONS: Use a half sheet for this drill. Center the drill vertically so that you will have equal top and bottom margins. Center each line of the drill horizontally. Use double spacing.

Carl van der Voort & Company

announces the removal of its offices to the

PLAZA BUILDING   .

on January 9

Analysis of Vertical Centering

Lines on half sheet, 8½ x 5½"		33
Lines to be used in typing drill		7
Lines to be divided between top and bottom margins		26
	26 ÷ 2 = 13	
Therefore: top margin, 13 lines		
bottom margin, 13 lines		
Proof: 13 + 13 + 7 = 33		

What would be the top and bottom margins for this same problem if it were typed on paper 8½ x 11"?

10   Business men say that the typist must be able to do a day's work judged   1265
by business standards. The size of the pay check will depend on how much,   1341
as well as how well, the typist can type. It is not always true that the cham-   1422
pion speed typist is the champion office worker. When other things are equal,   1502
though, he who has expert skill in typing will be able to command a better   1577
place in the business world than he who has just average skill. Nowhere is   1654
speed more needed than in business, but there must be accuracy with the   1726
speed. Business does not quickly forgive the one who fails to prove his own   1804
work. Right results count. All else is worthless. *(667)*   1858

11   I am puzzled when I see students work wildly to gain more speed in   1928
typing. They type faster and faster with no thought of right habits. The   2005
waste of uncontrolled speed seems not to worry them. I think speed is the   2081
outcome of exact typing habits. I know that frantic work seldom produces   2156
worthy outcomes. Most students know this to be true, yet they go on put-   2231
ting their faith in quantity rather than quality practice. If we wish to add to   2313
our speed in typing, we should type with less drive for speed. Controlled   2389
typing does not mean that we should write fewer words a minute; it means   2462
that we should get rid of the jerks in typing and keep the carriage move-   2536
ment constant and even. *(702)*   2560

12   Teachers say that it is not easy to get students to analyze and improve   2634
their technique to the point where they will always be able to type with con-   2712
trol. It may be that most students do not know just how to analyze their   2787
typing habits. Surely, all of us have the urge to do our best work at all   2863
times. There is that in each of us which makes us want to excel in whatever   2941
we do. It should not be hard, then, to interest each student in the work of   3019
building his typing skill on correct habits of copy-reading, on mastery of   3084
finger movement, and on the ability to hold thought firmly to the work that   3160
is being done. *(615)*   3175

13   Most students must overcome the tendency to type in jerks. This is one   3250
of the first hurdles they must surmount when they try to acquire typing skill.   3329
All students know that in typing it is a waste of time to lift the eyes from   3407
the line, but some will not work to get rid of this habit even when they know   3485
that it stands in the way of gaining the prize of expert skill. It is a waste of   3568
time to take timed test after timed test when no study is made of errors and   3645
no corrective drills are practiced. All students know that this is true, yet   3724
many fail to do the daily checking and listing of errors which such a study   3800
demands. Errors are overcome when remedial thinking precedes corrective   3874
drill practice. *(715)*   3890

14   Overcome wrong ways of typing and your skill will be greater, your joy   3963
in your work more lasting, and your work more in demand. Overcome wrong   4037
ways of thinking, and you will enrich your ability to serve and increase your   4115
power to achieve. The gauge of a man's greatness may be told in terms of   4191
what he overcomes. Each must judge for himself what must be overcome.   4263
The first question is "What?"; the next, "How?" Then, before corrective   4345
practice starts, comes the task of right thinking. It is a task worth a man's   4426
best thought. No price can be set on the prize which waits for him who will   4504
overcome. Power shall be his because "He that overcometh shall inherit."   4582
(692)

Review Practice 14

DIRECTIONS: Set the marginal stops for a sixty-space line. Have a top margin of one and a half inches. Use single spacing. Type each line twice. Double-space after the second typing of each line.

```
4f$f /;3/4; 5f%f 1/2;1/4; 3d#d ¢;@; 2s"s 1/2;1/4; 5f%f 6j_j 1/2;1/4; ¢;@;

"Happiness is not the end in life; character is."--Beecher

Ship car #259,537 on order #104; car #260,681, on #105.

Use the asterisk (*) for footnotes; the / for fractions.

The poor man will quickly mix a dozen jugs of black veneer.
```

Exercise 14

DIRECTIONS: Set the marginal stops for a sixty-space line. Adjust the tabular stop for a five-space indentation. Have a top margin of one and a half inches. Use double spacing. Type the exercise *once to a sheet*. If time permits, retype the exercise.

All letters of the alphabet are used in this paragraph.

	STROKES
There is a harvest time when all reap what they have	55
sown. This is just as true for you in the classroom as it	115
is for the man on the farm. Take learning to type, for ex-	176
ample. In every practice period, you forge the chain of	234
habits which make for success or failure. To be sure of suc-	297
cess, you must organize your effort so that you can quickly	357
forge a chain of right habits.	387

Syllable intensity, 1.25 *

Optional Exercise 14

Measurement paragraph. All letters of the alphabet are used in this paragraph.

	STROKES
It is amazing how few of us are free from handicaps.	55
Some of us fight doubt or fear or lack of faith in ourselves,	118
just as others fight poverty or the lack of training. Handi-	181
caps are quite common, but they do not need to harm one; only	243
the lack of will to do stands in the way of success. If you	305
have a handicap, use it for success and not as an excuse for	366
failure.	374

Syllable intensity, 1.25

Drill on Centering

Centering is not new to you. The directions for each drill and exercise you have typed called for the correct centering of the material on the page. To center vertically, you must place half of the material to be typed above the center of the page and half below the center of the page. The problem of horizontal centering is simply the problem of placing half of the material to be typed, to the left of the center of the page and half to the right of the center of the page.

Paper 8½ x 11″ has sixty-six writing lines of eighty-five pica spaces each. Half sheets, therefore, have thirty-three lines.

---

* Syllable intensity is found by dividing the total number of syllables in the paragraph by the total number of words. Measurement paragraphs have a syllable intensity of 1.25. This provides material of uniform difficulty by which to measure progress.

INSTRUCTIONAL BLOCK IX
MANUSCRIPT TYPING

A title page is usually given to a manuscript. This display page contains (1) the title of the book or the article and (2) the name of the author. Other information is added to the title page of a book which is to be published. For example, turn to the title page of this text. Note that, in addition to the title of the book and the name of the author, the name of the publisher and the place of publication are given. The copyright date may be given on the title page, or it may be given on the following page.

Simple border designs may be used with title pages. Ornate designs are not in good taste. Simplicity of form and arrangement is desirable in all typed material. Border designs may be made through the use of the following symbols and letters:

The period	.
The colon	:
The quotation mark	"
The number sign	#
The apostrophe	'
The dollar mark	$
The asterisk	*
The small letter	x
The small letter	o

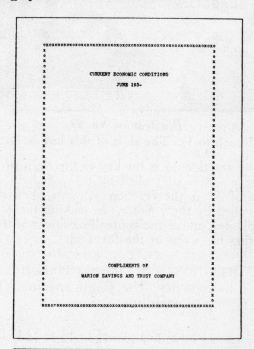

Combinations of these characters may be used to form attractive and artistic designs.

It is important that you provide equal top and bottom margins in laying out the title page. Plan your work according to the tabulation check list.

In the following work use 8½ x 11″ paper. After completing each budget of work, clip or bind the pages together in booklet form. Specific working directions are given with each exercise.

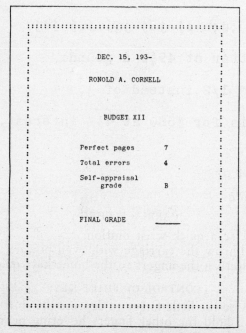

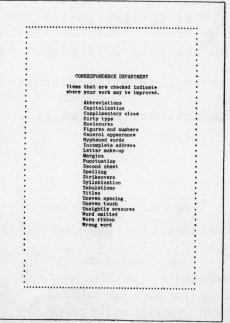

Illustration No. 47, Border Designs

Control of ½ and ¼, ¢ (cent or cents) and @ (at)

Locked-Key Drill. Study the illustrations and directions carefully. Through the locked-key drill, initiate the new reaches.

Illustration No. 39
Reach to ½. The shift of this key is ¼.

The fraction ½ is the key to the right of the letter *p*. It is controlled by the *;* *finger*. The shift of ½ is the fraction ¼; this likewise is controlled by the *;* *finger*. In making the reach to this key, move the controlling finger without twisting the wrist or the forearm.

Illustration No. 40
Reach to ¢ (cent or cents). The shift of this key is @ (at).

The key to the right of the semicolon is ¢. The shift of the ¢ is the special character @. This key is controlled by the *;* *finger*. Move the little finger one space to the right without moving the other fingers from their home position.

DIRECTIONS: Set the marginal stops for a sixty-space line. Have a top margin of one and a half inches. Use single spacing. Type each line twice. Double-space after the second typing of each line.

```
j ;j  ;½;  ;½;  j ;j  ;½j  ;¼;  ;¼j  5½%  5¼%  3½%  3¼%.6½%  6¼%  ;½;  ;¼;

j ;j  ;¢;  j¢j  j¢j  ;@;  j@j  j@j  15¢ each  ;¢;  j¢j  j@j  j@j  j@j  j¢j

The price is 29¼¢ each.  We quote butter at 49¾¢ a pound.

When typing with several carbons, use 1/2 instead of ½.

The interest rate is 5½%.  His note is for $580 at 4½% interest.
```

LESSON 14
Technique Guide

POSITION AT THE TYPEWRITER

1. Lean slightly from the hips toward the typewriter.
2. Keep your shoulders erect.
3. Keep your feet on the floor.
4. Keep your body well balanced.
5. Hold your eyes on the copy.
6. Keep the fingers well curved.

CARRIAGE THROW

7. Use a quick wrist motion.
8. Throw the carriage with even power.
9. Return the fingers to the home keys quickly.

CONTROL OF SHIFT KEYS

10. Use the little finger to depress the shift key; hold the other fingers hovering near the home position.

BUDGET XIII
Corrective Drills for *a*, *r*, *s*, *u*, and *w*

DIRECTIONS: Set the marginal stops for a seventy-space line. Use single spacing. Type each line twice. Double-space after the second typing of each line.

```
Appalachian acquaintance approximate analyzable approach Australia
robber repose remark relief restrain refresh revere regular reprove
seasickness self-seeking self-possession short-sighted son-in-law
unscrupulous unpunctual jujuism judge unsullied unnatural unsuited
wealth when sown wreck snows waste wrath waltz waxen waxwork west
```

Sentence Practice

DIRECTIONS: Use a different sentence in each practice period. Type the sentence five times. Set the marginal stops for a seventy-space line. Use double spacing.

STROKES FOR EACH SENTENCE

The check dated March 29 was for $357.60 in full payment of bill #148.	74
An ounce of practice is worth more than a pound of preaching.	62
Fear God and keep His commandments; this is the whole duty of man.	69
Go on and make errors and fail, but get up again and go on.—Brackett	71

Corrective Drill Paragraphs

DIRECTIONS: Set the marginal stops for a seventy-space line. Adjust the tabular stop for an indentation of five spaces. Use single spacing. Type one corrective drill paragraph in each practice period. Alternate the paragraphs in the various practice periods.

o key   Of what does success consist? Not of just making money or spending money; not of rising to fame on the broken lives of others. Success consists in doing good to one's fellow men and in being true to one's highest beliefs. Every day opportunity stands "outside your door," and bids you wake and rise to fight and win. Once you have won, new opportunities to go up higher in the scale of doing will come to you. You are expected to show the quality of vision which will cause you to recognize opportunities as they come.

p key   Purpose is prized by all thoughtful people. Promotion persists in following that person who exhibits persuasive personality and who keeps his objective plainly in mind. Probably no part is of more importance in promoting success than quietly but pleasantly to push persistently on. To prove this point, try to plan your work toward a certain purpose and see if it does not possess more practical application than you would have thought possible.

Five-Minute Timed Writing Practice

DIRECTIONS: Set the marginal stops for a seventy-space line. Adjust the tabular stop for an indentation of five spaces. Use double spacing.

STROKES

If you ask a high school boy why he is going to school, he is likely to	73
tell you that it is because he wants to get an education. It may be that just	153
what "getting an education" means is not clear to him, but he thinks that it	232
has something to do with getting passing grades in his studies, and he is sure	311
that it has quite a lot to do with getting a diploma at the end of four years.	390
Getting a diploma is not the goal. Most pupils can expect their high-school	469
diplomas at the end of four years, but education is a continuous process.	543
Each day brings new problems to be solved. It is in the solving of these	619
problems that growth, which is education, is realized.	674

Syllable intensity, 1.30

Colon Control

The colon (:) is the shift of the semicolon key and is controlled by the *; finger*. Depress the shift key with the *a finger* and strike the semicolon key. This will give, through the use of the shift, the colon (:). *Two spaces follow the colon.*

Review Practice 13

DIRECTIONS: Set the marginal stops for a sixty-space line. Have a top margin of one and a half inches. Use single spacing. Type each line twice. Double-space after the second typing of each line.

lazy zeal hazy size quit zone next zeal open size zeal quit

up-to-date two-by-four well-to-do son-in-law six-cylinder

John Zilbandy saw the quick vamp fixing the high trapeze.

A SUCCESS RECIPE: Study, think, plan, and work.

MY PLEDGE: the best work of which I am capable every day.

Exercise 13

DIRECTIONS: Set the marginal stops for a sixty-space line. Adjust the tabular stop for a five-space indentation. Have a top margin of two inches. Use single spacing. Type the exercise *once to a sheet.* Double-space between the paragraphs. A spacing rule which must always be observed is that single-spaced material requires double spacing between paragraphs. If time permits, retype the exercise.

All letters of the alphabet are used in this exercise.

	STROKES
THE TIME: the winter of the year 1866-67.	46
THE PLACE: just a little machine shop in the outskirts	106
of the city of Milwaukee.	133
THE SCENE: three middle-aged men, each quietly working	193
on his pet invention but expecting little more than a small	253
measure of fame or fortune.	279
THE AMAZING OUTCOME: the first practical typewriter.	369

Optional Exercise 13

All letters of the alphabet are used in this exercise.

	STROKES
To Christopher Latham Sholes, who was born in Columbia	61
County, Pennsylvania, on February 14, 1819, goes the honor	123
of being the central figure in the invention of the first	181
practical typewriter.	203
The naming of the typewriter had been quite as long a	260
job as the evolution of the machine itself. Sholes may not	321
have expected to revolutionize writing, yet he knew that the	382
correct naming of his invention was important. He called it	444
a "type-writer."	462

[30]

Exercise 93

DIRECTIONS: Type the following title page for a small booklet of poems. Center each line. Type a simple border design exactly two inches from the top, sides, and bottom of the page.

SELECTED POEMS

Compiled by

Robert Sidney Grant

Exercise 94

A pamphlet or book having chapters or other divisions should contain a table of contents. This is a brief list of the divisions or the items making up the pamphlet or book, typed in the order of their appearance.

DIRECTIONS: Type the following table of contents in two columns. Center the copy vertically. Determine the correct placement of the marginal stops and the tabular stop for the second column by the use of the tabulation steps given on page 102. Use double spacing.

	Page
The Boomerang	1
Mask	2
April Rain	3
It Isn't the World—It's You	4
A City Park	5

Exercise 95

In typing a poem, capitalize the first word of each line. Center the longest line unless this line is of such disproportionate length that centering it would give an unbalanced appearance to the completed page. If consecutive lines rhyme, they should be aligned. If the rhymes alternate, or follow at specific intervals, indent the rhyming lines to the same extent.

DIRECTIONS: Center the poem vertically. Center the longest line in order to get the correct horizontal placement. Use double spacing, with triple spacing between the title and the first line of the poem. Indent every other line of the poem two spaces.

THE BOOMERANG

When a bit of sunshine hits ye
  After passing of a cloud,
When a bit of laughter gits ye
  And ye'r spine is feelin' proud,

Don't forget to up and fling it
  At a soul that's feelin' blue,
For the minute that ye sling it
  It's a boomerang to you.
    —Captain Jack Crawford

Exercise 96

DIRECTIONS: Center the poem vertically. Center the longest line in order to get the correct horizontal placement. Use double spacing, with triple spacing between the title and the first line of the poem and between the stanzas. Begin all lines flush with the left margin.

MASK

At heart I am a stricken thing.
You would not think so, would you?
And if you looked for such deceit,
You could not find it, could you?

I have clothed my heart in mirth,
With brilliant colors flying.
But down inside my funny heart
A little child is crying.
    —Margaret Anne Keller

Exercise 97

DIRECTIONS: Center the poem vertically. Center the longest line in order to get the correct horizontal placement. Use double spacing, with triple spacing between the title and the first line of the poem and between the stanzas. Indent every other line of the poem two spaces.

APRIL RAIN

It is not raining rain for me,
  It's raining daffodils;
In every dimpled drop I see
  Wild flowers on the hills.

The clouds of gray engulf the day
  And overwhelm the town;
It is not raining rain to me,
  It's raining roses down.

It is not raining rain to me,
  But fields of clover bloom,
Where any buccaneering bee
  Can find a bed and room.

A health unto the happy,
  A fig for him who frets!
It is not raining rain to me,
  It's raining violets.
    —Robert Loveman

Fixation Practice 12
Control of *6* and __ (underscore), and / (diagonal) and ¾

Locked-Key Drill. Study the illustrations and directions carefully. Through the locked-key drill, initiate the new reaches.

Illustration No. 37
Reach to 6-__ (underscore)

Illustration No. 38
Reach to / (diagonal) -¾

The figure *6* is in the top row of keys just one step above the letter *y*; the underscore (__) is the shift of the figure *6*. The *j finger* controls these keys.

The diagonal (/) is below *;* and is controlled by the *; finger*. The shift of the diagonal is the special character ¾. On some models of typewriters, the shift of the diagonal is the interrogation point (?). If you are using a typewriter with the latter keyboard arrangement, your drill will be *;?;* instead of *;¾;*. The diagonal is used in typing fractions.

Give a quick, decisive blow to the center of the key; avoid changing the position of the hand.

DIRECTIONS: Set the marginal stops for a sixty-space line. Have a top margin of one and a half inches. Use single spacing. Type each line twice. Double-space after the second typing of each line.

To Underscore: When underscoring a word, back-space (depress the back-spacer, No. 27) to the first letter of the word to be underscored, and strike the underscore once for each letter in the word. When underscoring an entire sentence, write the entire sentence, move the carriage back to the first letter to be underscored, depress the shift lock (No. 28), and strike the underscore once for each letter in the words to be underscored. Form the habit of spelling each word as you strike the underscore. Do not underscore a punctuation mark or the space between words.

When typing a number of upper-case characters in succession, depress the shift lock (No. 28). When the shift lock is used, the little finger need not be kept on the shift key. To release the shift lock, depress the shift key.

```
jy6j jy6j sw2s jy6j j6_j jy6j jy_j sw2s jy6j jy_j jy6j jy_j

2s 6j 3d 91 4f 7j 5f 8k 2s 0; 5f -; 3d 6j 5f 6j 3d 7j 6j 6j

1 2 6 126 3 8 5 385 4 1 7 417 5 1 9 519 6 2 8 628 3 6 0 360

;/; ;¾; aza ;/; ;¾; aqa j/; j¾; fza ;/; j¾; sxs j/; j¾; ;/;
```

The <u>interest</u> <u>rate</u> is 6¾%. The <u>fraction</u> you mean is 5/6.

LESSON 13
Technique Guide

The correct use of the tabular key will save time and thus increase your typing output. Hold the tabular key (do not strike it) with the controlling finger until the carriage has completed its movement; keep your eyes on the copy; hold your hand in the correct keyboard position.

Exercise 98

DIRECTIONS: Center the poem vertically. Center the longest line in order to get the correct horizontal placement. Use double spacing, with triple spacing between the title and the first line of the poem and between the stanzas. Indent every other line of the poem two spaces.

IT ISN'T THE WORLD—IT'S YOU

You say the world is gloomy,
   The skies are grim and gray,
The night has lost its quiet,
   You fear the coming day?
The world is what you make it,
   The sky is gray or blue
Just as your soul may paint it;
   It isn't the world—it's you!

Clear up the clouded vision,
   Clean out the foggy mind;
The clouds are always passing,
   And each is silver lined.
The world is what you make it—
   Then make it bright and true,
And when you say it's gloomy,
   It isn't the world—it's you!

Exercise 99

DIRECTIONS: Center the poem vertically. Center the longest line for the horizontal placement. Use double spacing with triple spacing between the title and the first line of the poem.

A CITY PARK

Timidly

Against a background of brick tenements

Some trees spread their branches

Skyward.

They are thin and sapless,

They are bent and weary—

Tanned with captivity;

And they huddle behind the fence

Swaying helplessly before the wind,

Forward and backward,

Like a group of panicky deer

Caught in a cage.

—Alter Brody

BUDGET XIV

Corrective Drills for *b*, *h*, *d*, *j*, and *m*

DIRECTIONS: Set the marginal stops for a seventy-space line. Use single spacing. Type each line twice. Double-space after the second typing of each line.

```
barbarous bribery brambles bugaboo barbecue barber barbarity break
hairbrush hothouse household half-hearted hemisphere hemorrhage
deductions displeased deserved disdained disagreed disadvantage
Judith judicial judicious jugular jugulate junior jurisprudence
maximum mummify murmur mature martyrdom mesmerism matchmaker mystic
```

Sentence Practice

DIRECTIONS: Use a different sentence in each practice period. Type the sentence five times. Set the marginal stops for a seventy-space line. Use double spacing.

	STROKES FOR EACH SENTENCE
Accept access to an actually accurate account of the accident.	63
Improper impromptu impressions impart impractical impulses.	60
Contradict the contrary contractor, but control his contribution.	66
Expect expense if expert experience is expended in experimentation.	68
Assign the assessments to the assistant assessor for assortment.	65

[121]

LESSON 12
Technique Guide

In all of your typing, emphasize the following correct technique:

1. Curved fingers.
2. Quick key release.
3. Relaxed, but not sagging, wrists.
4. Eyes on the copy.
5. Rhythmic typing — the passing from one stroke to another with evenness.
6. Quick, well-controlled carriage return.
7. Accurate control of the tabular key.

Manipulation Drill

Repeat the manipulation drill, Carriage Return and Tabular-Key Control, given with Lesson 6, page 18. Compare your present score with that which you made when you were studying Lesson 6. The difference between the two scores will indicate your increased skill.

Review Practice 12

DIRECTIONS: Set the marginal stops for a sixty-space line. Have a top margin of one and a half inches. Use single spacing. Type each line twice. Double-space after the second typing of each line.

```
4f 8k 2s 9l 3d 0; 5f 7j 5f 7j 2s 9l 5f 7j 3d 0; 4f -; 5f 7j

4f$f 8k'k 2s"s 9l(l 3d#d 0;)); 5f%f 7j&j 2s"s -;*; 5f%f 7j&j

The sum of 14 and 9 and 5 and 10 and 38 and 57 and 75 is 208.

The $1,000 Marx & Co. 5% bond (Series B) is due February 15.

Mr. J. V. Quick was amazed at the long part he had to play.
```

Exercise 12

DIRECTIONS: Set the marginal stops for a sixty-space line. Adjust the tabular stop for a five-space indentation. Have a top margin of one and a half inches. Use double spacing. Type the exercise twice on the same sheet.

All letters of the alphabet are used in this exercise.

	STROKES
It was Henry Mill, an English engineer, who was the	57
first man known to have had the amazing idea of the type-	115
writer. No model of his machine is known to exist, yet	172
on January 7, 1714, he was granted a patent by Queen Anne.	233

Optional Exercise 12

DIRECTIONS: Have a top margin of seven single spaces.

All letters of the alphabet are used in this exercise.

	STROKES
The first American patent on a typewriter was given	55
in 1829 to William Austin Burt, of Detroit. There was just	120
one model of this quaint machine and it was destroyed by	177
fire. Working from the original patent and other papers,	236
others made a full-sized model and exhibited it in 1893.	292

[28]

Corrective Drill Paragraphs

DIRECTIONS: Set the marginal stops for a seventy-space line. Adjust the tabular stop for an indentation of five spaces. Use single spacing. Type one corrective drill paragraph in each practice period. Alternate the paragraphs in the various practice periods.

q
key

Mental quickness is a quality which will always help greatly in answering questions and solving problems. Queer questions often require just quickness of thought to keep one from being considered inadequate. For example, to draw designs in applique was clearly a queer quiz question to test the quality of reasoning, yet it was used in an intelligence test recently. Quick as a flash, one student saw the quarters of a square in an antique quilt her grandmother had. She quickly sketched in the design for the applique, thus scoring high on the quiz.

r
key

The ability to reason is always a real power. Rush and hurry are not conducive to proper reasoning, for reasoning requires deliberation. To reason well relieves one of many of the haphazard results of a hasty judgment poorly expressed. The one who can reason has the power to adjust himself to any situation; he will reflect credit on himself in any crisis. Lack of power to reason can mar the work of the most careful person. To be able to reason really well shows not only a great degree of intelligence, but also the ability to use that intelligence.

Five-Minute Timed Writing Practice

DIRECTIONS: Set the marginal stops for a seventy-space line. Adjust the tabular stop for an indentation of five spaces. Use double spacing.

STROKES

I know a man who gave work as a messenger to an honor graduate of a   69
high school. The boy was put at this work so that he could learn the rou-   145
tine organization of the offices of the firm. The boy thought that he was a   223
skilled bookkeeper and felt that his skill was not being correctly used. He   301
was not an expert in values, though, for he failed to see that bookkeeping   376
technique was just one of the skills the employer wanted. Still more than   452
that skill, the boy had to have the right attitude toward his work, and he   527
needed to see in the calls from each office a chance to learn procedure and   603
routine. His failure was in thinking that the work of the messenger was   677
beneath one skilled in bookkeeping routine.   721

Syllable intensity, 1.30

Exercise 100

In referring to footnotes, use superior figures in the text. Place the figure after the punctuation mark, if any, but do not space between the punctuation mark and the figure. If a reference figure is used with a quoted excerpt, it should stand at the end of the quotation. Number the references to footnotes consecutively throughout an article or a chapter in a book. The footnotes must appear on the same page as that on which the reference figures appear. Separate the footnotes from the text by a line extending approximately two inches from the left margin. Indent a footnote five spaces. Type footnotes with single spacing, but double-space between them. Observe, in the following copy, how a footnote should be typed when reference is made to a published book.

DIRECTIONS: Set the marginal stops for a sixty-five-space line. Adjust the tabular stop for an indentation of five spaces. Use double spacing. Leave a two-inch top margin. Make the corrections indicated in the manuscript. Leave a one-inch top margin on the second page; type the figure *2* in the center of the line; and space up two double spaces before typing the first line of the second page.

Exercise 11

DIRECTIONS: Set the marginal stops for a sixty-space line. Adjust the tabular stop for a five-space indentation. Have a top margin of one and a half inches. Use double spacing. Type the exercise twice on the same sheet.

All letters of the alphabet are used in this exercise.

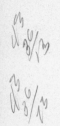

STROKES

An old motto reads, "Ability is the poor man's wealth."   62

If that is true, luck must be the lazy man's excuse. Many   124

young men blame bad luck for their failure just because it   183

is such an easy alibi to give. Ability, not luck, conquers.   244

Optional Exercise 11

All letters of the alphabet are used in this exercise.

STROKES

Let me name just a few techniques of typing which need   57

to be emphasized in your daily work. Correct fingering, eyes   120

on the copy, quick carriage throw, correct position, relaxed   181

wrists, rhythmic typing--these give typing power.   230

Fixation Practice 11
Control of 5-% and 7-&

Illustration No. 36, **Reach to 5-% and 7-&**

Locked-Key Drill. Study the illustration and directions carefully. Through the locked-key drill, initiate the new reaches.

The figure *5* is above and slightly to the left of the letter *t*; the symbol % (per cent) is the shift of the figure *5*. These characters are controlled by the *f finger.*

The key above *j* is the letter *u*. The key above *u* is the figure *7*, and the shift of the figure *7* is *&*, the sign for *and*, used in company or partnership names.

Figures have no context. They must be absolutely accurate. Learn them thoroughly.

DIRECTIONS: Set the marginal stops for a sixty-space line. Have a top margin of one and a half inches. Use single spacing. Type each line twice. Double-space after the second typing of each line.

f5f f5f f%f f%f 191 f5f k8k f%f k'k f5f f%f f5f f%f ;0; f5f

j7j j7j j&j j&j f5f j7j d3d j7j d#d j&j f5f j7j f%f j&j j7j

two 2 three 3 four 4 five 5 seven 7 eight 8 nine 9 ten 10

The Roberts & Mills' check isn't for this bill #157,570.

Bond & Morgan's 5% note, due February 15, is for $7,500.

In placing the superior figure for a reference to a footnote, turn the cylinder toward you approximately one-half of a line space; type the figure without releasing the cylinder; then return the cylinder to its line position.

When two footnotes contain references to the same work and follow each other without any intervening footnote, use *Ibid.*, the abbreviation for *ibidem* (meaning, in the same place), and the exact page number for the second footnote.

TRAIT ANALYSIS

What are the ~~qualities~~ *factors* which ~~condition~~ *affect* success in business?

A study of the causes of failure indicates that more workers fail because of lack of desirable traits than because of lack *of* skill.

If one is to be a successful stenographer, typing skill is needed; so is skill in taking and transcribing dictation. Even with these skills, though, many stenographers fail to achieve outstanding success in their work. Why? The difficulty is *Frequently* ~~usually traceable to~~ *caused by a lack of the* ~~some weakness in~~ personal traits *which make for success.*

One study of secretarial duties and traits ~~is that~~ *was* made by Charters and Whitley. A part of their study deals with personality as a factor in the success of the secretary. The following quotation will help you to understand how the data for this study were gathered:

> "A *considerable* number of employers ~~were~~ interviewed *were held* in order to find the secretarial qualities in which employers are especially interested, the things which secretaries do which please them or particularly irritate them, the reasons for discharge, the qualities in which they would like to improve their present secretaries, and so on."[1]

From the analysis of the reports of these interviews, traits were determined. In order to define what these traits mean, the list of suggestive trait-actions given in the study is used as a means of focusing attention in classroom work upon the actions which express the traits.

Build these into your daily work habits. Accuracy in typing is not enough, important though that is; you must be accurate in work habits, too.

---

1. W. W. Charters and Isadore B. Whitley, *Summary of Report on Analysis of Secretarial Duties and Traits*, Service Bulletin No. I, New York: National Junior Personnel Service, Inc., 1924, p. 46.

Fixation Practice 10
Control of *3-#* and *0-)*

Illustration No. 35, **Reach to *3-#* and *0-)***

Locked-Key Drill. Study the illustration and directions carefully. Through the locked-key drill, initiate the new reaches.

The figure *3* is above *e*, and the # (the number sign) is the shift of the figure *3*. This key is controlled by the *d finger*.

The cipher (*0*) is above the letter *p*; the shift of the cipher is) (the right parenthesis). This key is controlled by the *; finger*.

In making the reach, move the finger straight forward. Do not twist the elbow, the wrist, or the forearm. Curve the finger and give a quick, forceful blow to the center of the key.

DIRECTIONS: Set the marginal stops for a sixty-space line. Have a top margin of one and a half inches. Use single spacing. Type each line twice. Double-space after the second typing of each line.

```
de3d de3d de#d de#d lo9l de3d lo(l de#d ki8k de3d de#d de3d

;p0; ;p0; de#d ;p); ;p); de3d ;p0; de3d ;p0; de#d ;p); ;p);

1 2 4 124 1 3 8 138 1 3 9 139 1 3 0 130 1 4 0 140 1 0 3 103

ten (10) three (3) thirty (30) forty-nine (49) twenty (20)

Hall's order #143 (dated March 30) amounts to $298.30.
```

LESSON 11
Technique Guide

The control of the figures offers no special difficulty. The reaches are merely extended letter reaches. The new element involved in controlling the figures is learning the length of the reach. The direction is the same as that to the intervening letter control. Bring to your practice of figure drills the same type of well-controlled stroke that you use with the letter keys. Control the figures by touch. No other way of practicing will bring real typing power.

Review Practice 11

DIRECTIONS: Set the marginal stops for a sixty-space line. Have a top margin of one and a half inches. Use single spacing. Type each line twice. Double-space after the second typing of each line.

```
4f$f 3d#d 8k'k 2s"s 9l(l 3d#d 0;); -;*; 3d#d -;*; 2s"s 0;);

The sum of 4 and 9 and 3 and 10 and 12 and 38 and 24 is 100.

Is West-Hall's $1,000 bond (Series #1-A) due January, 1948?

"Day by day, in every way, I am getting better and better."

Joe packed my sledge with five dozen boxes of nice quail.
```

Trait Desired   *all caps*

Accuracy

(Ranked first by 86 per cent of the employers interviewed)

The secretary

1. Does not make mistakes in typing.
2. Does not make mistakes in computing.
3. ~~Gets the~~ spelling and pronunciation ~~of~~
   people's names ~~right.~~ *correctly.*
4. Pays attention to detail. *s*
5. Files material under the proper heading. *s*
6. Does not make mistakes in keeping records
   and data.
7. Gets the exact information asked for.
8. Does not lose papers.
9. Does not make mistakes in transcribing dictation.
10. Does not "guess" when information is desired. *x*
11. Sees that every letter is perfect before it
    goes out.
12. *13.* Checks all work. *Does not send out a letter unsigned.*
14. *13.* Does not make mistakes in proof reading.
15. Checks ~~up on~~ names, dates, and figures when
    copying written material.
16. Does not let letters go out unstamped.
17. Never ~~gets~~ the wrong address on a package.[2]
    places

---

2. Ibid., pp. 48 and 49.

Exercise 101

DIRECTIONS: Set the marginal stops for a sixty-five-space line. Adjust the tabular stop for an indentation of five spaces. Use double spacing. Leave a two-inch top margin. Make the corrections indicated in the manuscript. Leave a one-inch top margin on the second page; type the page number in the center of the line; and space up two double spaces before typing the first line.

Courtesy   *all caps*

(Ranked fifth *b* ~~hy~~ 71 per cent of the employers interviewed)

Courtesy is that something within the individual which sets

him apart. It is one of the *earmarks* ~~trademarks~~ of the successful. Courtesy

means thoughtfulness *to* ~~of~~ others; *i*~~I~~t means the doing of little things

in a *gracious* ~~happy~~ way. Each of us has within his own heart and mind the

seed of courtesy. Like a tender plant, it must be ~~watered and~~ cul-

tivated constantly in order that it may flower into a definite

trait of personality.

LESSON 10
Technique Guide

Think each word vigorously; this will set up a strong stimulus to type. Keep the carriage moving smoothly and continuously; this will develop rhythm, or continuity, in typing. Slam the mental door in the face of all intruding thoughts; this will develop concentration. The habit of concentrating, attending vigorously to the work to be done, is essential to success in typing. Begin now to set up this correct habit. It will pay rich dividends.

Manipulation Drill

Repeat the manipulation drill, Paper Insertion, given with Lesson 2, page 10. Compare your present score with that which you made when you were studying Lesson 2. The difference between the two scores will indicate your increased skill in the handling of paper. Do not be satisfied until you use in your daily work the most efficient method of handling paper.

Review Practice 10

DIRECTIONS: Set the marginal stops for a sixty-space line. Have a top margin of one and a half inches. Use single spacing. Type each line twice. Double-space after the second typing of each line.

NOTE: The quotation mark precedes the question mark if the latter applies, not to the quotation, but to the sentence containing the quotation. See line four of the following drill for an illustration of this rule.

```
4f 8k 2s 9l 4f -; $f 'k "s (1 "s *; 2s 9l 4f -; $f 'k "s (1

The sum of 14 and 9 and 2 and 18 and 12 and 48 and 9 is 112.

both next size page quiz next jump size paid such view more

Isn't it much better just to "wear out" than to "rust out"?

Do you have skill?  Apply it quickly, then, to this work.
```

Exercise 10

DIRECTIONS: Set the marginal stops for a sixty-space line. Adjust the tabular stop for a five-space indentation. Have a top margin of one and a half inches. Use double spacing. Type the exercise twice on the same sheet.

NOTE: At the end of a quotation, a period or a comma should always precede the quotation mark.

All letters of the alphabet are used in this exercise.

	STROKES
It was in 1492 that he set sail into the vast unknown,	57
there to find a new land. He never gained much reward for	117
his amazing trip, but what of that? He had conquered fear;	178
he had experienced "the joy of discovery."	220

Optional Exercise 10

All letters of the alphabet are used in this exercise.

	STROKES
The joy of discovery can be experienced by each of us.	57
Not new lands to be conquered, but "self" to be brought in	119
subjection. This is a real man's task. It calls for zeal	180
to discover weaknesses and for courage to overcome them.	236

[25]

Suggestive Trait-Actions

The secretary

1. Meets people well.
2. Makes people feel at ease.
3. Is pleasant and gracious over the telephone and to callers.
4. Does not leave visitors standing in the office.
5. Says "Thank you" and "Please" to everyone. *(space)*
6. Does not slam the doors in a rude way.
7. Does not interrupt a conversation without ~~a~~ *saying* "Pardon me."
8. Does not go into *an* office, ~~where~~ the door *of which* is closed, without knocking (unless it is an entrance office).
9. Does not ^bang^ the receiver of a telephone.
10. Is not curt and ungracious to janitors, messenger boys, expressmen, etc.[1]

Courtesy pays. It oils the wheels of human contacts and makes them move ~~so very~~ much more smoothly. If we are honest with ourselves, we must admit that, for the most part, none of us *is* ~~are~~ any too easy to live with. Each of us is so ~~anxious~~ *eager* to attain his own ends, ~~that~~ he fails to notice when he is rudely elbowing the one who stands next *to* ^him; ~~E~~ach is so bent upon his own pleasure, ~~that~~ he forgets to notice he is ignoring his neighbor; ~~E~~ach is so eager for his own gain, ~~that~~ he fails to see that he is needlessly hurting another. Apply courtesy, though, and the whole situation changes.

It is the most natural thing in the world to meet courtesy with courtesy. When a request is made in a manner which suggests that a favor is being done the one ~~who asks~~ *from whom the request comes,* the most usual response is the gracious one. The same request made in another way has the power to arouse the deepest resentment.

Failure is often ~~due to~~ *caused by the* lack of ~~this~~ social intelligence--the *total of the* qualities which make for happy human contacts. Sometimes workers learn only after bitter experience that courtesy is an asset.

---

1. W. W. Charters and Isadore B. Whitley, Summary of Report on Analysis of Secretarial Duties and Traits, Service Bulletin No. I, New York: National Junior Personnel Service, Inc., 1924, p. 51.

Exercise 9

DIRECTIONS: Set the marginal stops for a sixty-space line. Adjust the tabular stop for a five-space indentation. Have a top margin of one and a half inches. Use double spacing. Type the exercise twice on the same sheet.

All letters of the alphabet are used in this exercise.

STROKES

It is in the attitude to each day's work that I would   57

try to excel if I were in school again. Others might excel   119

in quick evasion, but none should excel me in just one thing   180

--my zeal to lift thought to a high plane and hold it there.   240

Optional Exercise 9

All letters of the alphabet are used in this exercise.

STROKES

Most of us guess too much. What we need is to face facts   61

squarely. Do we do our best work at all times, or do we just   124

lazily expect chance to take care of our lives? We should   185

rule chance out, face facts, plan our work, and work our plan.   247

Fixation Practice 9
Control of *2-"* and *9-(*

Illustration No. 34, **Reach to** *2-"* **and** *9-(*

Locked-Key Drill. Study the illustration and directions carefully. Through the locked-key drill, initiate the new reaches.

The figure *2* is in the top row of keys above *w*; the shift of the figure *2* is the quotation mark ("). This key is controlled by the *s finger.* In making the reach, you need not hold the other fingers of the left hand rigidly in their home position. The *d* and *f fingers* should be permitted to move slightly.

The figure *9* is above *o*; the left parenthesis is the shift of *9*. This key is controlled by the *l finger.*

Figures must be typed with absolute accuracy. Learn the controls. If you hesitate in making figure reaches, additional practice is needed.

DIRECTIONS: Set the marginal stops for a sixty-space line. Have a top margin of one and a half inches. Use single spacing. Type each line twice. Double-space after the second typing of each line.

sws s2s s2s k8k s2s s"s s2s s"s k8k s2s k'k s"s s2s s"s s2s

lol 191 191 s2s 191 s"s l(l f4f 191 f$f l(l s2s 191 s"s l(l

1 9 19 1 2 12 4 1 41 8 1 81 2 8 28 4 8 48 2 9 29 1 9 19 219

The "(" is just half of the complete mark you will use later.

What is the sum of 4 and 8 and 2 and 9 and 1? The sum is 24.

[24]

This exercise summarizes the best practice in manuscript typing. You will find it worth while to apply the following instructions when you type your own work. Study each paragraph of this exercise carefully. This is not merely an exercise to be typed; it is a source of information which will be of help in your own typing work.

DIRECTIONS: Set the marginal stops for a sixty-space line. Use single spacing with double spacing between paragraphs. Leave a two-inch top margin. Number all pages after the first at the top. Make a carbon copy for your own use.

MANUSCRIPT TYPING

1. Manuscripts should be typed with double spacing, on paper of uniform size, preferably 8½ x 11 inches. Only one side of the paper should be used.

2. A duplicate copy of each manuscript should be made for future reference. The duplicate is also a protection if the original manuscript is lost.

3. The correct margins for manuscripts bound in various ways are given in the following paragraphs.

    a. If the manuscript is to be bound at the side, leave a two-inch left and a one-inch right margin.

    b. If the manuscript is to be bound at the top, leave a three-inch top margin on the first page and a two-inch top margin on each succeeding page. Leave at least a one-inch margin at the left, the right, and the bottom of the page.

    c. If a manuscript is not to be bound, leave a one-inch margin at the left, the right, and the bottom of each page, a two-inch top margin on the first page, and a one-inch top margin on each succeeding page.

    Exception: The bottom margin may be one line narrower to avoid carrying the last line of a paragraph to the succeeding page, or to avoid leaving a hyphened word at the end of a page. It may be wider in order to avoid leaving only one line of a paragraph on a page.

4. The title, or heading, should be centered and typed in capital letters approximately two inches from the top of the first page. A period should not be placed after a title, but a question mark or an exclamation point should be used when one is appropriate.

Note: Do not underscore the title if it is typed in capital letters, nor place it in quotation marks unless it is a quotation. The use of capitals gives sufficient emphasis.

5. Leave three single spaces between the title and the first line of the copy.

6. In manuscript typing, use the underscore as a sign for the printer to set the word, or words, in *italic type*.

7. Quoted titles of books, periodicals, and manuscripts are usually italicized.

Note: It is correct, but not the best practice, to enclose the title of a book in quotation marks. Use italics for the title of a book, and quotation marks for the names of chapters or subdivisions of the same book.

8. The pages of a manuscript should be numbered in Arabic numerals, not Roman. The number may be omitted from the first page since the title indicates the page. Leave three single spaces between the number and the first line of composition.

    a. If the manuscript is to be bound at the side, place the number an inch from the top of the page, and (1) center it horizontally or (2) type it an inch from the right edge of the paper.

    b. If the manuscript is to be bound at the top, place the number an inch from the bottom of the page and center it horizontally.

    c. If the manuscript is not to be bound, place the number an inch from the top of the page and center it horizontally.

9. In referring to footnotes, use superior figures in the text. Place the figure after the punctuation mark, if any, but do not space between the punctuation mark and the figure.

    a. If the figure refers to a footnote

Fixation Practice 8
Control of *4-$* and *8-'*

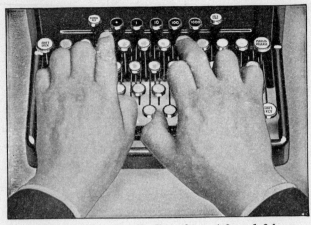

Illustration No. 33, Reach to *4-$* and *8-'*

Locked-Key Drill. Study the illustration and directions carefully. Through the locked-key drill, initiate the new reaches.

The key above the letter *f* is *r*; this you have already learned. The key above *r* is the figure *4,* and the shift of the figure *4* is *$* (the dollar sign). The *f finger* controls these keys.

The letter *i* is above *k* and is controlled by the *k finger*. The figure *8* is above *i*; the *'* (apostrophe) is the shift of *8*. Hold the *k finger* in the air; mentally associate the new controls with this finger. In making the reaches, lift the *j finger* slightly, but do not permit any of the fingers to move with the *k finger* as it moves to the upper row of keys. Keep the fingers curved.

DIRECTIONS: Set the marginal stops for a sixty-space line. Have a top margin of one and a half inches. Use single spacing. Type each line twice. Double-space after the second typing of each line. (In a series of figures in which the period or comma is used, do not space after the mark of punctuation.)

```
frf fr4f fr$f f4f f$f kik f4f f$f kik f4f f$f f4f f$f f4f

kik ki8k ki'k k8k k'k f4f k8k f$f k'k f4f k8k f$f k'k k8k

4 8 48 $ 4 $4 8 4 84 $848 f4f k8k f$f k'k $4.48 $8.48 848

Our sales are $48.48; the total sales for the day are $484.

Doesn't the girl have to get to the office at eight o'clock?
```

LESSON 9
Technique Guide

Speed in typewriting has little or no commercial value without a high degree of accuracy. The emphasis in all your typing must be on accuracy. Speed will come as a result of intelligent practice. Well-directed practice is the only "royal road" to success in typewriting.

Review Practice 9

DIRECTIONS: Set the marginal stops for a sixty-space line. Have a top margin of one and a half inches. Use single spacing. Type each line twice. Double-space after the second typing of each line.

NOTE: The small letter *l* is used for the figure *1*. In a series of figures in which the comma or the period is used, do not space after the mark of punctuation. See the third line for the use of the period in a series of figures.

```
4f$f 8k'k 4f$f 8k'k wsxs ol.l 4f$f 8k'k qaza p;j; 4f$f 8k'k

1 4 14 1 8 18 4 8 48 4 1 41 8 4 84 8 1 81 1 4 8 148 8 4 84

Mr. P. C. Quinn's bill, due May 8, amounts to $184.81.

lax six put vex box six cap mix wax pay box was fix put six

gaze quit maze quiz raze quit maze quiz next ship quiz maze
```

which gives credit for a quotation, it should stand at the end of the quotation. The figure should not be placed after the colon used to introduce the quoted matter.

b. If reference to the work of an author is made in the text, but no quotation from the work is used, place the figure indicating the footnote immediately after the author's name. The title of the work referred to will appear in the footnote.

c. Number the footnotes consecutively throughout an article or a chapter in a book.

d. The footnotes must appear at the foot of the same page as that on which the reference figures appear. In planning the manuscript page, leave sufficient space at the foot of the page for the footnotes. Separate the footnotes from the text by a line extending approximately two inches from the left margin.

e. It is important to arrange the footnotes correctly.

(1) A footnote must be given the same number as that used for the reference in the text.

(2) Indent the footnote five spaces. In typed manuscripts, the number preceding the footnote need not be elevated; that is, made a superior figure. If the number is not elevated, a period (.) may be placed after the number. This practice, however, is not uniform.

(3) Single-space footnotes, but double-space between them.

(4) When reference is made to a published book, the footnote should be typed as follows: the author's name, including his Christian name or initials, followed by a comma; the title of the book, underscored and followed by a comma; the place of publication, followed by a colon; the name of the publisher, followed by a comma; the date of publication, followed by a comma; and the exact pages of the book to which reference is made, followed by a period.

(5) When reference is made to a published article, the footnote should be typed as follows: the author's name, including his Christian name or initials, followed by a comma; the title of the article, placed within quotation marks and followed by a comma; the name of the periodical in which the article is published, underscored and followed by a comma; the volume number, typed in capitalized Roman numerals and followed by a comma; and the page reference, typed in Arabic numerals.

(6) When two footnotes contain references to the same work and follow each other without any intervening footnote, use *Ibid.*, the abbreviation for *ibidem* (meaning, in the same place), and the exact page number for the second footnote.

10. Place quotation marks and other marks of punctuation as follows:

a. A period or a comma at the end of a quotation should precede the quotation mark.

b. A semicolon or a colon should follow the quotation mark.

c. A question or an exclamation mark at the end of a quotation should stand first if it applies to the quotation, and not to the sentence containing the quotation. The quotation mark should stand first if the question or the exclamation mark applies to the sentence containing the quotation, and not to the quotation.

d. When a quotation consists of several paragraphs, a quotation mark should be placed at the beginning of each paragraph and at the end of the quotation.

LESSON 8

Be on guard mentally against making errors in typing. Some errors are caused by awkwardness or lack of finger control, but far more errors are caused by lack of mental control. To correct an error, discover and eliminate the faulty technique causing it.

Mere repetition of stroking is not effective; it is not how many times the stroke is made, but the quality of the stroking, that brings improvement.

In each practice period you should try to single out one technique for a special improvement drill. The stroking, carriage return, insertion of the paper, shifting for capitals, use of the tabular key, etc., are techniques which need to be studied carefully.

Review Practice 8

DIRECTIONS: Set the marginal stops for a sixty-space line. Have a top margin of one and a half inches. Use single spacing. Type each line twice. Double-space after the second typing of each line.

```
qaza p;-; wsxs ol.l edcd ik,k rfvf ujmj tfbf yjnj gfjh -;*;

lazy quit zeal hazy quit size next zone quit zeal size open

well-to-do up-to-date one-half two-thirds son-in-law one-half

John Zilbandy saw the quick vamp fixing the high trapeze.

A two-thirds price reduction is given by the up-town store.
```

Exercise 8

DIRECTIONS: Set the marginal stops for a sixty-space line. Adjust the tabular stop for a five-space indentation. Have a top margin of one and a half inches. Use double spacing. Type the exercise twice on the same sheet.

All letters of the alphabet are used in this exercise.

	STROKES
Most fears are just as foolish as they can be. Life is	59
good; success is possible for all except the lazy. What is	120
there to fear? We must know that we have quite enough skill	183
to do some work well; then we must find that work and do it.	243

Optional Exercise 8

All letters of the alphabet are used in this exercise.

	STROKES
Be your best in all you do. Train yourself to work with	60
quick zeal. Begin this training now; the best place in which	123
to do it is just where you are. Make no excuses; accept no	184
defeats as final. Give your best to all that you do.	238

[22]

Ten-Minute Timed Writing Practice

DIRECTIONS: Set the marginal stops for a seventy-space line. Adjust the tabular stop for an indentation of five spaces. Use double spacing.

When a quotation consists of several paragraphs, a quotation mark should be placed at the beginning of each paragraph and at the end of the quotation.

THRIFT

STROKES

Thrift is a many-sided topic, yet too often we hear of thrift as it relates 77
to money only. Success stories have told us how money grows at four or six 154
per cent. This has tended to make us penny wise; it has caused us to forget 232
that life is more than money and that eyes always held to the ground can 305
never see the stars. We should not reject the idea of thrift as including the 385
saving of money; we should try, though, to realize that in the building of a 462
life other phases of thrift are of equal importance. This point of view is ex- 543
pressed by one high-school boy in the paragraphs which follow. *(606)* 606

"Our thrift drive has just ended. We are one hundred percenters in our 682
room; each student is now a weekly depositor in the school savings bank. 755
This success is due quite largely to Bob, our class president. He is a most 834
excellent persuader. His zeal for 100% membership in all school drives has 912
gained for him a place on most of the school committees. All the teachers 988
beam on him, and most of the students think him great. He was at his best 1064
in this last campaign as he urged the value of thrift on us. *(519)* 1125

"The other day I began to think that even Bob has feet of clay. I got a 1203
new view on thrift, too. Our typing teacher had explained the problem and 1279
assigned the work to be done. After a few minutes of half-hearted work, 1353
Bob sat back with folded arms, saying to the teacher that he would just rest 1431
a while. In a short time he asked me whether the work should be typed 1503
with single or double spacing. Eagerly I told him what the teacher had said 1582
to all of us. Another minute of puzzled inspection of the problem was fol- 1659
lowed by a noisy talk with the pupil in front of him. Finally the teacher 1735
came to answer his questions and to repeat the instructions given before Bob 1813
had begun to rest. *(707)* 1832

"Of course, I am glad that our class can be 100% in every school activity. 1912
Bob surely deserves a lot of credit for his zeal, too. I wish, though, he would 1995
become eloquent about the value of thrift in things other than merely school 2072
savings. There must be more to thrift than just depositing nickels in the 2148
school savings bank. What of thrift in the use of time? Such thrift might 2227
cause us to listen more carefully to the explanations our teachers give. Per- 2307
haps then our teachers would not be compelled to repeat their directions 2380
two or three times during each lesson. Of course, thrift in the use of money 2459
is a good thing. That is one way to make certain that there will be money 2535
to spend later. Thrift in the use of time, though, must be just as important, 2615
for it calls for using each minute as it comes and using it wisely. *(851)* 2683

"Some good persuader should start a drive for thrift in the use of energy, 2760
too. Most of us seem to have the activity craze. There must be something 2837
doing. Just what that something is, does not seem to matter so much if there 2916
is excited movement to it. To be calm and quiet is akin to being one of the 2994
unburied dead; it is a state to be avoided at all costs. I do not know how 3071
there can be most earnest thinking when there is such constant motion; yet 3146
not often do we hear anything said about thrift in the use of our energy." 3222
(539)

The thought of thrift in the use of energy is excellent. It suggests that 3300
competition and trial by combat need no longer rule our lives. It throws out 3379
organized contests as essential to progress. It shifts the goal from beating 3458

Optional Exercise 7

All letter reaches previously practiced are used in this paragraph.

Tests come daily to all of us. We expect to   48

find them in texts, but do we not just as often have   101

them in our contacts with others? More failures are   156

caused by lack of social grace than lack of skill.   206

Fixation Practice 7

Control of *q*, hyphen (-), asterisk (*), and *z*

Illustration No. 31

Reach to *q*, hyphen (-), and asterisk (*)

Illustration No. 32, Reach to *z*

Locked-Key Drill. Study the illustrations and directions carefully. Through the locked-key drill, initiate the new reaches.

The letter *q* is above *a* and is controlled by the *a finger*. Make the movement without twisting the elbow or turning the wrist.

The hyphen (-) is the end key at the right in the top row of the keyboard. It is controlled by the *; finger*. The asterisk (*) is the shift of the hyphen on most typewriters. On some typewriters, the special $\frac{3}{4}$ character is the shift of the hyphen.

The hyphen is used to form compound words and at the end of a line to indicate the division of a word. When the bell rings, it is a warning that there are six or seven more spaces before the carriage locks. If you are writing a word of one syllable when the bell rings, complete the word, and then start a new line. If you are writing a word of *more* than one syllable when the bell rings, complete the syllable, strike the hyphen (-) once, throw the carriage, and complete the word on the next line. *Do not lift the eyes from the copy.*

The dash is made with two hyphens, spacing neither before nor after.

The letter *z* is in the first row of keys, below the letter *a,* and is controlled by the *a finger*. In making the reach, keep the fingers curved; give a quick, decisive blow to the center of the key. Avoid changing the hand position.

DIRECTIONS: Set the marginal stops for a fifty-two-space line. Have a top margin of one and a half inches. Use single spacing. Type each line twice. Double-space after the second typing of each line.

aqa fqa quit aqa quit acquit quack quick quack que

;p; aqa ;-; que ;-; aqa ;*; que ;*; fqa j*; que j*;

aza fza size aza size amazed sizes amaze sized aza

one-half three-fourths up-hill top-heavy one-half

Men do not realize how great thrift is.--Cicero

[21]

a rival in a game to winning over one's own past best record. The world   3533
might be better if the yardstick of comparison could be made to measure   3605
strength, not by the marks set by others, but by those set by the one whose   3681
progress is being measured. Some day we may acquire the power to do our   3755
best just for the joy of doing our best; then we shall not need a track meet   3832
to cause us to break records. *(1179)*   3862

Let us practice thrift in saving money, thrift in the use of time, and   3935
thrift in the use of energy. Let us excel in all that we do just for the joy of   4017
doing our best. The best prize, when all is said and done, comes not from   4093
beating the other fellow, but, rather, from making our past record the yard-   4170
stick of comparison and going far beyond what we have done in the past.   4242
When such is the attitude, acquiring thrift is a daily challenge. *(447)*   4309

Syllable intensity, 1.30

BUDGET XV

Corrective Drills for *f*, *k*, *g*, and *l*

DIRECTIONS: Set the marginal stops for a seventy-space line. Use single spacing. Type each line twice. Double-space after the second typing of each line.

```
four-footed forefather fateful forgetful football forfeit fitful

kick kept Kirk lack lake kink kill pink keep rink link rake sink

grade grateful grudging gorgeous gurgling exaggerating aggregating

lastingly legible legalize loyalty literal lifelessly likely liable

one 1 two 2 three 3 four 4 five 5 six 6 seven 7 eight 8 nine 9 ten 10
```

Sentence Practice

DIRECTIONS: Use a different sentence in each practice period. Type the sentence five times. Set the marginal stops for a sixty-five-space line. Use double spacing.

STROKES FOR
EACH SENTENCE

Energy will do practically anything that can be done in this world.   68

He who does little for others does just as little for himself.   63

What is the sum of 3 and 8 and 9 and 2 and 7 and 5 and 6 and 40?   66

The lazy dog was always several jumps behind the quick brown fox.   66

It is necessary for one to be careful in everything that he does.   66

Corrective Drill Paragraphs

DIRECTIONS: Set the marginal stops for a seventy-space line. Adjust the tabular stop for an indentation of five spaces. Use single spacing. Type one corrective drill paragraph in each practice period. Alternate the paragraphs in the various practice periods.

A salesman's cause is lost as soon as he starts using sarcasm. His samples may satisfy, his seasonal goods may be the best, but the use of sarcasm is just that short-sighted exhibition of rudeness which leaves customers antagonized. Success in selling may not require submission to a strenuous course in salesmanship, but in every such course the prospective salesman is taught that tact and courtesy are essential to success in selling, and that sarcasm is a serious shortcoming of a salesman.

DIRECTIONS: Set the marginal stops for a fifty-two-space line. Have a top margin of one and a half inches. Use single spacing. Type each line twice. Double-space after the second typing of each line.

```
sxs fxs sxs six sxs six fix six fix wax six box six

;p; jp; apt ;p; put jp; pad lip ;p; apt put dip lap

box six put lax sip fix pay six pad lax put six pay

k,k k,k k?k sxs k,k sxs k?k fbf k,k sxs k?k k,k k?k

You expect six men, do you?  Did he put the box in?
```

(Space once after the comma.)

LESSON 7

Technique Guide

Do you have a clean-cut and quick get-away stroke? Does your finger deliver the blow to the center of the key without following the key on its downward movement? Are your movements well controlled, your wrists and forearms practically motionless? Do you keep your eyes on the copy from which you are typing? Does your finished work have an even appearance, indicating an even distribution of force back of each stroke? Are you typing as smoothly as possible? Are you doing your best work on every assignment?

Review Practice 7

DIRECTIONS: Set the marginal stops for a fifty-two-space line. Have a top margin of one and a half inches. Use single spacing. Type each line twice. Double-space after the second typing of each line.

```
rf ,k ws mj vf ol xs ik ed yj bf .l cd p; tf nj ?k

ship next page keep next hope trip copy next plan

If he is to go up in it, is he to be in it at six?

Will they have that girl from your shop stop here?

Excel in thinking if you would excel in your work.
```

(Space once after the comma.)

Exercise 7

DIRECTIONS: Set the marginal stops for a fifty-two-space line. Adjust the tabular stop for a five-space indentation. Have a top margin of one and a half inches. Use double spacing. Type the exercise twice on the same sheet.

All letter reaches previously practiced are used in this paragraph.

	STROKES
Too many of us set our eyes on the big things	48
we expect to do and forget to do the little things	99
that come each day. Is not life, though, mostly	149
little things with a big event just now and then?	199

[20]

It is just as important for typing students to think as it is for them to strive for top-rate typing scores. Very often students wait until they have obtained a position before they start to think, but it is then too late to begin *t* to do a thing which should have been established as a habit long before the *key* position was taken. Begin now to train yourself zealously to think through every problem. Make extra effort to see that you understand each typing assignment. The question of accuracy in interpreting directions cannot be overlooked. It will pay as rich dividends as increased typing speed.

Five-Minute Timed Writing Practice

DIRECTIONS: Set the marginal stops for a seventy-space line. Adjust the tabular stop for an indentation of five spaces. Use double spacing.

STROKES

Business education has been making use of the survey. Many studies	70
have been made of the young worker in business. Small and large centers	144
have made their local inquiries and have found some amazing facts. One of	220
the first things to be learned is the fact that local problems do not vary much	300
except in details. The true point of difference is in the judging of the facts	381
which have been brought out by the surveys and the seeming lack of desire	455
to base action on the facts learned. It may be that in the use of facts life pre-	539
sents its greatest test for all of us. After all, it is neither knowing nor know-	623
ing that we know that truly counts, but it is doing as we know that scores.	699
The use of facts and not the mere knowing of facts, then, is the measure of	776
our strength.	790

Syllable intensity, 1.30

Exercise 103

DIRECTIONS: Set the marginal stops for a sixty-five-space line. Adjust the tabular stop for an indentation of five spaces. Use double spacing. Leave a two-inch top margin on the first page. On each succeeding page leave a one-inch top margin and center the number of each page at the top.

INTRODUCTION

Methods and materials of instruction in commercial education are undergoing a significant development. That remedial instruction is receiving widespread consideration in schools is indicated by recent educational literature. This tendency is particularly evident in the field of typewriting.

This study is an analysis of the errors made in a first-, a second-, and a third-semester class in typewriting of Schenley High School, Pittsburgh, Pennsylvania, to determine the persistence and the kind of errors common to the work and to the classes studied.

Learning to typewrite presents four major problems according to Dr. Book.[1] His classification of problems is as follows:

1. Getting the copy.
2. Typing without omissions or errors.
3. Learning to manipulate the machine.
4. Acquiring finger dexterity and correct technique for quickly striking and releasing the keys.

This thesis is concerned only with the second problem listed by Dr. Book, the problem of typing without omissions or errors. Present practice in teaching typewriting is to give drill for the group as a whole as far as the students of the group have common difficulties, and to try to adapt the drill to the needs of individuals as far as their difficulties differ from the group problems. It is essential, then, to find common difficulties of the class in order that class drill may be corrective.

Bailey[2] studied the weighting of speed and accuracy factors in typewriting. The study resulted in the conclusion that employers attach less importance to speed

---

[1] William F. Book, *Learning to Typewrite*, New York: Gregg Publishing Company, 1925, p. 168.

[2] Florence D. Bailey, *Weighting of Speed and Accuracy Factors in Typewriting*, Thesis, University of Iowa, 1930.

Optional Exercise 6

All letter reaches previously practiced are used in this paragraph.

STROKES

(Type the exercise twice. Use double spacing.)

```
Few men owe their failure to foes other than       47
the foe within.  Few fail through lack of ability.  99
We can all make our lives just what we will through 152
the thoughts we think and the work we do.          193
```

Corrective Drill Practice

In each lesson check all completed work. In doing this, train yourself to circle each word in which an error has been made. Finding the error is important; equally important, however, is the remedial thinking and the corrective drill practice which should be a part of each day's work and which should follow the listing of the errors made.

After each exercise has been completed, list the errors on the bottom of the same sheet. For example, if, in typing the word for, you type it flr, you will write with pencil, *l for o*.

Corrective drill practice for the errors can be done with the keys locked. Make the finger reaches, as, *lol* for the error listed above; then practice the words in which the errors were made. Corrective drills must be built to fit your own needs. Measurable improvement will come as the result of this remedial thinking and corrective drill practice.

Fixation Practice 6
Control of *x*, *p*, comma (,), and interrogation point (?)

Illustration No. 28, Reach to *x*

Illustration No. 29, Reach to *p*

Illustration No. 30
Reach to comma (,) and interrogation point (?)

Locked-Key Drill. Study the illustrations and directions carefully. Through the locked-key drill, initiate the new reaches.

The letter *x* is below *s* and is controlled by the *s finger*. In making the reach to *x*, do not attempt to hold the other fingers of the hand rigidly in their home positions. Keep the fingers curved and the *a finger* poised above its home position. Lift the other fingers slightly. This will give greater freedom to the movement to *x*.

The letter *p*, controlled by the *; finger*, is above the *;*. In making the reach to the letter *p*, move the finger straight forward. Do not twist the elbow, the wrist, or the forearm.

The comma (,) is below and slightly to the right of *k*. On most typewriters, the interrogation point (?) is the shift of the comma. On some models of typewriters, the shift of the comma is the comma. If you are operating such a typewriter, you will need to change the instructions for controlling the key for the interrogation point. On the typewriters having the double comma key, the interrogation point is the shift of the diagonal, the last key to the right in the first row of keys, and is controlled by the *; finger*.

Curve the finger and give a quick, forceful blow to the center of the key; immediately snatch the finger back toward the palm of the hand, and bring it to its home position. Do not permit the hand to get out of correct alignment with the keyboard. *Eliminate unnecessary hand movement.* The fingers must do the work.

and accuracy as a basis of measurement of typists' ability than has been thought.

Carmichael[3] studied the effect the element of time had upon accuracy. He reached the conclusion that the difference between the results achieved by the double-period schools and the results achieved by the single-period schools is not great enough to justify the use of the double period for typewriting.

Ford[4] studied errors in typewriting from the standpoint of spelling and compared the errors with the Ayres Spelling Scale. She found a slight gain in accuracy for second-year over first-year students on the first 350 words in the Ayres Scale.

A most comprehensive study of errors was made by Lessenberry[5] in an analysis of 63,000 errors listed from weekly timed tests and daily class papers and sent in from all states of the United States. This study lists adjacent key control and vowel confusion as the major types of errors.

Morrison[6] evaluated errors in typewriting on the basis of business men's opinions, classifying them under letters mailable without correction, mailable after correction, and unmailable. The results of this study show that some errors are more serious than others.

Ostrey[7] evaluated methods and mechanical equipment in typewriting. One of the elements of his study was to determine the relative frequency of errors and to rank the letters according to the frequency of use and to the frequency of errors. He concluded that it is possible to determine, in a general way, the nature and distribution of errors, from which reasonable deductions may be made leading to remedial procedure.

Stone[8] studied thirty pupils to determine the common errors made by beginning pupils and to discover what effect corrective drill had in eliminating errors. The records of eight failing pupils were eliminated from the study, thus leaving only twenty-two pupils for whom data were listed. She found that speed improved without much inaccuracy under the classroom procedure of individual analysis of errors and corrective drill practice.

[3] Vernal H. Carmichael, *Objective Measurement of Typewriting of High School Commercial Pupils in Indiana,* Thesis, Indiana University, 1929.

[4] Gertrude Catherine Ford, *A Study of Typewriting Errors,* Thesis, University of Washington, 1928.

[5] D. D. Lessenberry, *Manual for Twentieth Century Touch Typewriting, Complete,* Cincinnati: South-Western Publishing Company, 1929.

[6] Noble Brewer Morrison, *An Evaluation of Errors in Typewriting,* Thesis, University of Iowa, 1930.

[7] J. Method Ostrey, *A Critical Analysis of Letter Sequences as a Basis for Proving Criteria for the Evaluation of Methods and Mechanical Equipment in Typewriting,* Thesis, University of Nebraska, 1929.

[8] Ruby M. Stone, *A Study of Typewriting Errors Made in the Beginning Classes of Monroe High School, Monroe, Michigan,* Thesis, University of Michigan, 1928.

OPTIONAL BUDGET XVI

In completing the work of this optional budget, you have an opportunity to plan a booklet of instructions which will be of help to you in your personal typing. Look through the text carefully up to this page. Note the instructions or the exercises which you want to keep in your personal manual of instructions on typing. The problems listed below are suggestive. Add to these as your interest dictates.

DIRECTIONS: Use full sheets of paper. You are to have absolute freedom in determining the set-up of each problem. Try to show your mastery of arrangement as well as of typing technique. This booklet will be returned to you for your own use. Put in it the instructions you want to keep for later use.

Suggested Problems

1. Technique guides, Lessons 2 to 14 inclusive.
2. Rules for vertical and horizontal centering, page 33.
3. Manipulation drills:
   a. Page 34. d. Page 41.
   b. Page 36. e. Page 42.
   c. Page 40. f. Page 43.
4. Summary of spacing instructions, page 44.
5. Daily check on fundamental habits, page 46.
6. Syllabication, page 48.
7. Summary of the set-up of the business letter, page 79.
8. Style Letters:
   No. 1, page 60.   No. 8, page 90.
   No. 2, page 64.   No. 9, page 93.
   No. 3, page 65.   No. 10, page 94.
   No. 4, page 67.   No. 11, page 97.
   No. 5, page 75.   No. 12, page 99.
   No. 6, page 82.   No. 13, page 109.
   No. 7, page 88.
9. Arabic and Roman numerals, page 73.
10. Check list for tabulation, page 102.

Carriage Return and Tabular-Key Control, Manipulation Drill

Time: Thirty Seconds

Purpose of the Drill. Two sources of waste of time and typing power are the inaccurate control of the tabular key and the sluggish return of the carriage. This drill will help you to overcome these faults.

DIRECTIONS: Set the marginal stop for the left margin at 15. Set tabular stops at 40 and 65. Use single spacing. If you are operating a typewriter which has a left carriage throw, use Drill a. If you are operating a typewriter which has a right carriage throw, use Drill b.

Drill a: When the command to begin is given, type the word *the* at the left margin; depress the tabular key and hold it down until the carriage stops; then type the word *the* again; depress the tabular key and again type the word *the*. Throw the carriage and repeat the operation until time is called. The word *the* should be typed three times to a line and should be perfectly placed in the three columns.

Drill b: Follow the directions for *Drill a,* except type the word *his* instead of the word *the.*

SCORE: Your score will be the number of words correctly typed in columns. Record your score in order that you can determine your progress when you compare the present score with the score you make in later tests.

Exercise 6

DIRECTIONS: Set the marginal stops for a fifty-two-space line. Adjust the tabular stop for an indentation of five spaces. Have a top margin of one and a half inches. Use double spacing. Type the exercise as shown below.

All letter reaches previously practiced are used in this paragraph.

	STROKES
It is just as easy to form a good habit as a	47
bad one. It is just as hard to break a good habit	99
as a bad one. Form good habits in all that you do;	152
then you can let every habit work for you.	195
It is just as easy to form a good habit as a	242
bad one. It is just as hard to break a good habit	294
as a bad one. Form good habits in all that you do;	347
then you can let every habit work for you.	389

[18]

SPECIAL PROBLEMS IN TYPING BUSINESS LETTERS

You have learned the standard forms of business letters. In this instructional block, you are given the opportunity of studying the problems in adapting the standard forms of letters to office customs. Study these adaptations of forms carefully.

BUDGET XVII
Drill Emphasizing the Shift-Key Control

DIRECTIONS: Set the marginal stops for a seventy-space line. Use single spacing. Type each line twice. Double-space after the second typing of each line.

Albert Vaughn, Paul Jones, and Carl Baxter are on the football squad.
The teacher asked Frank, Henry, Walter, George, and Eric to help him.
Don Irwin's twin brothers, Oren and Loren, will go to school at Yale.
Nolan Morris invited Kenneth, Ronald, and Sam to visit him in Quincy.
John Underwood needs to practice words using the letters X, Y, and Z.

Corrective Drill Paragraphs

DIRECTIONS: Set the marginal stops for a seventy-space line. Adjust the tabular stop for an indentation of five spaces. Use single spacing. Type one corrective drill paragraph in each practice period. Alternate the paragraphs in the various practice periods.

u
key
    Do not demur when you are called upon to be useful. Rather, seize each opportunity as just one more chance to show how useful you can be. Unfortunate is he who is unwilling to serve, unstable in friendship, and uninterested in community problems. It is quite unfair that society should be burdened with an individual of little use. If he can be made to realize his own weaknesses, ultimately he may cease to undervalue his debt to society and may experience the urge to adapt himself to his opportunities. In such a case his usefulness becomes his own joy and his place in society unquestioned.

v
key
    Every photogravure of Paradise Valley fails to reveal the exquisite colors of the sky and the vegetation. The Valley is a vista of velvet green, and everywhere is visible a lavish variety of wild flowers. The heavy grays and browns have vanished and given way to vigorous blues, lovely lavenders, and vermilions. Just above the clouds, Mount Rainier can be hazily seen, its peak covered with ice. Paradise Valley is exquisite; but you will have to be there in springtime, as I was, to appreciate it fully.

Five-Minute Timed Writing Practice

DIRECTIONS: Set the marginal stops for a seventy-space line. Adjust the tabular stop for an indentation of five spaces. Use double spacing.

STROKES

	STROKES
Change is the whole keynote of progress. We scrap the good for that	71
which is better. That which is good in one age must give place to that	144
which better fits the needs of a later time. Look at business writing. For a	225
long time men were content to write with the quill pen. Times changed;	298
life began to be speeded up. The quill pen did not fit in with our amazing	375
energy. A new device for business writing had to be found. When the need	452
was felt, the man with his plan soon appeared. Thus came the typewriter.	527
It was clumsy at first, but now it will write faster than our fingers have yet	607
been able to move. We cannot use its full speed. Our next work should be	684
to improve in the use of the typewriter we have. It is in this failure to work	765
to capacity that we find our greatest waste. We build time-saving machines,	843
but we fail to develop our best use of these machines.	898

Syllable intensity, 1.30

LESSON 6
Technique Guide

Correct position at the typewriter is important. The way you sit has much to do with the way you type. Then, too, correct posture aids in correct breathing, which greatly increases your resistance to fatigue. Carefully review the instructions given on page 3. Students sit more often too close to the typewriter than too far from it. Determine the most comfortable position consistent with the development of correct habits, and assume that position every day.

Review Practice 6

DIRECTIONS: Set the marginal stops for a fifty-space line. If you are using 40 as the centering point, set the marginal stops at 15 and 71. Have a top margin of one and a half inches. Use single spacing. Type each line twice. Double-space after the second typing of each line.

```
rfvf ujmj tfbf yjnj asws ;lol edcd ik;k ol.l gfhj

jay fib cad lay nab cad but may cad jay fib can

but may can you may why but can yet boy can you

You can do good work if you think that you can.

It is well to think and to act as well as we can.
```

Tabular-Key Controls

The tabular mechanism is used for paragraphs, special lines, and tabulated column work. It consists of the tabular key (No. 22), the tabular rack (No. 23), the tabular stop (No. 24), and the tabular scale (No. 25).

The location of the tabular key (No. 22) is not the same on all typewriters. You will notice that in Illustration No. 25 this key is controlled by the *f finger*. In Illustrations No. 26 and No. 27 the tabular key is controlled by the *; finger.*

The margin release (No. 26) is used in writing outside the marginal lines without a readjustment of the stops.

Illustration No. 25
Reach to Tabular Key
UNDERWOOD, MODEL 6;
L. C. SMITH

Illustration No. 26
Reach to Tabular Key
REMINGTON; ROYAL; UNDERWOOD,
MODEL 5; WOODSTOCK

Illustration No. 27
Reach to Tabular Key
NOISELESS TYPEWRITER

Illustrations and instructions are given on pages V to IX for the different typewriters. The operating technique is practically the same for all typewriters, the greatest difference being in the location of the tabular key itself. First, know the mechanism of the typewriter you are using; then, carefully study the mechanism of the other typewriters.

Exercise 104

DIRECTIONS: Set the marginal stops for a fifty-space line. Type the following letter in the modified block form with the closing lines indented to the position for the complimentary close and blocked in that position (see Style Letter No. 9 on page 93). Leave seven single spaces between the date and the inside address. Use single spacing and open punctuation.

Mrs. W. C. Bayne 1164 Ridgeway Avenue Plainfield, New Jersey Dear Madam: Our cashier has called to our attention a notation on the heading of your bill, requesting us to change your account from Bess R. Thomas to Mrs. W. C. Bayne. (P) In making changes in charge accounts, we always require the customer to sign a new application card. We do this to protect the customer no less than to protect ourselves. (P) Please fill in the enclosed application card, sign, and return it to this office as soon as possible. When this card has been returned to us, your account will be changed as you have requested. Yours very truly JOHN WANAMAKER (Dictated by N. B. Jameson) Credit Manager Enclosure No. 30 *(539–95)*

Exercise 105

DIRECTIONS: Set the marginal stops for a forty-space line. Type the following letter in the modified block form with five-space paragraph indentations and the closing lines indented to the position for the complimentary close and blocked in that position (see Style Letter No. 10 on page 94). Since a letterhead is not used, the heading contains the complete address of the writer. Type the street number and name on the tenth line from the top of the sheet so that the date will be in the correct position. Leave seven single spaces between the date and the inside address. Use single spacing and open punctuation. The signature *Mrs. W. C. Bayne* should be typed in parentheses four single spaces below the complimentary close.

Observe that a personal name representing a corporation requires the use of the salutation *Gentlemen.*

The spaces between the complimentary close and the typed signature are left for the penwritten signature, Bess Thomas Bayne. This letter illustrates the correct method for a married woman to use in signing a business letter.

1164 Ridgeway Avenue Plainfield, New Jersey (current date) John Wanamaker Ninth Street New York, N. Y. Gentlemen: I am enclosing the application card for a change in my charge account. This account should be changed from the name of Bess R. Thomas to Mrs. W. C. Bayne. (P) Since I am not opening a new account but merely changing the name in which the account is to be used, I assume that the references given at the time I originally opened the account with you will be sufficient. If additional references will be necessary before the change is made, please let me know. Very truly yours (Mrs. W. C. Bayne) Enclosure *(469–83)*

Exercise 106

DIRECTIONS: Set the marginal stops for a fifty-space line. Type the following letter in the modified block form with the closing lines indented to the position for the complimentary close and blocked in that position (see Style Letter No. 9 on page 93). Leave seven single spaces between the date and the inside address. Use single spacing and open punctuation.

Mrs. W. C. Bayne 1164 Ridgeway Avenue Plainfield, New Jersey Dear Madam: Your charge account, which was formerly on our books under the name of Bess R. Thomas, has been changed, in accordance with your request, to Mrs. W. C. Bayne, 1164 Ridgeway Avenue, Plainfield, New Jersey. (P) The former charge coin #68934 has been changed to coin #83710-Y. (P) Please call and return to us the old coin and obtain the new one. If you cannot call in person for this new shopping coin, please return the old one to us, and we shall immediately send you the coin for your new charge account. Yours very truly JOHN WANAMAKER (Dictated by N. B. Jameson) Credit Manager *(520–91)*

Exercise 107

DIRECTIONS: Set the marginal stops for a sixty-space line. Type the following letter in the modified block form with the attention line centered on the sheet, the second paragraph of quoted material indented in block form five spaces on the left and the

Work that is well done is its own reward.   43

(At the end of a sentence, the period is followed by two spaces.)

Life is just. It will give us all we earn.   89

Wise use of time will make for wiser living.   135

Move forward; leave the low levels to others.   181

Optional Exercise 5

have must view like with when this list whom   45

The time we devote to work is never lost.   88

Lives grow through making wise use of time.   133

Giving is more than getting. Give more.   175

Fixation Practice 5
Control of *y*, *b*, and *c*

Locked-Key Drill. Study the illustrations and directions carefully. Through the locked-key drill, initiate the new reaches.

Illustration No. 23, **Reach to** *y* **and** *b*

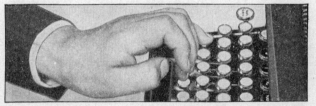

Illustration No. 24, **Reach to** *c*

The letter *y*, controlled by the *j finger*, is above the letter *h*. In making the reach to *y*, hold the hand in its correct keyboard position, straighten the *j finger*, and make the reach without changing the hand position.

The letter *b* is below the letter *g* and is controlled by the *f finger*. Make a direct reach from *f* to *b*. Do not attempt to hold the *d* and *s fingers* over their home keys, but let them move slightly. The *a finger* should be held in its position to act as a guide in bringing the other fingers back to the home position.

The letter *c* is below and slightly to the right of *d* and is controlled by the *d finger*. In making the reach to *c*, hold the *a finger* curved over its home position, but permit the other fingers to move with the controlling *finger d*. This will give greater freedom of movement to the *d finger*. Move the *d finger* diagonally from its home position to *c*.

DIRECTIONS: Set the marginal stops for a forty-five-space line. Have a top margin of one and a half inches. Use single spacing. Type each line twice. Double-space after the second typing of each line.

```
jjj jyj jay jay jjj day jay hay jay jyj say

fbf fbf bad fib fbf big fib fbf bag fbf big

dcd cad cad bid cad act did cad his cad dcd

jay fib lay can bag may cad big can big may

back year come year both come back year cold
```

(Hit the center of the key with a swift, controlled stroke. Release the key quickly.)

right, and the closing lines indented to the position for the complimentary close and blocked in that position. Leave five single spaces between the date and the inside address. Use single spacing and open punctuation. Type the dictator's name in the position for the reference initials. Observe that the letter in this exercise is the same as Style Letter No. 15 in the illustration. This letter is to be arranged in exactly the same form.

American Engineering Society 3856 Marchand Street Milwaukee, Wisconsin Attention Purchasing Agent Gentlemen: Our sales manager has just handed me a message straight from the shoulder. Here it is: (P) The American Engineering Society should have a copy of our new pamphlet, "Visible Purchase Control." The sales record card of this society shows that, although Fidex visible card records are now being used in other departments, one of the most important departments, the purchasing department, has been overlooked. (P) "Visible Purchase Control," which is the pamphlet our sales manager wants you to read, has been carefully prepared and explains in an interesting, concise way the methods that simplify and multiply the usefulness of the vital records that are so essential to the success of a progressive purchasing department. (P) If you want a copy of this pamphlet, just make a note of the fact on the lower margin of this letter and return the letter to us. The rest will be up to us. We will do our part without obligating you in any way. Yours very truly (Dictated by C. A. Neeley, Jr.) Manager, Systems Department *(963–159)*

Exercise 108

DIRECTIONS: Set the marginal stops for a fifty-five-space line. Type the following letter in the modified block form with the attention line centered horizontally and the closing lines indented to the position for the complimentary close and blocked in that position. Use paragraph subjects typed in capitals, for those paragraphs beginning "Quantity," "Price," and "Terms." Leave six single spaces between the date and the inside address. Use single spacing and open punctuation. Type the dictator's name in

Style Letter No. 15—Modified Block Form with Centered Attention Line and Indented Quotation

the position for the reference initials. Observe that the letter in this exercise is the same as Style Letter No. 16 in the illustration. This letter should be arranged in exactly the same form.

De Luxe Furniture Company 2354 Euclid Avenue Cleveland, Ohio Attention Purchasing Agent Gentlemen: In answer to your recent letter making inquiry as to the best price we can quote on 300 pairs of hinges, we quote you as follows: (P) QUANTITY: 300 pairs hinges, like sample #714, flat back, 3" joint, left leaf 1½", right leaf 1¾". (P) PRICE: Net price of $50 for the lot. (P) TERMS: C.O.D. (P) We shall be glad to receive this initial order from you. Immediate shipment of the 300 pairs of hinges can be made. (P) We do not believe that you can duplicate this quotation elsewhere. We have these hinges in stock and are willing to quote you an attractive price in order to dispose of them promptly. Very truly yours (Dictated by L. C. Walleck) Manager, Sales Department *(611–108)*

in a diagonal line with the letters *u* and *j*. Make the reach without twisting the hand and

without moving the other fingers from their home positions.

Illustration No. 21, Reach to *i* and *v*

Illustration No. 22, Reach to *w* and *m*

DIRECTIONS: Set the marginal stops for a forty-space line. Have a top margin of one and a half inches. Use single spacing. Type each line twice. Double-space after the second typing of each line.

```
kik frf kik fir kik sir kik his kik sir

fff fvf jnj fvf van fvf van fvf van fvf

sws sow fws how sws who sws vow sws now

jmj mow jmj mid jmj mow jmj ham jmj dim

from wish from this vial wish vial mail
```

(Let the finger make the reach. Avoid all forearm movement. Type with an even touch and an even speed.)

LESSON 5

Technique Guide

You are learning to type by touch. This means that you are developing the skill of typing without looking at the hands or the keyboard. Control of all operating parts also should be by touch. When throwing the carriage, *hold your eyes on the copy*. This makes possible the reading of notes or copy without any interruption in the typing.

Review Practice 5

DIRECTIONS: Set the marginal stops for a forty-five-space line. If you are using 40 as the centering point, set the marginal stops at 18 and 69. The extra six spaces are added at the right so that the bell will ring for the end of the writing line. Have a top margin of one and a half inches. Use single spacing. Type each line twice. Double-space after the second typing of each line.

```
ed uj tf ol as nj vf ik ws mj vf ik ws mj tf

did how aim vow him did vow him who sir vow

if he is to go in it he is to do so as if we

Don will give the rent for August to Jake.

Mr. Vaughn will move into his new home soon.
```

(Sit erect. Keep the feet on the floor. Curve the fingers. Use a forceful snatch stroke.)

Exercise 5

DIRECTIONS: Set the marginal stops for a forty-five-space line. Have a top margin of four double spaces. Use double spacing. Type the exercise twice on the same sheet. Leave an extra double space between the two writings.

WALLECK HARDWARE COMPANY
318-324 WABASH AVENUE
CHICAGO ILLINOIS

January 16, 193-

De Luxe Furniture Company
2354 Euclid Avenue
Cleveland, Ohio

Attention Purchasing Agent

Gentlemen:

In answer to your recent letter making inquiry as to the
best price we can quote on 300 pairs of hinges, we quote
you as follows:

QUANTITY: 300 pairs hinges, like sample #714,
           flat back, 3" joint, left leaf 1½",
           right leaf 1¼".

PRICE: Net price of $50 for the lot.

TERMS: C. O. D.

We shall be glad to receive this initial order from you.
Immediate shipment of the 300 pairs of hinges can be made.

We do not believe that you can duplicate this quotation
elsewhere. We have these hinges in stock and are willing
to quote you an attractive price in order to dispose of
them promptly.

                              Very truly yours

                              L. C. Walleck
                              Manager, Sales Department

LCWalleck:MGH

Style Letter No. 16—Modified Block Form
Containing Inverted Paragraphs with
Subjects Typed in Capitals

Optional Exercise 109

DIRECTIONS: Set the marginal stops for a fifty-five-space line. Type the following letter in the modified block form with the attention line centered horizontally and the closing lines indented to the position for the complimentary close and blocked in that position. Indent the description of the order (second paragraph) five spaces on the left and the right, and type it in block form. Type each financial reference (fourth paragraph) on a line by itself, indenting it five spaces on the left. Leave six single spaces between the date and the inside address. Use single spacing and open punctuation. Type the dictator's name in the position for the reference initials:

Walleck Hardware Company 318-324 Wabash Avenue Chicago, Illinois Attention Mr. L. C. Walleck Gentlemen: In accordance with your recent quotation, please enter our order #156 as follows: (P) 300 pairs of hinges with flat back, 3" joint, left leaf 1½", and right leaf 1¼". (P) We note that your terms are C.O.D. We want to ask you to extend to us the usual terms of thirty days net on open account. In addition to our ratings in Dun's and Bradstreet's, we are listing the following references in case you want further information about our financial condition: (P) First National Bank, Cleveland, Ohio. Belknap Hardware Company, Louisville, Ky. Republic Iron Company, Pittsburgh, Pa. (P) If you can accept our order on open account, please make shipment as soon as possible. Yours very truly (Dictated by H. J. Martin) Purchasing Agent *(696)*

BUDGET XVIII

Drill Emphasizing Figures and Symbols

DIRECTIONS: Set the marginal stops for a seventy-space line. Use single spacing. Type each line twice. Double-space after the second typing of each line.

STROKES FOR
EACH SENTENCE

	STROKES FOR EACH SENTENCE
The sum of 38 and 27 and 14 and 92 and 60 and 52 and 84 and 73 is 440.	71
The 17,800# of 11/16" round #1920 steel was shipped in PRR car #281453.	78
Will the Lee Service Company's 6% bond for $1,000 be due May 4, 1957?	78
This heater has 36½ feet of #50 Waterton gauge ¾-inch copper tubing.	71
The asterisk (*) refers to the footnote, "Vol. IX, No. 6, July, 1932."	80

Corrective Drill Paragraphs

DIRECTIONS: Set the marginal stops for a seventy-space line. Adjust the tabular stop for an indentation of five spaces. Use single spacing. Type one corrective drill paragraph in each practice period. Alternate the paragraphs in the various practice periods.

LESSON 4
Technique Guide

Points for special emphasis: (1) Quicken the key release. (2) Return the finger to its home position after completing the stroke. (3) Hold the eyes on the copy when throwing the carriage. (4) Quicken the throw of the carriage. (5) Eliminate excess wrist motion.

Review Practice 4

DIRECTIONS: Set the marginal stops for a forty-space line. Have a top margin of one and a half inches. Use single spacing. Type each line twice. Double-space after the second typing of each line.

(Reach-stroke review.)   `rf uj ed .l tf ol as nj tf ol gf hj nj`

(Phrase drill.)   `to go; as of; so as to go; so as to do;`

(Easy word drill.)   `and old not and old got and lot old got`

    `not got for lot and for the got ask one`

(Sentence rhythm drill.)   `Don and Joe got the old net for the lad.`

Exercise 4

DIRECTIONS: Set the marginal stops for a forty-space line. Have a top margin of four double spaces. Use double spacing. Type the exercise twice on the same sheet. Leave an extra double space between the two writings.

	STROKES
`to go at an or he do an as of us to go`	39
`sold take done told done talk done told`	79
`Dr. North had to go to the lake shore.`	120
`Nat sold the house to Dr. J. N. Hart.`	162

(Space once after a period used with an abbreviation.)

Optional Exercise 4

	STROKES
`offer often total other often total other`	42
`The total sales for the store are good.`	83
`Jane had a large dog at the other house.`	125
`Dr. Hoke sent to the store for the goods.`	168

(Use directions for preceding exercise.)

Fixation Practice 4
Control of *i, v, w,* and *m*

Locked-Key Drill. Study the illustrations and directions. With the keys locked (as directed for preceding fixation drills), practice the reaches given.

The letter *i*, controlled by the *k finger*, is above the letter *k*. In making the reach to *i*, the *j finger* should be lifted slightly to give greater freedom of movement to the *k finger*.

The letter *v*, controlled by the *f finger*, is below and to the right of *f*. The reach should be made without change of hand position.

The letter *w*, controlled by the *s finger*, is above the letter *s*. In making this reach, hold the *a finger* in its home position but lift the *d* and the *f fingers* slightly so that you will have greater freedom in making the reach to *w*.

The letter *m*, controlled by the *j finger*, is below and to the right of the letter *j*. This key is

All of us must work. That is certain. The question is: How will we work? We can work willingly, or we can work lazily; we can work with the determination to win, or we can work with the attitude of "just getting by."

w key How we work has almost as much to do with the outcome of our effort as what work we do. Each day brings opportunities for us to learn how to do better the life work we have to do. If we learn well from these daily opportunities, we can expect to achieve great things, for great things can always be done by willing workers.

x key If I wish to be known as expert, I must exert my whole thought to extend my experience in as many ways as possible. I must mix experience with judicious choosing and avoid becoming lax in my thinking. Errors are quite too expensive to minimize. Errors will tax the patience of the employer who expects me to exercise excellent skill in all my work.

Five-Minute Timed Writing Practice

DIRECTIONS: Set the marginal stops for a seventy-space line. Adjust the tabular stop for an indentation of five spaces. Use double spacing.

STROKES

Just what outcomes do you expect from your daily class work? Have you	75
taken time to vision the end result of all your effort? This end result should	157
be kept before you all the time. If you are a beginning student in shorthand,	237
you should know some of the problems of the end product of your study.	308
Many of the errors made in the transcript class have their start in the first	387
few weeks of work in shorthand. If in the early study you learn to read for	465
thought rather than words, you will be laying a solid base for the end skill	542
—the ability to transcribe quickly and surely that which has been taken in	618
dictation. Do you want this outcome? You can make sure that you will get	696
it, for outcomes are inevitable. Each minute of our lives, whether filled with	777
thought or with lazy dreaming, gathers the forces that lead to an outcome.	851

Syllable intensity, 1.30

The Inverted Paragraph Style of Letter

The inverted paragraph style of letter is a semi-block form, usually typed with single spacing. This style of letter is very infrequently used in business. Its chief claim to distinction is its unusual appearance, which claims the attention of the reader. This form of letter is not a good style for use in routine office correspondence, but it may be used to advantage for special sales or advertising letters.

In this form the first line of each paragraph is written flush with the left margin, and all succeeding lines of the paragraph are indented a uniform number of spaces, usually five.

After typing the inside address, the salutation, and the first line of the first paragraph, reset the left marginal stop at the five-space indention point. When it is necessary to begin the paragraph at the outside margin, depress the margin release and back-space to the point of the outside margin.

The inverted paragraph may be used when several paragraphs in a letter have subjects. Note the inverted paragraphs in Style Letter No. 16 on page 135. This method of typing the paragraphs makes reference to them convenient. The subjects may be typed in capital letters, or they may be typed in small letters and then underscored.

Exercise 110

DIRECTIONS: Set the marginal stops for a fifty-space line. Adjust the tabular stops so that you can quickly and accurately indent for the closing lines. Type the following letter in the inverted paragraph form. Leave four single spaces between the date and the inside address. Use single spacing and open punctuation. Observe that the letter in this exercise is the same as Style Letter No. 17 in the illustration on page 137. This letter should be arranged in exactly the same form.

Observe the special way in which the reference initials are typed in this letter. Note also, in the last paragraph of the letter, the use of the single hyphen with a space before and after it to indicate the dash. This method of typing the dash is contrary to the general practice, but it is used in some offices. Miss Harriet Moore Sohns Rathskin Apartments Nashville, Tennessee Dear

Exercise 3

DIRECTIONS: Set the marginal stops for a forty-space line. Have a top margin of four double spaces. Use double spacing. Type the exercise twice on the same sheet. Leave an extra double space between the two writings.

STROKES

led use lad she dug fed use lad she due 40

head else deal dead head else deal held 80

as he; as he has; as he has had a deal; 120

Jake had a hard fall. He fell here. 158

Optional Exercise 3

STROKES

(Note that directions for the preceding exercise are to be used for each optional exercise.)

far led jug ask had fur lad jag ask has 40

hear sure deal fear lead head sale hear 80

grade large grade heard large shall usual 122

Jake heard he had as large a sale as Fred. 166

Fixation Practice 3
Control of *t*, *o*, and *n*

Locked-Key Drill. Study the illustrations and directions. With the keys locked (as directed for Fixation Practice 2, page 11), practice the reaches given below.

The letter *t* is in the row of keys above the home keys. It is controlled by the *f finger*. The reach is forward in a diagonal line to the right. The letter *o* is above *l* and is controlled by the *l finger*. In making this reach, do not hold the other fingers of the hand rigidly in their home positions; but the correct alignment of the hand with the keyboard must be maintained. The fingers must be curved, and the controlling finger must move diagonally.

The letter *n* is below *h* and is controlled by the *j finger*. This reach calls for a short downward left movement. Hold the other fingers in their home positions.

Illustration No. 19, **Reach to *t* and *o***

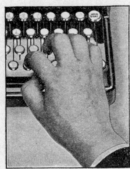

Illustration No. 20, **Reach to *n***

DIRECTIONS: Set the marginal stops for a forty-space line. Have a top margin of one and a half inches. Use single spacing. Type each line twice. Double-space after the second typing of each line.

ftf ftf jhj ftf the ftf the juj atf the

the fat had the get had the let fat get

lll lol ftf lot lot l.l faf lol ftf lol

old ago lot ago lot old got lot old out

jnj jnj and jnj and jnj not jnj not jnj

(Type the entire drill with even rhythm and with equal force behind the strokes. Avoid jerks; emphasize rhythmic control.)

[13]

Miss Sohns: One of our neighbors, a merchandising leader, has made the slogan, "It's smart to be thrifty," a real "buy" word. (P) The Hotel Regis-Plaza has proved, too, that comfort, convenience, and good taste need not be high-priced. We give our guests such conveniences as radio, both tub and shower bath, servidor, and circulating ice water at as low a price as $3.50 a day. (P) If you are thrifty with your time, you will find the convenient location of the Hotel Regis-Plaza an added advantage. For instance, coming in from Philadelphia by the Pennsylvania Railroad you walk through our private tunnel right from the station to the hotel. Eight large department stores are within a few minutes' walk of the hotel. It is merely a short walk to any one of twenty-six theatres, too. (P) For your convenience a special reservation card is enclosed. Drop it into the mail a day or two in advance of your visit to New York—all you need do is to check the rate you wish to pay and the date of your arrival. We shall have a comfortable room ready for you. Very truly yours Ralph Harvey, Manager Enclosure *(1092–186)*

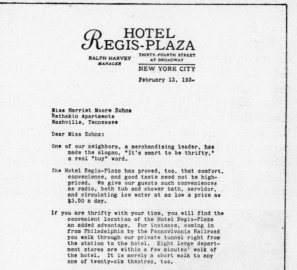

Style Letter No. 17—Inverted Paragraph Form

Exercise 111

DIRECTIONS: Set the marginal stops for a fifty-space line. Type the following letter in the inverted paragraph form, same as that of Style Letter No. 17. Leave five single spaces between the date and the inside address. Use single spacing and open punctuation.

Mr. Thomas L. Smith Principal, Senior High School Tacoma, Washington Dear Sir: At the recent convention of the National Education Association, one of the outstanding features of the program was the universal interest that was expressed in the radio and its connection with the schools of our country. (P) Successful efforts to place radio receiving sets in schools have been made in Atlanta, Georgia, Columbus, Ohio, and many other places. Hundreds of other cities are looking for practical methods of accomplishing the same purpose. (P) The time has come for a radio to be placed in every school room in Tacoma, and the *Sun-Telegraph* is heading a campaign to accomplish this purpose. (P) We would like to send a representative to tell you about our plan. A ten-minute talk will be sufficient. When will it be most convenient for a representative to call at your office? Very truly yours (Dictated by Wm. N. Robson) THE SUN-TELEGRAPH *(846–131)*

Exercise 112

DIRECTIONS: Set the marginal stops for a fifty-five-space line. Type the following letter in the modified block form with five-space paragraph indentations. Leave four single spaces between the date and the inside address. Use single spacing and open punctuation. Observe that the letter in this exercise is the same as Style Letter No. 18 in the illustration on page 138. This letter should be arranged in exactly the same form.

Mr. John W. Carthew The Hebert Company Monroe, Louisiana Dear Sir: It required six months for us to gather and condense into a 28-page pocket-size booklet all the information the shipper needs for the selection, packing, sealing, and shipping of corrugated fibre shipping boxes. (P) This booklet shows how to seal

Shifting For Capitals

Each key has two characters, the lower case or small character, and the upper case or capital. To type a capital controlled by a finger of the right hand, depress the left shift key (No. 20) with the *a finger*. To type a capital controlled by a finger of the left hand, depress the right shift key (No. 21) with the *; finger*. Stretch the little finger to the shift key; keep the other fingers hovering near their home positions. Hold the shift down until the key has been struck and released. If the capital letter is above the line of writing, the shift key was not firmly depressed, or it was released too quickly.

Study Illustrations Nos. 17 and 18, read the instructions for shifting, and practice the shift drill. Avoid unnecessary hand movements; *stretch* the little finger to the shift key.

Practice the drill in this way: Depress the left shift key; strike the *u* key; release the shift key; return the *u finger* to the home key; at the same time return the *a finger* to its home key. Follow this technique in typing other capitals.

Illustration No. 17, Control of Left Shift Key

Illustration No. 18, Control of Right Shift Key

Supplementary Shift Key Drill

(This is not to be handed in for a grade.)

Uaj Uaj R;f R;f Jaj Jaj F;f F;f Uaj R;f

F; Ja D; Ka S; La D; Ka R; Ua A; S; La D;

LESSON 3

Technique Guide

There is rhythm in everything you do, even in the way you walk and in the way you talk. There must be rhythm in your typing, too. This does not mean that the same interval of time must elapse between all strokes. Rhythmic typing means keeping the carriage moving continuously and smoothly; it means eliminating the jerks in typing. Type rhythmically.

Review Practice 3

DIRECTIONS: Set the marginal stops for a forty-space line. Have a top margin of one and a half inches. Use single spacing. Type each line twice. Double-space after the second typing of each line.

(Shift key review.)   F; F; R; Ja Ua La D; Ka F; Ja A; S; La

(Finger reach review.)   rf gf uj hj ed .l as ;l ed uj rf .l ed

led fed she led ask she due led ask led

Sue fed her; he asked her; Sue led her;

(At the end of a sentence, the period is followed by two spaces.)

Fred had Sue led here. He had her fed.

[12]

every sort of corrugated box, how to pack various commodities conformably to transportation regulations, how to select the proper style of box construction, and how to specify just what you require when you are ordering boxes or packing supplies. (P) We shall be glad to mail you a copy of this useful little book with our compliments and to supply, without cost or obligation, any further information you may wish to have. Just check and mail the enclosed card at once, while you have it in hand. Yours very truly THE BOYD & TODD PAPER CO. (Dictated by H. M. Sampson) Enclosure (P) Our consultation and package designing service is also free as the card indicates. It has made important improvements and savings for hundreds of shippers. Why not make use of it? Where you buy your packing room supplies makes no difference—you are welcome to the service. *(1075-171)*

Exercise 113

DIRECTIONS: Set the marginal stops for a sixty-space line. Type the following letter in the indented form with paragraph indentations of ten spaces. Leave three single spaces between the date and the inside address. Type the dictator's name and his official title on one line. Write the postscript in the same form as that used in Style Letter No. 18. Use single spacing and open punctuation.

Miss Edna M. Johnson 3768 Brandon Road Pittsburgh, Pa. Dear Miss Johnson: For the Public Health Contest conducted annually by the United States Chamber of Commerce, the Public Health Committee of the Chamber of Commerce is now preparing its report for next year. (P) Last year this city made the satisfactory grade of seventh. If possible we would like to show further advancement for next year. With that end in view, the committee is inviting the cooperation of all industrial, commercial, welfare, civic, relief, and other organizations, associations, clubs, etc., to report on any activities pertaining to health examinations, nursing, medical advice, supplies distributed, or other features in any way connected with health conservation and preservation service to employees, members, or the public generally. (P) If there is

Style Letter No. 18—Letter Showing One Method of Typing a Postscript

any doubt as to whether any functions performed may be regarded as included in the activities to be reported, please submit particulars thereon and the committee will endeavor to embody the report in an appropriate classification. (P) Your cooperation in furnishing such data as you may have will materially aid in advancing the high standing that this city has already attained. Very truly yours PUBLIC HEALTH COMMITTEE Frederick Marshall, Secretary (P) If you are reporting to the City Council or to any other local authority, it will not be necessary to duplicate the report for us. *(1277-197)*

Exercise 114

DIRECTIONS: Set the marginal stops for a sixty-space line. Type the following letter in the modified block form with the closing lines indented to the position for the complimentary close and blocked in that position (see Style Letter No. 9 on page 93). Type the third paragraph, which is a quotation, in the block form with a five-space indentation at the left and the right. Leave four single

Optional Exercise 2

STROKES

(In typing an optional exercise, use the same directions as those given for the preceding exercise of the same lesson.)

lug fag all ask jar fur had has lad sad   40

rush dusk hush jugs dash lark hard lurk   80

a lass had a sad fall; dad has a flag;   119

all lads had dark jugs; dad had a jar;   157

Fixation Practice 2
Control of *e*, period (.), and shift keys

Locked-Key Drill

a. Depress the carriage release and move the carriage as far as it will go to the left. This will lock the keys.

b. Place the hands in the home position, fingers curved. Assume the alert typing position.

c. Quickly and lightly strike each key which you have used. *Race* the fingers in this stroking.

Alternate the left- and the right-hand controls.

d. Study Illustrations Nos. 15 and 16 and the instructions given for the reach to *e* and the period (.). Practice making the reach to the new locations. After each reach, quickly return the controlling finger to its home position. Develop a quick, well-controlled stroke.

Illustration No. 15, Reach to *e*

Illustration No. 16, Reach to Period (.)

The letter *e* is above *d* and is controlled by the *d finger*. In making the reach to *e*, lift the *f finger* slightly, but do not move it with the *d finger* to the row of keys in which *e* is located. Mentally associate the new control with the controlling finger. Hold the *d finger* in the air. Think *d-e-d*.

The period (.) is below *l* and is controlled by the *l finger*. In making the reach to the period (.), hold the little finger on its home key; lift the other fingers slightly. This will give greater freedom to the finger movement. As you look at the *l finger*, establish a relation between that finger and the period (.).

DIRECTIONS: Set the marginal stops for a forty-space line. Have a top margin of one and a half inches. Use single spacing. Type each line twice. Double-space after the second typing of each line.

ddd ded jhj ded fed jhj ded juj fed jhj

1.1 ded led 1.1 ded 1.1 ded led 1.1 fed

fed led fed led use led fed led fed use

(Hold the eyes on the copy. Do not look up at the end of the line.)

led she fed use led she due fed led she

head fake dead rake head lead sale deed

spaces between the date and the inside address. Use single spacing and open punctuation.

Dr. Earl O. Beatty Principal, Long Academy Omaha, Nebraska Dear Dr. Beatty: The Charters and Whitley study, *Analysis of Secretarial Duties and Traits,* is perhaps the best source of secretarial traits that you can find. This book is published by Williams & Wilkins, Mount Royal and Guilford Avenues, Baltimore, Maryland. (P) I have before me a summary of this study. The summary is published by the National Junior Personnel Service, Inc., at 70 Fifth Avenue, New York City. From it I quote the following: (P) Compilation revealed 871 differentiated duties. The median number of duties performed by the individual secretary was about 130. Three-fourths of the secretaries, however, performed less than 210 duties each. (P) As interesting as the list of duties is, I find a study of the table showing the vocational traits of secretaries even more helpful. I enclose a copy of Table 4 that shows the trait and its rank. Perhaps you can make some use of this information until you obtain a copy of the book. (P) Let me know if there is anything more that I can do to help you or your teachers in the curriculum revision which you are now making. Yours very truly William Bradford Murray Associate Professor of Education Enclosure *(1166–182)*

Enclosure for Exercise 114

DIRECTIONS: Type the following copy in tabulated form, using four columns. The first and third columns will contain the names of the traits; the second and fourth columns, the numbers representing the frequency ranking. Center the copy vertically and horizontally. Use single spacing with a triple space between the main heading and the secondary heading and a double space between the secondary heading and the columns. Type the main heading in capitals. Do not type the punctuation marks. Plan this tabulation according to the tabulation check list, page 102.

VOCATIONAL TRAITS OF SECRETARIES
Frequency Ranking

Accuracy, 1; Responsibleness, 2; Dependability, 3; Intelligence, 3; Courtesy, 5; Initiative, 5; Judgment, 5; Tact, 8; Personal Pleasantness, 9; Personal Appearance, 9; Interest in Work, 11; Speed, 11; Reticence, 13; Adaptability, 14; Businesslikeness, 14; Neatness, 14; Memory, 17; Good Breeding, 18; Poise, 19; Self-confidence, 19; Graciousness, 21; Honesty, 21; Health, 21; Industriousness, 21; Executive Ability, 25; Loyalty, 25; Pleasant Voice, 25; Orderliness, 28; Grooming, 28; Alertness, 30; Drive, 30; Ambition, 32; Curiosity, 32; Forcefulness, 32; Foresight, 32; Thoughtfulness, 32; Thoroughness, 37; Willingness, 37; Modesty (Not Conceit), 39; Originality, 39; Patience, 41; Resourcefulness, 41; Self-control, 43; Versatility, 43; Fairness, 45; Self-respect, 45; Sense of Humor, 45

BUDGET XIX
Drill Emphasizing Figures and Symbols

DIRECTIONS: Set the marginal stops for a seventy-space line. Use single spacing. Type each line twice. Double-space after the second typing of each line.

	STROKES FOR EACH SENTENCE
What is the sum of 48 and 56 and 32 and 29 and 17 and 80 and 63 and 9?	72
Claim 253-A-7 is for the shortage of 1,846# of steel on Invoice 981-YB.	77
The asterisk (*) refers to the third item: 4¼ lbs. cheese @ 21¢ a lb.	75
"Give to your work the best you have!" is advice each should follow.	74
These are the H. P. Wright & Company's 6%, $1,000 bonds (due 2/1/50).	78

LESSON 2

The following basic plan of organization is used for each of the following lessons in Instructional Block I:

	Approximate Time		*Approximate Time*
1. Brief finger gymnastic drill	2 minutes	4. Check of papers, remedial	
2. Review practice	8 "	practice, etc.	5 minutes
3. Exercise	20 "	5. Fixation practice	10 "

The time given to each part of this lesson outline may be increased or lessened as conditions make necessary.

Technique Guide

As you check your completed work, inspect the page for evidence of unequal power behind the different strokes. If the page has light and dark letters, you are not giving equal power to the strokes. Detect the weak strokes; through finger gymnastic and stroking drills, strengthen the weak fingers. Develop the habit of giving equal power to the stroking of all keys.

Paper Insertion, Manipulation Drill

Time: Fifteen seconds. If your teacher cannot time you for this drill, use a watch with a second hand and time yourself.

The purpose of this drill is to show how you can improve your skill in inserting the paper in, and removing it from, the typewriter. Read the directions before beginning the drill.

DIRECTIONS: Place six sheets of paper on the desk, to the left of your typewriter. Turn the sheets endwise to the typewriter so that the left hand can readily grasp the center of the sheet on the side toward you. When the signal to begin is given:

1. Twirl a sheet of paper to a normal writing position.

2. Using the paper release lever, remove the sheet quickly and place it on the desk.

3. Continue inserting and removing the paper, a sheet at a time, until time is called.

SCORE: The score will be the number of sheets inserted, removed, and placed on the desk. Record your score so that you can compare it with scores made in later tests.

Review Practice 2

DIRECTIONS: Set the marginal stops for a forty-space line. Have a top margin of one and a half inches. Use single spacing. Type each line twice. Double space after the second typing of each line.

```
fff jjj faf j;j frf juj fgf jhj frf juj

fasdf j;lkj afsdf ;jlkj fasdf j;lkj frf

fur jug rug fur jug ask rug had ask fur

dug lad fur has fur lad has jug had ask

has rug had lad fur ask had lug far jug
```

(Have the fingers curved and poised lightly over the keys ready for a quick, decisive "snatch" stroke.)

Exercise 2

DIRECTIONS: Set the marginal stops for a forty-space line. Have a top margin of four double spaces. Use double spacing. Type the exercise twice on the same sheet. Leave an extra double space between the two writings.

	STROKES
jug fur ask jug had rug has all jug had	40
had rug jar lug has lad rug ask lag fur	80
furl hard furl glad hard asks glad rush	120
a lad has a dark jug; all lads had rugs;	160

(Space once after the semicolon.)

[10]

Corrective Drill Paragraphs

DIRECTIONS: Set the marginal stops for a seventy-space line. Adjust the tabular stop for an indentation of five spaces. Use single spacing. Type one corrective drill paragraph in each practice period. Alternate the paragraphs in the various practice periods.

y
key
Youth is a precious possession. Many people would be willing to hazard almost anything to recapture their youth of yesterday, but youth cannot be acquired in any such way. Youthful energy rightly directed is a joy; put to the wrong use, youthful energy is tragedy. It is a pity that there seems to be no way to have youthful energy yoked to the wisdom which comes from experience. Seemingly this cannot be. Youth must go on enjoying its own gaiety, heedless of wasted time and of lost opportunities.

z
key
Zeal and zest are words with which to conjure. The people with zeal are usually the ones who expect much of life and set out to make their expectations come true. Zeal means "ardent and active interest—enthusiasm, fervor." Zest connotes joy in doing. These are qualities of most great men. The lazy worker is never a zealous worker. The hazy thinker has little zest for his problem. Zeal and zest, lazy and hazy; by which pair of words shall you be known?

Five-Minute Timed Writing Practice

DIRECTIONS: Set the marginal stops for a seventy-space line. Adjust the tabular stop for an indentation of five spaces. Use double spacing.

	STROKES
Today we are masters of machines, but slaves to wrong thinking. We do	74
not have dominion over ourselves. We let greed, envy, and jealousy cripple	150
us. We cheat a little here, get by a little there, and bluff our way through	229
when we should think our way through our problems. As we think, so we	301
act; as we act, so we become. These wrong qualities of mind enslave us.	375
We who might have been masters are slaves to the commonplace, and slaves	449
we remain until we learn that the power to excel comes only through right	523
thinking. When we fully realize this, our ships will come in laden with the	601
tea, spices, and silks of lasting success.	644

Syllable intensity, 1.30

Exercise 115

DIRECTIONS: Set the marginal stops for a fifty-space line. Type the following letter in the block form (see Style Letter No. 8 on page 90). Indent the tabulated material in the body of the letter five spaces on the left and the right. Center the line *Additional Credit* and leave a double space before and after it. Study carefully the placement of this copy before you begin to type the letter. Leave four single spaces between the date and the inside address. Use single spacing and open punctuation.

The Dixon Motor Company 618 W. Sixteenth Street Youngstown, Ohio Attention Mr. Fred Lisfelt Gentlemen: A credit memorandum is being sent you to cover the following adjustment of your account:

Credits	$53.63
Charges	25.57
Balance	$28.06

Additional Credit

Freight (See receipt enclosed.)	$ 3.23
Express	.74
Cash discount	1.27
Total credit due	$33.30

This credit memorandum makes the final adjustment required by the return of the goods shipped you on your order #469. If there are any further details about which you would like information, please let us know. Yours very truly DETROIT ACCESSORIES COMPANY (Dictated by Milton L. Crawford) Manager, Adjusting Department Enclosure *(504–73)*

Exercise 1

DIRECTIONS: Set the marginal stops for a forty-space line. Have a top margin of four double spaces. Use double spacing. Type the exercise twice as shown. The entire exercise, not the single line, is the problem. Do not repeat the line. Leave an extra double space between the two writings of the exercise.

		STROKES
fur jug fur jug rug fur had jug fur jug		40
jug had fur jug had jug ask fur ask jug		80
ask lad ask rug had jug ask rug had fur		120
a lad has a jug; dad had a rag rug;		157
fur jug fur jug rug fur had jug fur jug		197
jug had fur jug had jug ask fur ask jug		237
ask lad ask rug had jug ask rug had fur		277
a lad has a jug; dad had a rag rug;		312

Optional Exercise 1

With each lesson an optional exercise is given. In typing this exercise, use the same directions as those given for the preceding exercise of the same lesson. Your teacher will give you instructions as to whether the optional exercise is to be typed or used as an extra assignment in providing for different levels of ability. If the optional exercise is used, it constitutes a test of the skill developed in typing the preceding drills and exercise.

	STROKES
rug had ask fur had lad rug had jug ask	40
jar has rug fad all far ask lug lag dug	80
dad has a rag rug; a lad had a jar;	116
a lass has a fur; dad had a glass jar;	154

[9]

Two-Page Letters

All letters of more than **275** words should be written on two or more pages. The margin at the bottom of the first page should be as wide as the left margin. The last paragraph of the first page should contain at least two lines, and the first paragraph of the second page should have at least two lines. Avoid ending a page with a hyphenated word. The heading for the second page should begin two inches from the top of the page and should show the name of the person or the company to which the letter is being written, the page number, and the date. The second page heading should be typed, beginning at the left margin, in one of the two following styles:

(1)

The H. S. Closson Company   2   January 15, 193-

(2)

McMasters & Lee, Inc.
Page 2
August 3, 193-

Leave four single spaces between the second page heading and the first line of the body of the letter. Complete the typing of the letter as you would if you were finishing it on the first page.

Exercise 116

DIRECTIONS: Set the marginal stops for a sixty-space line. Type the following letter in the single-spaced indented form (see Style Letter No. 2 on page 64). Type the word MENTOR in the fourth paragraph in capitals with two spaces between the letters; center the word horizontally. Leave four single spaces between the date and the inside address. Use open punctuation. For the second page use one of the styles of headings illustrated above.

Mr. E. C. Patterson 1294 Ridgeway Street Charleston, W. Va. Dear Mr. Patterson: Can you solve this riddle? (P) What is strikingly different, yet fundamentally the same? What is more costly than ever, yet costs less? (P) The answer is a six-letter word representing delightful entertainment, authentic information, and superlative reading pleasure for you during all of next year: (P) MENTOR (P) This information is particularly interesting to you just at this time, because your subscription expires with the next issue. (P) We live in an era of swift, dramatic change. The *Mentor* keeps just a step ahead of the procession. Things which are worth while deserve worth-while settings. No expense has been spared in making the *Mentor* a worth-while magazine. It comes to you in rich new dress, modern type, sparkling covers, and with illustrations by America's leading artists. It brings to you romance and achievement, travel and all the arts, personalities and places, news stories of history and science, brilliant comments on current topics. It is a real reporter of life in all the ages. The *Mentor* brings you into contact with the most versatile, interesting, and prominent writers of the day, men and women whose very names are indications of magic. You meet such people as Emil Ludwig, Radclyffe Hall, John Erskine, Will Durant, Princess der Ling, Havelock Ellis, Abbe Ernest Dimnet, Heywood Broun, Konrad Bercovici, Galli-Curci, and hundreds of other delightful writers. (P) Your *Mentor* is now far more costly, much more expensive, to edit and print. It costs YOU less than ever, however; so much less, in fact, that you get two years' subscription for the former price of one year's. (P) Because the *Mentor* is so expensive to produce, strictly limited editions are being printed. Only one news stand in ten is being supplied. The way in which to assure yourself of a copy every month is to place your order at once. (P) Just check and sign the enclosed order form and mail it today. We will pay the postage. Cordially yours (Dictated by David R. Blaine) Director, Subscribers' Bureau *(2058–316)*

Fixation Practice 1
Control of *r*, *u*, *g*, and *h*

Illustration No. 13, **Reach to *r* and *u***

The new reaches initiated in this drill are first-finger reaches. They offer no finger-control difficulty. You can quickly learn the direction and distance of each reach. Carefully study the following:

The letter *r* is above the *f* position and is controlled by the *f finger*. The letter *u* is above the *j* position and is controlled by the *j finger*. Make the reach without moving the other fingers from their home keys. Develop the *snatch stroke*. Think the reach from the *f* position to the *r* location and from the *j* position to the *u* location.

Always keep your eyes on the copy when typing. This is very important.

DIRECTIONS: Set the marginal stops for a forty-space writing line. If the center is 40, the left marginal stop will be set at 20 and the right marginal stop at 66. Have a top margin of eight single spaces. Use single spacing. Type each line of the drill twice. Double-space after the second typing of each line.

```
fff frf jjj j;j faf frf j;j frf faf frf

jjj juj faf j;j juj faf juj faf juj juj

frf juj fur fur fff jjj faf j;j jar fur
```

Illustration No. 14, **Reach to *g* and *h***

Leave the paper in the machine while you study the illustration showing the control of the letters *g* and *h*. After studying the illustration and the instructions which follow, type the remainder of the drill on the same sheet of paper, double-spacing after the second typing of each line.

Note the relation between the *f* position and the *g* location, and between the *j* position and the *h* location. Close your eyes and finger the reach from *f* to *g* and back to *f*; finger the reach from *j* to *h* and back to *j*. Make the reach without moving the other fingers from their home positions.

There must be no constriction of hand muscles. The finger must make its movement to the new control without disturbing the general alignment of the hand with the keyboard.

```
fff jjj faf j;j fgf juj fgf juj fgf j;j

fdf jkj frf jhj frf jhj fgf jhj faf j;j

fur jug fur jug fur jug had fur jug had
```

Insert a new sheet of paper and type the entire six lines of the drill without referring to the illustrations or the instructions for making the reaches. Type each line twice. Double-space after the second typing of each line.

Exercise 117

DIRECTIONS: Set the marginal stops for a sixty-space line. Type the following letter in the single-spaced indented form (see Style Letter No. 2 on page 64). Leave four single spaces between the date and the inside address. Use open punctuation. You will observe that this letter has a long postscript which will have to be continued on a second page. Type the postscript in the form used in Style Letter No. 18 on page 138. Do not forget to type the proper heading on the second page.

Mr. Martin L. Ayres 2513 Observatory Road Cincinnati, Ohio Dear Sir: From the enclosed card you will see that we are reserving for your desk or pocket a memorandum pad, fashioned of genuine hand-finished two-tone lambskin, with a renewable filler. (P) Your name will be embossed in gold, and the pad will be forwarded at once, upon the return of the card with the blanks filled. (P) We are taking this means of bringing a simple plan to the attention of those who want to quit work some day. By this plan they can provide, for later years, a guaranteed income which cannot be outlived! (P) It does not matter whether your present income is large or just above the average. If you will follow the plan, you will have, when you are ready, an income which will enable you to retire. (P) The full details of this plan, which combines savings, investment, and protection, will gladly be sent without obligation. You need simply make the request for further information on the enclosed card. Very truly yours (Dictated by Robert L. Hartman) Vice President Enclosure (P) The plan calls for setting aside merely a few dollars a month. The minute the first premium deposit is made, most money worries begin to disappear. Even if you should become totally and permanently disabled, you would not need to worry about the premium deposits. We would make them for you. (P) Nor should the loss of your regular income cause you to worry about other expenses. We would mail you a good-sized monthly check, even though you might be disabled for many years. (P) The plan shows you how you can become financially independent; how you can retire on an income; how you can provide money for emergencies, money to leave your home free of debt, money for other needs. (P) The plan is simple, reasonable, and logical. The minute you learn about it you will realize why it accomplishes such desirable results for hard-working, forward-looking people who know what they want and are ready to make definite plans to get it. (P) There is no obligation. Just fill out and return the enclosed card, and we shall supply the details as they apply to you personally. *(2012–343)*

Exercise 118

DIRECTIONS: Set the marginal stops for a sixty-space line. Type the following letter in the modified block form with five-space paragraph indentations and the closing lines indented to the position for the complimentary close and blocked in that position (see Style Letter No. 10 on page 94). Since Mr. Munson's official title is long, it should be typed on a line by itself. Make two carbon copies of this letter. Leave five single spaces between the date and the inside address. Use single spacing and open punctuation.

The notation appearing below the following letter is to be typed on the two carbon copies only. After you have typed the letter, do not remove it from the typewriter, but turn the sheets back to the top. Then place a blank sheet of paper against the paper table and turn the letter forward, two lines below the reference initials. If the blank sheet of paper has been correctly placed in the machine, it will be between the ribbon and the original copy of the letter. Type the notation with single spacing and a five-space indentation, below the reference initials. Do not type the word *Notation*. The copy will appear on the two carbon copies of the letter, but not on the original. One carbon copy will be given to Mr. Hughes, and the other will be retained for the files.

Mr. C. A. Munson Superintendent of Shipments Pittsburgh Coke Company Pittsburgh, Pennsylvania Dear Sir: We have your letter in regard to the handling of PCC Cars 875 and 1202, the last report on which indicated that they were empty at New Castle on February 9 and 10, respectively. (P) We find that Car 875 was moved from New Castle to McKees Rocks on February 13. From this point it was moved to Dickerson Run on February 14 and was delivered to the Pennsylvania Railroad at Summit Transfer on February

LESSON 1

Reread the pre-typing information given on pages 1 to 6. Note, also, the following:

1. Use half sheets of paper.

2. Adjust the paper guide so that the center of the paper will be at the center of the scale.

3. Six single line spaces make a vertical inch, and ten thumb spaces make a horizontal inch for typewriters having pica type. For typewriters having elite type, twelve thumb spaces make a horizontal inch. Paper 8½ x 11″ has sixty-six lines of eighty-five pica spaces each. Half sheets, 8½ x 5½″, have thirty-three lines.

4. Finger gymnastics should be used daily for not more than one or two minutes. For Lesson 1, practice Finger Gymnastic Drills 1, 2, 3, and 4, given on the inside front cover of this text.

Review Practice 1

DIRECTIONS: Use a forty-space line. Set the left marginal stop 20 spaces to the left of the center of the paper, and the right marginal stop 26 spaces to the right. The extra six spaces are added to the right so that the bell will ring for the end of the writing line. If you are using 40 as the centering point, set the marginal stops at 20 and 66.

Insert a half sheet of paper, twirling it in so that the top edge comes approximately one space above the line scale (No. 19). Since the drill has five two-line groups with an extra space between groups, you should have an inch and a half (nine spaces) for the top margin. Adjust the line-space regulator for single spacing. All single-spaced material must have double spacing between paragraphs. Double-space, therefore, after each two-line group in the drill.

```
                    Use a half sheet of paper, 8½ x 5½″.


        fasdf j;lkj fasdf j;lkj fasdf j;lkj fasdf
        fasdf j;lkj fasdf j;lkj fasdf j;lkj fasdf


        afsdf ;jlkj afsdf ;jlkj fasdf j;lkj afsdf
        afsdf ;jlkj afsdf ;jlkj fasdf j;lkj afsdf


        fff jjj faf j;j fff jjj faf j;j fff jjj
        fff jjj faf j;j fff jjj faf j;j fff jjj


        faf j;j fsf jlj fsf jlj fff jjj fsf jlj
        faf j;j fsf jlj fsf jlj fff jjj fsf jlj


        fff jjj fdf jkj fdf jkj faf j;j fdf jkj
        fff jjj fdf jkj fdf jkj faf j;j fdf jkj
```

To assist you in arranging Review Practice 1 on the page, the drill is shown above exactly as you should type it. The lines are numbered in the left margin to assist you in noting the spaces in the top and bottom margins and between groups. The ruler shows the length of the paper in inches. Note that there are six single line spaces to a vertical inch.

16. (P) Car 1202 was moved from New Castle to New Castle Junction on February 12; from New Castle Junction to McKees Rocks on February 13; and from this point to Dickerson Run on February 14. It was delivered to the Pennsylvania Railroad at Summit Transfer on February 16. (P) You will note that these cars were delayed slightly at New Castle and at Dickerson Run. The cause for the delay is being investigated. We shall let you hear from us further in connection with this matter as soon as we have completed the investigation. Yours very truly J. L. O'Toole Supt., Freight Transportation *(990–167)*

Notation

Mr. Hughes: Will you please investigate the delay of these cars at New Castle and Dickerson Run and let me know the reason for the delay. At the same time see that it is thoroughly understood by all concerned at these points that the PCC cars must be given prompt movement in the future. J. L. O'Toole

Formal and Informal Letters

The formal or the informal style of letter is used for official letters, formal social invitations and acceptances, or purely personal letters. The inside address is typed at the left margin four single spaces below the complimentary close. If the writer's address is not engraved on the stationery, it must be included in the heading of the letter. Study carefully Style Letter No. 19. Compare it with Style Letter No. 5, page 75.

Exercise 119

DIRECTIONS: Set the marginal stops for a fifty-space line. Type the following letter in the formal style. Type the date two inches from the top of the sheet and leave six single spaces between the date and the salutation. Use single spacing. Observe that the letter in this exercise is the same as Style Letter No. 19 in the illustration. This letter should be arranged in exactly the same form.

My dear Judge Hughes: You have doubtless noticed that very serious charges of dishonesty have been made in connection with the production of aircraft. (P) Because of the capital importance of this branch of the military service, I feel that these charges should be thoroughly investigated and with as little delay as possible, in order that the guilty, if there be any such, may be promptly and vigorously prosecuted and that the reputations of those whose actions have been attacked may be protected, in case the charges are groundless. (P) I requested the Department of Justice to use every instrumentality at its disposal to investigate these charges, and, with the approval of the Attorney General, I am writing to beg that you will act with him in making this investigation. I feel that this is a matter of the very greatest importance, and I sincerely hope that you will feel that it is possible to contribute your very valuable services in studying and passing upon the questions involved. Cordially and sincerely yours, (Woodrow Wilson) Hon. Charles E. Hughes 9 Broadway New York City *(987–162)*

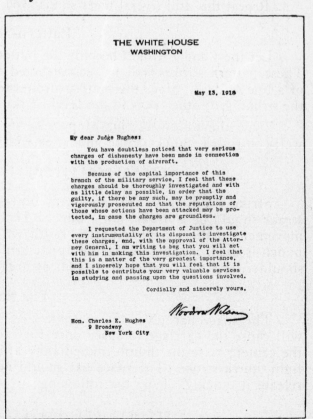

Style Letter No. 19—Formal and Informal Style

[143]

Illustration No. 12

Method of Returning the Carriage (Right Throw)

2. Right-Throw Typewriters: Curve the *j* and *k* fingers, bracing them with the thumb, and extend the hand to the line-space and carriage-return lever; *throw* the carriage, striking the lever at the second joint of the fingers.

Get the hand back in position, ready to start writing, by the time the carriage has been returned to its left margin. Learn to return the carriage rhythmically and in one count: count one, throw the carriage; count two, begin typing the next line.

The exact amount of power necessary for the carriage return may vary with different typewriters. If the throw is too forceful, an uneven left margin may result. Similarly, too little power may cause an uneven left margin. In practicing the carriage throw, determine the exact amount of power necessary; then try to use the same force for each carriage return.

Carriage-Return Drill

1. Depress the carriage release and move the carriage to approximately 50 on the scale.
2. Place the hands on the home keys; hold the eyes on the illustration of the carriage return.
3. Throw the carriage quickly, using a forceful movement of the wrist. Quickly return the hand to its home position.
4. Repeat this drill several times so that you will initiate the correct movements in returning the carriage. The repetition of the drill many times *in the same best way* will develop the correct habit. Determine the exact amount of power necessary for the carriage throw. The use of too much or too little power for the carriage return shows faulty technique. Eliminate all waste movement of the elbow or the forearm.

Pattern-Stroke Drill

Let the *f* and *j* strokes become the patterns after which all other strokes are modeled. These pattern strokes will be reconstructed frequently by the use of *fff jjj* at the beginning of a line of drill. Since the pattern strokes set the model for all stroking, you should bring the stroking of other keys to the level of skill set by the pattern strokes.

Type the following line of pattern strokes, with special emphasis upon a clean-cut, well-controlled, quick stroke and release of the key:

```
fffjjjfffjjjfffjjjfffjjjfffjjjfffjjjfff    (Throw the carriage.)
```

Strike the keys swiftly and with uniform power behind all strokes. Each repeated stroke should be a *stroke,* not a punch. If the finger is stiffened and held rigidly without movement at the second joint, the result will be a punch instead of a stroke. Whenever a punch is used, the muscles of the upper arm contract, tension comes into the forearm and shoulder, and the rigidity of movement greatly retards the development of skillful typing.

The Space Bar

The space bar (No. 17) is controlled by the *right thumb only*. The use of this bar will cause the carriage to space once for each stroke. Curve the thumb and hit the bar in the center; raise the thumb immediately after the stroke has been made. This should be a light, quick stroke. The space bar should not be depressed the full distance. Strike and release it quickly. Type the following:

```
fff jjj fff jjj fff jjj fff jjj fff jjj

fasdf j;lkj fasdf j;lkj fasdf j;lkj fasdf
```

BUDGET XX

Address and Salutation Forms

Business Persons

PARTNERSHIP: Talbott & Cook (address). Gentlemen:

MARRIED WOMAN: Mrs. E. C. Baker (address). Dear Madam: *or* My dear Mrs. Baker:

NOTE: A wife never shares her husband's official title.

SINGLE WOMAN: Miss Esther C. Forbes (address). My dear Miss Forbes:

SINGLE WOMEN: Misses Alice and Gertrude Morgan (address). Ladies:

Misses Johnson and Fleming (address). Ladies: *or* My dear Miss Johnson and Miss Fleming:

MIXED FIRM: Spencer & Weir (address). Dear Sir and Madam:

Professional Persons

COLLEGE PRESIDENT: President R. M. Gage (address). Dear Sir: *or* My dear President Gage:

DEAN (Academic): Dean G. H. Alderman (address). Dear Sir: *or* My dear Dean Alderman:

PROFESSOR: Professor Everette Leigh Hunt (address). Dear Sir: *or* My dear Professor Hunt:

DOCTOR: Dr. O. R. Moore or O. R. Moore, M.D. (address). Dear Sir: *or* My dear Dr. Moore: but never, Dear Doctor:

BISHOP (whether Roman Catholic or Protestant): The Right Reverend Joseph L. Morton, D.D., Bishop of Rhode Island, Providence, Rhode Island. Right Reverend and Dear Sir: *or* Right Reverend Bishop: *or* Sir:

RABBI: Dr. Stephen S. Morley *or* Rabbi Stephen S. Morley (address). Dear Sir: *or* Dear Rabbi Morley:

PROTESTANT CLERGYMAN: The Reverend Horace S. George (address). Sir: *or* Dear Sir:

PRIEST: Very Reverend John Laws (address). Dear Reverend Father:

MOTHER SUPERIOR: Mother M. Baptiste, Superior (address). Dear Mother Superior:

SISTER SUPERIOR: Sister M. Angela, Superior (address). Dear Sister Superior:

SISTER: Sister M. Theresa (address). Dear Sister:

BROTHER: Brother Charles Boromeo (address). Dear Sir:

Important Officials

THE PRESIDENT: The President, Washington, D. C. Sir: *or* Mr. President:

THE VICE PRESIDENT: The Vice President *or* The Honorable (name), Vice President of the United States, Washington, D. C. Sir:

MEMBER OF THE PRESIDENT'S CABINET: The Secretary of State, Washington, D. C. Sir:

AMBASSADOR: The American Ambassador, American Embassy, London. Sir:

SENATOR (United States): The Honorable Chester H. Wilderman, United States Senate, Washington, D. C. Sir: *or* Dear Sir:

GOVERNOR: His Excellency The Governor, Lansing, Michigan *or* The Honorable (name), Governor of Michigan. Your Excellency: Sir: *or* Dear Sir:

MAYOR: The Honorable (name), Mayor of (give the city). Sir: *or* Dear Sir: *or* (more intimately) Dear Mr. Mayor:

ASSOCIATE JUSTICE OF THE SUPREME COURT: The Honorable (name), Associate Justice, United States Supreme Court, Washington, D. C. Sir: *or* Dear Sir:

JUDGE: The Honorable (name), Justice of the Superior Court, Court House (address). Sir: *or* Dear Sir:

CONSUL: The Belgian Consul (address). Sir: *or* Dear Mr. Consul:

NOTE: Funk & Wagnalls' *New Standard Dictionary of the English Language* gives additional forms of address under the word "Form."

Stencils

Through the use of stencils, several hundred copies of typewritten material may be made available in a comparatively short time. The typing and running of the stencil necessitate a familiarity with the materials and equipment used in this procedure.

Type the material to be stenciled so that you can definitely estimate the length of stencil required and may accurately place it on the stencil sheet.

Clean the type thoroughly. Remove all ribbon lint or any other accumulation before typing the stencil. Use a stiff brush to remove the ribbon ink which may have dried on the type.

Adjust the ribbon lever for stenciling. The ribbon mechanism must be completely disengaged so that the type will strike against the stencil itself.

Naming the Fingers

The fingers are named according to their home key positions. The forefinger of the left hand is called the *f finger* because its home key position is the letter *f*. The finger next to the *f finger* is called the *d finger*. Next to the *d finger* is the *s finger*, and the little finger on the left hand is called the *a finger*. The fingers of the right hand are the *j finger* (the right forefinger), the *k finger*, the *l finger*, and the *; finger* (the semicolon finger).

Stroke and Release of Key

After contact between the controlling fingers and their home keys is established, an important phase of your learning will be an intelligent understanding and an accurate use of the *snatch stroke*. The snatch stroke is a quick, decisive, forceful blow to the center of the key, with an immediate release. The finger does not follow the key but is swiftly pulled back toward the palm of the hand. This is a combination of extended-finger and hand-snatch stroke and requires little wrist or forearm movement. The hands cannot be kept motionless, but all up-and-down movement of the wrists and all in-and-out movement of the elbows should be eliminated.

Stroking Drill with Keys Locked

1. Depress the carriage release and move the carriage as far as it will go to the left. This will lock the keys.

2. Place the hands, with the fingers curved, in the home position. Hold the fingers slightly above, not resting on, the home keys. Assume the correct typing position.

3. Strike each key of the home row rapidly and lightly. This will not give a complete key stroke, for the keys will be locked, but it will help to develop a quick key release.

4. With the keys locked, alternate the left-hand and the right-hand strokes. Flick all keys quickly and lightly.

Carriage Return

After a line of typing has been completed, the carriage must be returned to the left margin for the next line. This carriage return must be a quick throw, not a slow pushing or drawing of the carriage. This throw must be made through the use of the line-space and carriage-return lever (No. 18). As the carriage is returned with a throw, this lever automatically spaces the paper forward in position for the succeeding line. Make the carriage throw a wrist movement. Return the hand to the home position immediately; keep it parallel with the keyboard, palm down. Study the instructions on this and the following page.

Illustration No. 11

Method of Returning the Carriage (Left Throw)

1. Left-Throw Typewriters: Extend the left hand, palm down, fingers bracing one another, to the line-space and carriage-return lever; *throw* the carriage, striking the lever with the first finger between the first and second joints.

Get the hand back in position, ready to start writing, by the time the carriage has been returned to its left margin. Learn to return the carriage rhythmically and in one count: count one, throw the carriage; count two, begin typing the next line.

The exact amount of power necessary for the carriage return may vary with different typewriters. If the throw is too forceful, an uneven left margin may result. Similarly, too little power will cause an uneven left margin. In practicing the carriage throw, determine the exact amount of power necessary; then try to use the same force for each carriage return.

[5]

Typing the Stencil

Insert the porous cushion sheet between the stencil sheet and its backing according to the directions printed upon the folder containing them. In typewritten work the cushion sheet *should never be omitted*. Its use prevents the cutting out of letters.

Place the top edge of the impression paper, which is to receive the copy, at the corner marks indicated on the stencil sheet, in order to determine how far down on the stencil sheet the first line of copy should be typed. The numbers at the sides serve as a guide to arrive at this point. Note the number of the line opposite the desired starting point of printing, such as the date line, etc. This number may be noted when the stencil sheet is placed in the typewriter as the place at which the stencil should begin. These marginal numbers serve also to assist in keeping the stencil straight in the typewriter.

Take the backing, the cushion sheet, and the stencil sheet, and place them in the typewriter so that the backing sheet is next to the platen of the typewriter. Use a quick, decisive, snatch stroke, striking the letters with equal force.

Precaution: When it is necessary to roll back the cylinder to any determined writing position or to make an insertion or correction in the material already typed, the loose ends of the stencil sheet and the backing sheet must be held firmly together while the rolling is being done. This prevents the wrinkling of the cushion sheet or the stencil sheet.

Making corrections: When an error is made in typing the stencil, it may be corrected by the use of mimeotype correction fluid. Roll the stencil forward so that the line on which the error is made is clear of interference; then gently rub the error with the smooth rounded end of the brush handle. This closes the perforations of the stencil and prevents the fluid from running through to the backing sheet. Pour (do not squeeze) a small quantity of the fluid on a piece of paper and, with the brush, make a single application which will lay a thin coating over the error. Allow the fluid to set for a few seconds and then type in the correction, using a normal type of stroke.

The Printing Operation

When you are ready to run the stencil, remove the cushion sheet and attach the stencil to the cylinder of the mimeograph. Hook the buttonholes over the buttons and, by holding both of the lower corners of the stencil sheet with the hands, draw the narrow part of the buttonholes snugly against the button shanks; then fasten the lower end of the stencil clamp.

Care must be used in spreading the stencil smoothly over the surface of the ink pad. If the stencil sheet becomes overlapped or wrinkled, it can be raised and respread on the ink pad without risk of injury. Do not pull this sheet, however, because an uneven strain may distort the alignment of the typewritten material. Wrinkles can be removed by the use of the finger tips applied to the extreme side margins of the stencil sheet.

If you use stencil paper which does not extend to the stencil clamp, lay on the inking pad a piece of blank paper of sufficient length to extend from under the bottom of the stencil sheet. This permits clamping, as described in the second paragraph above.

The stencil may be cleaned and filed for future use. To clean a stencil, lay it between two sheets of absorbent paper (regular stencil paper or a newspaper) and rub it gently. File it between clean sheets of paper so that the stencil will not stick to the paper.

Complete information about handling the mimeograph machine, which you are to use, will be furnished by the nearest supply office handling the equipment. Booklets containing this information are available for free distribution. Study the instructions carefully and learn how to operate the mimeograph machine quickly, accurately, and without waste of effort. Stencil work is part of the daily routine of many offices. Be prepared for it!

Exercise 120

DIRECTIONS: Type stencils of the following letter and its enclosure. Run fifteen copies of these stencils.

(From New York City, current date)

The time has come for radio to take stock of itself. More and more a great national broadcasting chain like ours is becoming of public service. One of the surest ways of finding out what the public wants is to ask its leaders. (P) It is in this spirit of asking, for the improvement of our service to the public, that we request you to give your answers to the questions which are listed on the enclosed sheet. Please give us, also, a brief resume of any constructive thoughts you may have about radio broadcasting, which are not covered by the questions. (P) If you so desire, your answers to these questions will be held in confidence; otherwise, we shall probably use them with the answers of others as a basis for making public the results of our research into the public reaction toward radio broadcasting. Sincerely yours (Signed) P. F. Beckwith, Manager NATIONAL BROADCASTING COMPANY (Enclosure)

NOTE: The signature will be written on the stencil so that each letter will not need to be personally signed. Use a stylus for writing the pen signature.

be eight to ten inches from the base of the type-writer and from an inch to an inch and a half to the right of the center of the keyboard. The letter *k* should point to the center of the body.

3. Body Position: Hold your body in an alert position; lean slightly forward from the hips.

4. Shoulders: The shoulders should be erect without being rigid.

5. Arms and Elbows: Let the arms hang easily at the sides, the elbows a little in front of a vertical line from the tips of the shoulders. The distance of the elbows from the side of the body depends upon the proportional length of the little fingers. If the little fingers are quite short, hold the elbows away from the body; if the little fingers are in proportion to the other fingers, hold the elbows near the body.

6. Wrists: There should be a gradual slope from the back of the hands to the tips of the elbows. This position avoids arched wrists, yet it does not permit the hand to rest on the base of the typewriter.

7. Fingers: Curve the fingers until the tips are an inch to an inch and a half from the palm of the hand.

8. Thumbs: Curve the right thumb and hold it above, but not on, the space bar (No. 17). The left thumb is not used in operating the type-writer keyboard; curve it and keep it out of the way of the fingers and of the right thumb.

9. Feet: Let the feet rest on the floor in front of the chair, one foot in advance of the other. This helps to give body balance.

10. Eyes: While typing, hold the eyes on the copy. This will eliminate breaks in reading the copy.

The correct typing position is the position of the sprinter—the alert, well-controlled, ready position. Maintain this correct position while typing.

Home Key Position

The home keys for the left hand are **a, s, d, f**; for the right, **j, k, l, ;.**

Illustration No. 8, Home Keys

Illustration No. 9, Home Key Position

1. Place the little finger of the left hand on the first key of the second row; this is the *a* key. Let the other three fingers cover the three succeeding keys, the *s, d,* and *f* keys. Have the fingers curved, and hold them *slightly* above, but not on, the home keys.

2. Place the little finger of the right hand on the key which is *next to that at the end* of the second row; this is the *;* (semicolon) key. Let the other three fingers cover the three preceding keys, the *l, k,* and *j* keys. This will leave the two center keys uncovered. Have the fingers curved, and hold them *slightly* above, but not on, the home keys.

3. Practice assuming the correct typing position and quickly and accurately placing the hands in the correct position on the keyboard.

Illustration No. 10, Home Key Position
(Side View)

The tips of the fingers may touch the home keys lightly, but they should never rest upon them.

Enclosure for Exercise 120

Please give us your constructive criticisms on radio broadcasting. Help us to make broadcasting more helpful to others.

1. Is your general impression of the way in which radio broadcasting, on a national scale, is meeting its opportunity good or bad?

2. Should broadcasting deal more, or less, with news events?

3. If there are any fields of activity which radio broadcasting is neglecting, please name them.

4. Do you feel that any particular part of the country is being neglected?

5. Do you think there should be more speeches, more classical music, more popular music, more sketches, or more comedy?

6. Do you feel that international broadcasts are of special benefit and that they should play a greater part in programs?

7. Have you any suggestions as to the manner in which radio can play a better part in the support of religion, morals, and good conduct?

8. Do you feel that there is any particular period of the available broadcasting hours that is not used to the best advantage? If so, what part of the day or the evening?

Exercise 121

DIRECTIONS: Fill in the name, the address, and the salutation on the fifteen mimeographed copies of the letter given in Exercise 120, to be mailed to the addresses listed below. Use the current date. Consult the chart for the correct address and salutation of each letter. In filling in the date, the inside address, and the salutation, try to match the printing. If the typing is too dark to match the mimeographed copies, strike the letters lightly; if the typing is not dark enough to match the mimeographed copies, put a new ribbon in your typewriter.

Address an envelope for each letter; place each letter under the flap of its envelope and present them to your teacher for approval. When the letters have been approved, fold and mail them. On the typewritten copy of the original letter, type the name and the address of each person to whom a letter is mailed. This copy is for your files.

1. Mr. Charles Frank Turner
3154 East Overlook Avenue
South Pasadena, California

2. Mrs. Mary Hazel Albers
Secretary to the President
Eastern School for Girls
Memphis, Tennessee

3. The Honorable Russell Wilson
Mayor of Cincinnati
Cincinnati, Ohio

4. Miss Corinne Ernst
Berea, Kentucky

5. The Reverend Joseph Saunders, D.D.
First Baptist Church
Wickliffe, Ohio

6. Rabbi Samuel Goodman
Congregation Beth Jehuda
1167 Berkshire Road
Albany, New York

7. Dr. Wilbur C. Evers
Walsh Building
Dallas, Texas

8. Professor Paul Hulme
School of Education
Ohio State University
Columbus, Ohio

9. Very Reverend Robert I. Lynch
St. Ann's Church
Covington Road
Kansas City, Missouri

10. Smith & Reynolds
Attorneys-at-Law
Bohnett Building
Pittsburgh, Pennsylvania
Attention Mr. Roy Smith

11. President Walter Gibson
Presbyterian Theological Seminary
New Haven, Connecticut

12. The Honorable John H. Summers
United States Senate
Washington, D. C.

13. Address the governor of your state.

14. Address the mayor of your city.

15. Address the principal of your school.

Straightening the Paper

When it is necessary to straighten the paper, grasp it with the forefinger and the thumb of each hand and square the edges of the paper. In order to do this, use the paper release (No. 16). Follow the instructions given below.

UNDERWOOD: Partially depress the paper release with the heel of the right hand. Study Illustration No. 5.

ROYAL and WOODSTOCK: Pull the paper release forward with the little finger of the right hand.

REMINGTON: Push back the paper release by using the backs of the second and third fingers of the left hand.

L. C. SMITH: Pull the paper release forward with the little finger of the left hand. Study Illustration No. 6.

After straightening the paper, return the paper release to its regular position.

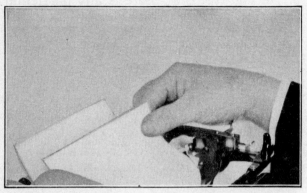

Illustration No. 5, Straightening the Paper
UNDERWOOD TYPEWRITER

Illustration No. 6, Straightening the Paper
L. C. SMITH TYPEWRITER

Removing the Paper

Operate the paper release according to the instructions given under *Straightening the Paper.* Remove the sheet with the other hand, grasping it at the center of the top. Practice inserting and removing the paper until you are entirely familiar with the movements.

Position at the Typewriter

Illustration No. 7
GEORGE HOSSFIELD, *World Champion Typist*

There are two positions to be used in the typing classroom. In the alert typing position, let the body lean slightly forward from the hips. The fingers should be poised above the home keys. The second position is the at rest, or relaxed, posture. When the hands are removed from the typewriter, the body should relax; the shoulders should drop against the back of the chair. The position should be one of ease and relaxation. This is the position you should use when not typing.

Illustration No. 7 shows the correct typing position. Study the illustration and the following instructions:

1. Height of Desk and Chair: The desk should be high enough to give approximately six to eight inches of space between the top of the knee and the frame of the typewriter. Consult your teacher if you feel that the desk and the chair assigned to you are not so suitable to your size as other equipment in the room would be.

2. Position of Chair: Place the chair so that when you are seated the front of your body will

MISCELLANEOUS OFFICE FORMS

Telegrams

Telegraph service offers a means of quick communication which is employed daily by business offices. The kind of service used depends to a large extent upon the length and the urgency of the message. The fast telegram is the standard service which takes precedence over all other messages. It gives immediate service. This is more expensive than any of the other types of service.

The Day Letter

Day letters are subordinated to full-rate telegrams in the order of transmission. They constitute a deferred day service at reduced rates. The cost of a fifty-word day letter is one and one-half times the cost of a ten-word telegram. This class of service is rapidly growing in popularity for longer messages which can stand the moderate delay involved in their subordination to full-rate telegrams.

The Night Message

Night messages are accepted until 2.00 A.M. for delivery at the beginning of the next ensuing business day. The cost is less than that for full-rate telegrams. Code language may be used. For short messages this is the cheapest over-night service.

The Night Letter

Night letters may be filed at any time during the day or night until 2.00 A.M. for delivery at the beginning of the next ensuing business day. The cost of a fifty-word night letter is the same as that for a ten-word telegram. This is the cheapest service available for messages of some length. It is widely used by business firms as an inexpensive substitute for the mails.

Preparation of the Message

In the upper left-hand corner of the telegraph blank, space is provided in which to indicate by a cross or a check mark the class of service desired. Care should be taken that the service desired is clearly indicated in the space provided.

The writing of telegrams is different from the writing of letters in that every word not essential to the clearness of the message should be omitted. In addresses, the words *East*, *West*, *North*, or *South* should be spelled in full. If the telegram is addressed to a transient, the name of the person in care of whom the addressee may be located, together with the street address, should be given. No charge is made for whatever information is required in the address to enable the telegraph company to identify and to locate the addressee.

Regardless of its length, the telegram should be typed double space. Unless they are requested and paid for, punctuation marks are not transmitted. It is important, therefore, that messages should be so phrased that their exact meaning is not dependent on punctuation marks. The word *stop* is frequently used to indicate the end of a sentence. When this word is used, it is counted as a word for which the regular charge is made. The signature, whether it is that of an individual or that of a company, should be typed. Incoming messages are typed in upper-case letters with-

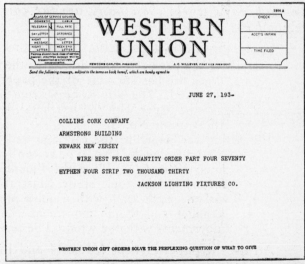

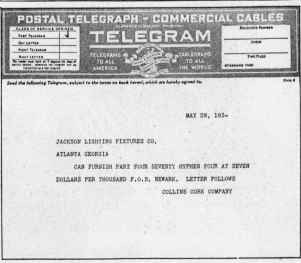

Illustration No. 48, Telegrams

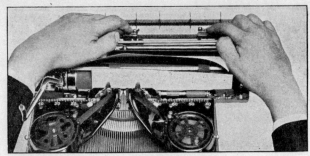

Illustration No. 2, Setting the Marginal Stops
ROYAL TYPEWRITER

Marginal Stops. The marginal stops (Nos. 10 and 11) control the width of the margins. The marginal stops can be set so that any desired margins can be obtained.

In setting the marginal stops, move the carriage so that the carriage-frame pointer is near the center of the margin scale; then move the marginal stops to the points desired on the margin scale. For today's work, set the marginal stops at 20 and 66.

Line-Space Regulator. Typed material may be spaced single, double, or triple. For ordinary purposes, however, triple spacing is seldom used. The spacing between lines is controlled by the use of the line-space regulator (No. 12). For today's work, adjust the line-space regulator for double spacing.

Inserting the Paper

Inserting the paper is an important detail; carelessness in this detail often results in a loss of time in the work of typists. The correct method of inserting the paper is given below. Master the method in every detail. You will thus eliminate waste movement. *In each day's work, consciously use the correct method of inserting the paper until this method has become a habit.*

Study the following specific instructions for inserting the paper:

1. Place the paper, turned endwise to the typewriter, on the desk to the left of the machine. Place the bottom edge of the paper near the typewriter, the top being to the left of the hand. The side to be written on must be uppermost.
2. Grasp the paper with the left hand, left thumb under the paper, fingers on top. Study Illustration No. 3.
3. Bring the paper to the carriage and drop it behind the cylinder (No. 4) and against the paper guide (No. 5); *at the same time* bring the right hand to the right cylinder knob (No. 13). Place the thumb well under the knob, with the first and second fingers on the top. Study Illustration No. 4.
4. Twirl the right knob with a quick movement of the fingers and the thumb. Make this a finger and thumb movement. Avoid twisting the elbow or making unnecessary movements with the wrist. The paper should be inserted with one twirl of the knob.

Adjust the paper clamps (Nos. 14 and 15) so that they will hold the left and right edges of the paper firmly against the cylinder.

Illustration No. 3, Inserting the Paper

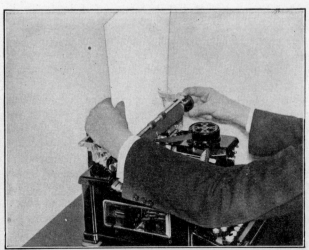

Illustration No. 4, Inserting the Paper

[2]

out punctuation marks. Some offices require that all outgoing messages be typed in the same way so that the clearness of the message may be checked. Usually the message is typed with punctuation marks as in any other piece of work. Familiarize yourself with the two forms and be guided in your office work by the wishes of your dictator.

Messages may be filed by telephone or sent by messenger to the telegraph office. The tolls will be charged to the subscriber's telephone bill if the message is filed by telephone. This filing and local delivery of messages by telephone is a modern cut in telegraphic correspondence which saves time and trouble. The original copies of messages telephoned should be kept in your own files along with the carbon copies of all telegrams sent by messenger. This will save time in checking the monthly bill and will provide exact copies for reference.

Methods of Counting Chargeable Words

All words, figures, and letters in the text of domestic messages are counted and charged for. Each initial is counted and charged for as one word. All groups of letters, when the letters are not dictionary words or combinations of dictionary words, are counted at the rate of five letters to a word. Figures, decimal points, punctuation marks, and bars of division, if they are transmitted, are counted, each separately, as one word. Write out all figures; otherwise, each figure will be counted as one word. For example, *20* will be counted as two words if the figures are used, but if it is written as *twenty,* it will be counted as one word. In groups consisting of letters and figures, each letter and each figure is counted as one word. For example, *A3C* will be counted as three words.

When there is more than one signature, each, except the last, is counted and charged for. For example, in the signature

Don Myers and Bob Harris

Don Myers and are extra words. Family signatures, such as *John and Emma,* however, contain no extra words. All words added to the signature are counted and charged for. For example, *John Brown, President,* contains one extra word. *Ltd.* and *Inc.,* however, are not counted as extra words because they are a part of the firm's name.

Illustration of the Method of Counting Chargeable Words

Counted as one word:

Abbreviations such as lbs., cwt., hhds., No., St., Ave.

All names of states such as New Jersey, New York, West Virginia, South Dakota.

Names such as McGregor, O'Connor, DuPont.

Marks of punctuation such as ( ), parentheses, " ", quotation marks.

Special abbreviations common to business transactions such as a.m., p.m., f.o.b., C.O.D., O. K., S.S.

Miscellaneous words such as cannot or can't, tomorrow, today, tonight, etc., if they are written without the hyphen.

Counted as more than one word:

Initials and names such as G. W. Brown (three words).

Abbreviations and names of railroads such as B&O (three words), New York, New Haven and Hartford Railroad (five words), PRR (two words).

NOTE: RR is the abbreviation of the word *Railroad* and is counted as one word only.

Miscellaneous words such as all right, post office, air mail (two words each).

BUDGET XXI

You are working for the Collins Cork Company of Newark, New Jersey. Carbon copies of all outgoing work from your office should be made. Do not type carbons for incoming mail.

Exercise 122
Regular Fast Telegram No. 1

DIRECTIONS: Indicate in the upper left-hand corner of the telegraph blank the service desired. In an office, three copies are made. The original copy is sent to the telegraph office, one carbon is filed, and the other carbon is held until a letter of confirmation is sent. Type the one copy. Your copy should be similar to the first telegram in Illustration No. 48.

(Telegram from Atlanta, Georgia)

Collins Cork Company Armstrong Building Newark, New Jersey Wire best price quantity order part four seventy hyphen four strip two thousand thirty JACKSON LIGHTING FIXTURES CO.

NOTE: The part number referred to in the telegram is 470-4. In order that this would be transmitted accurately, it was necessary to use the word *hyphen* to show that the number was 470-4 and not 474.

The Fundamentals of Typewriting

INSTRUCTIONAL BLOCK I
DEVELOPING KEYBOARD CONTROL

Typing power cannot be bestowed; it must be achieved. This text furnishes illustrations of correct practice procedures and organized materials of instruction. Your teacher will direct, stimulate, and challenge you in all your work. Teacher direction and text materials are effective aids, but responsibility for the development of typing power must be assumed by you, the student. This work, which you are now beginning, should therefore command your best effort. The success of your effort will depend, to a large extent, on the attitude you have toward the work. You must demonstrate the right attitude by the sincerity of your effort and the worth of your production. This is the daily challenge.

Principal Operative Parts of the Typewriter

You must be familiar with the operative parts of your typewriter. Some of these parts must be used in making the necessary machine adjustments before typing is begun; other parts will be used as a part of the typing operation. Learn these parts in the order of their use. When a part is referred to in the text, learn its name and its function by referring to the charts illustrating the different parts of the typewriter, shown on pages V to IX.

Machine Adjustments

Carriage-Release Lever. When the carriage-release lever (Nos. 1 and 2), is depressed, the carriage can be moved in either direction. When you depress the carriage-release lever, be certain to have a firm hold on the carriage in order to prevent loss of control. If the carriage of your typewriter has a thumb piece (No. 3), place your thumb around this machine part and depress the carriage release with one of your fingers.

Illustration No. 1, Use of the Carriage-Release Lever

Paper Guide. Locate on your typewriter the cylinder (No. 4), the paper guide (No. 5), the paper table (No. 6), the front or margin scale (No. 7), and the carriage-frame pointer (No. 8). Learn the use of each part. To determine the correct placement of the paper guide, follow the instructions given below.

1. Fold a sheet of 8½ x 11″ paper lengthwise, making a slight crease at the top to mark the center of the paper.

2. Depress the carriage-release lever and move the carriage so that the carriage-frame pointer is at the center of the margin scale.

3. Insert the paper so that the crease comes at the exact center of the type-bar guide (No. 9). The center of the paper will be inserted at 40 if your typewriter scale reads 0-80. It will be inserted at 43 if the scale reads 0-85.

4. Adjust the paper guide so that the left edge of the paper is even with the paper guide.

Exercise 123

Regular Fast Telegram No. 2

DIRECTIONS: Indicate in the upper left-hand corner of the telegraph blank the service desired. Type two copies. The original will be sent to the telegraph office, and the carbon will be filed in your office. A letter of confirmation will be written for this telegram. Your copy should be similar to the second telegram in Illustration No. 48.

(*Telegram from Newark, New Jersey*)

Jackson Lighting Fixtures Co. Atlanta, Georgia Can furnish part four seventy hyphen four at seven dollars per thousand f.o.b. Newark. Letter follows. COLLINS CORK COMPANY

NOTE: The abbreviation *f.o.b.* will be counted as one word.

Letters of Confirmation

It is customary to confirm a business telegram. This is done by mailing a copy of the telegram to the addressee, or by writing a letter of confirmation which quotes the message in full. The letter of confirmation provides a check on the telegram and is frequently used by business men to present additional information not easily given in a telegram.

Exercise 124

Letter of Confirmation for Telegram No. 2

DIRECTIONS: Single space with double spacing before and after the quoted telegram. Use open punctuation.

Jackson Lighting Fixtures Co. Atlanta, Georgia Gentlemen: In answer to your telegram asking for our price on a quantity order of Part #470-4, a strip of #2030 Fine Composition, we telegraphed you as follows:

"Can furnish part four seventy hyphen four at seven dollars per thousand f.o.b. Newark. Letter follows."

(P) We are glad to confirm this telegram and to say that we can make shipment of a reasonable quantity within two or three days after we receive your order. (P) We hope that you will give us your order as we are certain that you will be satisfied with this product. Yours very truly COLLINS CORK COMPANY (Dictated by S. C. Collins) Vice President *(531–93)*

Exercise 125

Regular Fast Telegram No. 3

DIRECTIONS: Type two copies of this telegram. If possible, reduce the message to twenty words. Count *p.m.* and *New York* as one word each.

Write a letter of confirmation to be signed by Mr. Collins. As the letter will be written entirely in the first person, the company signature will not be used. Type the official title, Vice President, four single spaces below the complimentary close. Use only your own initials for the reference initials.

S. L. Morrison 3909 K Street Washington, D. C. Meet me at the Willard at two p.m. Saturday. Must be in New York Monday. It is very important that I see you before I go. S. C. COLLINS

Exercise 126

Regular Fast Telegram No. 4

DIRECTIONS: Type two copies of this telegram. Reduce the message to ten words. Indicate the class of service desired.

Write a letter of confirmation. This is a company letter to be signed by Mr. Collins.

Superior Cork Company Lima, Ohio Please cancel order No. 280. It is impossible for us to wait longer for the material. COLLINS CORK COMPANY

Exercise 127

Night Letter No. 5

DIRECTIONS: Two carbon copies are to be made of this telegram. One copy is to be kept for your files and the other copy is to be sent to your salesman, Mr. Hale, at Terre Haute. As you are permitted fifty words in a night letter without extra charge, it is not necessary to omit any words from this message. No letter of confirmation is necessary when a copy of the telegram is sent.

Mr. T. F. Hale Terre Haute House Terre Haute, Indiana Park and Davis have given contract to Van Hussen of Armstrong Cork Company through T. E. Roberts. Get in touch with Van Hussen. Understand he will purchase all cork required. Wire if I can be of any assistance. S. C. COLLINS

THE L. C. SMITH TYPEWRITER

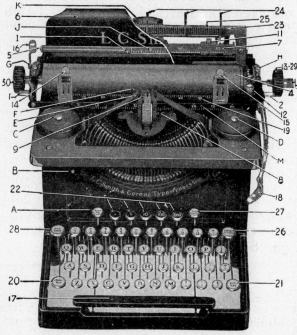

In the table of machine parts the first number for each part is the number assigned to that part in the discussion and in the illustration. The second number is the number by which that part is indicated in the wall charts published by the typewriter company.

1. 12L—Left Carriage-Release Lever
2. 12R—Right Carriage-Release Lever
3.   Thumb Piece (Not numbered in this illustration)
4. 26 —Cylinder
5. 15 —Paper Guide
6. 19 —Paper Table
7. 24 —Margin Scale
8. 30 —Carriage-Frame Pointer
9. 7 —Type-Bar Guide
10.   Left Marginal Stop (Not shown in this illustration)
11. 23R—Right Marginal Stop
12. 27 —Line-Space Regulator
13. 13R—Right Cylinder Knob
14. 11L—Left Paper Clamp
15. 11R—Right Paper Clamp
16. 16 —Paper Release
17. 1 —Space Bar
18. 31 —Line-Space and Carriage-Return Lever
19. 28 —Line Scale
20. 2L—Left Shift Key
21. 2R—Right Shift Key

22. 5 —Tabular Keys (The first key in this group is for the first tabular stop. The others are for additional tabular stops.)
23. 22 —Tabular Rack
24. 21 —Tabular Stops
25.   Tabular Scale (Not numbered in this illustration)
26. 33 —Margin Release
27. 32 —Back-Space Key
28. 3 —Shift Lock
29. 13R—Variable Line Spacer
30. 13L—Left Cylinder Knob
A. 4 —Ribbon Key
B. 6 —Ribbon-Shift Lever
C. 8L—Left Ribbon-Spool Lock Screw
D. 8R—Right Ribbon-Spool Lock Screw
E. 9 —Ribbon Carrier
F. 10 —Line-Space Finder
G. 14L—Left Cylinder Lock
H. 14R—Right Cylinder Lock
I. 17 —Paper-Guide Indicator
J. 18 —Paper-Guide Scale
K. 20 —Tabular-Stop Indicator
L. 25 —Variable Line Lock
M. 29 —Carriage Scale

A Standard Keyboard

Invoices

The work of the invoice clerk is of vital importance. Accurate billing greatly aids in prompt settlement of accounts due. The work is not peculiarly difficult if you have skill in operating the typewriter and if you have a "figure sense" which will make it possible for you to make the extensions without error.

The column headings on the bill forms indicate the position for the different amounts even though the rulings are often omitted from the printed form. (See the invoice on this page.) Before typing your invoice, study the wording of the column headings. The location of the figures in the proper columns makes it possible for the company or person to whom the bill is sent to interpret the figures accurately. You must be very careful to see that the items and the extensions are in the proper columns.

In typing tabulated work, make full use of all the special attachments of your typewriter, particularly the tabular mechanism. Set the tabular stops so that you can quickly indent to the exact position desired. Before setting the stops, scan the figures which are to go into each column and set the tabular stop at the position which will give the correct indentation for the greatest number of extensions. If your typewriter has the decimal tabulator keys, you can easily indent to the correct position for ten, hundred, thousand, etc. If your typewriter does not have the decimal tabular mechanism, you can space forward for one or two positions where necessary, or you can back-space for each additional spacing required. For instance, if you have a column of figures in which the hundred column is used most frequently, set the stop for that point; when it is necessary to use the thousand column, back-space once after indenting to the hundred position. Use your tabular stops for the main columns of figures. This effects a saving in time which will greatly increase your production.

Window Envelopes

Window envelopes are provided with transparent or cut-out openings in the lower center, through which the address typed on the letter, statement, or invoice may be seen. Such envelopes are used by many business offices for invoices and monthly statements, and by some offices for regular correspondence.

In the folding of correspondence for the window envelope, the important thing is to keep in mind that the complete address must show through the "window" space in the envelope. For full-page invoices or letters, fold from the top down fully two-thirds the length of the paper; then fold back the required distance to make the address come to the correct position. Only two folds are usually necessary for the window envelope. With half sheets, fold through the center, keeping the address in view. Insert with the address to the front of the envelope.

The SPECIALTY COMPANY
CINCINNATI, OHIO

Invoice No. B-6439

Date May 2, 193-   Cust. Order No. 350

Sold to Specialty Gift Shoppe
Steubenville
Ohio

SHIPPED VIA: Express   TERMS: Cash in 10 days; no discount

QUANTITY	DESCRIPTION	PRICE PER UNIT	AMOUNT
6 pr.	Book Ends, #339	$ 1.25 pr	$ 7.50
3	Desk Sets, #701	9.00 ea	27.00
2	Desk Sets, #703	12.00 ea	24.00
4 sets	Desk Pad Corners, #530	2.70 set	10.80
6	Paper Knives, #508	.30 ea	1.80
4	Paper Knives, #533	.75 ea	3.00
6	Pin Trays, #503	.60 ea	3.60
			$77.70

Illustration No. 49, Invoice

THE WOODSTOCK TYPEWRITER

In the table of machine parts the first number for each part is the number assigned to that part in the discussion and in the illustration. The second number is the number by which that part is indicated in the wall chart published by the typewriter company.

1. 9-32–Left Carriage-Release Lever
2. Right Carriage-Release Lever (Not numbered in this illustration)
3. Thumb Piece (Not used on this machine)
4. 5–Cylinder
5. 33–Paper Guide
6. 11–Paper Table
7. 13–Front or Margin Scale
8. 8–Carriage-Frame Pointer
9. 10–Type-Bar Guide
10. 1–Left Marginal Stop
11. 6–Right Marginal Stop
12. 28–Line-Space Regulator
13. 15–Right Cylinder Knob
14. 4–Left Paper Clamp
15. 14–Right Paper Clamp
16. 12–Paper Release
17. 22–Space Bar
18. 31–Line-Space and Carriage-Return Lever

19. 7–Line Scale
20. 23–Left Shift Key
21. 21–Right Shift Key
22. 19–Tabular Key
23. 3–Tabular Rack
24. 2–Tabular Stop
25. 3–Tabular Scale
26. 20–Margin Release
27. 25–Back-Space Key
28. 24–Shift Lock
29. 30–Variable Line Spacer
30. 29–Left Cylinder Knob
A. 18–Ribbon-Shift Lever
B. 27–Cylinder Detent Release Knob
C. 10–Ribbon Guide
D. 16–Ribbon-Spool Shaft
E. 17–Ribbon Spool
F. 18–Ribbon Cut-Out (for Stencil)
G. 34–Carriage-Tension Winder
H. 26–Ribbon Reverse

Check List for Invoice Work

1. Have pencil and paper ready for checking extensions, figuring discounts, etc.

2. Study the material so that you can type it accurately on the billhead.

3. Set the tabular stops for all main columns.

4. Duplicate copies of all invoices would be made in regular office work.

5. After abbreviations and in column tabulations where the ruling separates the dollars from the cents, you *may* omit all periods.

6. Use the following special abbreviations:
   " (quotation mark) for ditto, used as the sign of repetition.
   " (quotation mark) used to express inches.
   ' (apostrophe) used to express feet.
   # (number sign) used to express pounds.
   C used for hundred.
   M used for thousand.

7. Type all invoices single space unless there are only two or three items.

8. To rule with the typewriter:
   a. Use the underscore for the horizontal line.
   b. Raise or lower the line position by resetting the carriage through the use of the variable line space lever.
   c. Vertical rulings should be made by the use of the apostrophe or the colon.

9. To rule with pencil while the paper is still in the machine:
   a. Place the point of the pencil above the ribbon, firmly against the paper. Let the pencil rest on the ribbon mechanism, at the "V" point.
   b. For a horizontal line, depress the carriage release lever and move the carriage to the right. Keep a firm control of the carriage.
   c. To rule vertically, let the pencil rest on the ribbon mechanism; roll the carriage forward.

10. Check all work before mailing. Use window envelopes for the invoices.

You are working as invoice clerk for THE SPECIALTY COMPANY of Cincinnati, Ohio. Make a duplicate copy of each invoice for your invoice file. After your extensions have been approved by your teacher, fold and insert the invoice in a window envelope.

Exercise 128

Sold to Specialty Gift Shoppe, Steubenville, Ohio. Invoice No. B-6439. Customer order No. 350. Terms: Cash within 10 days. Shipped via express.

6 pr.	Book Ends, #339	$ 1.25	pr.
3	Desk Sets, #701	9.00	ea.
2	Desk Sets, #703	12.00	ea.
4 sets	Desk Pad Corners, #530	2.70	set
6	Paper Knives, #508	.30	ea.
4	Paper Knives, #533	.75	ea.
6	Pin Trays, #503	.60	ea.

NOTE: Observe that this is the same invoice as that illustrated in Illustration No. 49.

Exercise 129

Sold to H. Lee Jenkins, 1026 First St., South Bend, Indiana. Invoice No. B-6440. Customer order No. 22. Terms: 2%, ten days. Shipped via Railway Express.

1	Cigarette Box, #625	$ 6.00	ea.
2	Cigarette Boxes, #636	3.00	ea.
1	Humidor, #626	11.00	ea.
6	Ash Trays, #631	1.00	ea.
1	Tobacco Bowl, #635	4.50	ea.

Exercise 130

Sold to McCloy Stationers, Inc., State Street, Lexington, Ky. Invoice No. B-6441. Customer order No. 210. Terms: 5% from list price. Shipped via truck.

2	Double Ink Stands, #524	$ 6.00	ea.
1	Lamp, #902	15.00	ea.
2 doz.	Address Books, #900-E	1.00	ea.
6 pr.	Book Ends, #309	2.75	pr.
4	Roll Blotters, #536	.90	ea.
2	Comb. Memo. Pads, #512	$2.67\frac{1}{2}$	ea.

Exercise 131

Sold to Harris-McClintoc Company, Johnstown, Pa. Invoice No. B-6442. Customer order No. 176. Terms: Cash within ten days. Shipped via Pennsylvania Railroad.

3 doz.	Ash Trays, #637	$ .60	ea.
3 doz.	Incense Burners, #1115	.60	ea.
3 doz.	Cal. & Memo., #522	1.50	ea.
1 doz.	Ash Trays, #631	1.00	ea.
3 doz.	Match Holders, #632	1.25	ea.
3 doz.	Ash Trays, #627	1.00	ea.
3 doz.	Match Box Holders, #628	.60	ea.
6 pr.	Book Ends, #330	4.20	pr.
3 doz.	Incense Burners, #1113	2.00	ea.
3 pr.	Book Ends, #339	3.25	pr.
$\frac{1}{2}$ doz.	Candlesticks, #415	1.25	ea.
3	Vasettes, #110	1.20	ea.
2 doz.	Paper Knives, #516	.75	ea.
2 doz.	Paper Knives, #517	.90	ea.
2 doz.	Paper Knives, #518	.75	ea.

THE ROYAL TYPEWRITER

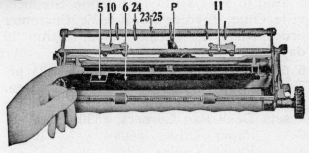

In the table of machine parts the first number for each part is the number assigned to that part in the discussion and in the illustration. The second number is the number by which that part is indicated in the wall charts published by the typewriter company.

1. 3–Left Carriage-Release Lever
2. 21–Right Carriage-Release Lever
3. Thumb Piece (Not used on this machine)
4. Cylinder
5. 32–Paper Guide
6. 34–Paper Table (Tilting)
7. 17–Front Scale
8. 18–Carriage-Frame Pointer
9. 28–Type-Bar Guide
10. 33–Left Marginal Stop
11. 38–Right Marginal Stop
12. 2–Line-Space Regulator
13. Right Cylinder Knob
14. Left Paper Clamp (Not used on this machine)
15. Right Paper Clamp (Not used on this machine)
16. 22–Paper Release
17. Space Bar
18. 4–Line-Space and Carriage-Return Lever
19. 27–Line Scale
20. 11–Left Shift Key
21. 12–Right Shift Key
22. 13–Tabular Key
23. 36–Tabular Rack
24. 35–Tabular Stop
25. Tabular Scale
26. 15–Margin Release

27. 9–Back-Space Key
28. 10–Shift Lock
29. 5–Variable Line Spacer
30. Left Cylinder Knob
A. 1–Line-Space-Disengaging Lever
B. 6–Left Ribbon Spool
C. 7–Ribbon Mechanism-Release Lever
D. 8–Ribbon Hand-Reverse Lever
E. 14–Plate Glass Protection Panel
F. 16–Color-Change and Stencil Lever
G. 19–Ribbon-Spool-Guard Door
H. 20–Right Ribbon Spool
I. 23–Paper-Bail Lift Lever
J. 24–Paper Scale
K. 25–Overhead Paper Bail and Scale
L. 26–Paper-Bail Roller
M. 29–Ribbon Vibrator
N. 30–Left and Right Card-Holding Points
O. 31–Paper-Guide Scale
P. 37–Center Stop Post with Indicator Arrow

BUDGET XXIII
Legal Documents

Many legal documents have become standardized in form and may be secured as printed copies to be filled in. A study of legal papers must be limited to a few of the special forms which will show the general arrangement of typical documents. It will then be easy for you to arrange other legal papers which you may have to type.

The typing of legal papers requires more accuracy than is required in the typing of any other papers, because the context *must* be clear and concise in order to avoid misunderstanding. Erasures must be definitely avoided. Great care must be used in punctuating accurately so that the meaning is made clear.

Most law papers are typed double space on legal paper 8½ x 13″ with left and right ruled margins. Always type within these vertical lines, leaving two or more spaces between the typing and the ruled line. The first line of typing begins approximately two inches (twelve single spaces) from the top of the paper. Type the page number at the bottom and center of each page. In some states, the first page is not numbered.

The Endorsement

Legal documents are usually bound in manuscript covers on which is typed information concerning the contents of the document. This information is called the *endorsement*.

How to fold, endorse, and bind the backing sheet:

1. Make approximately an inch fold at the top.
2. Fold the bottom edge of the backing sheet even with the top edge. Crease this fold neatly.
3. Place the bottom edge of the first fold even with the top of the sheet and crease. It is on the back of this fold that the endorsement will be typed.
4. Unfold the last crease, insert backing sheet in the typewriter, and type the endorsement as shown in Illustration No. 50.
5. Place the typed pages under the inch fold at the top of the backing sheet, and bind them, placing an eyelet at each side approximately one inch from the top and the sides.

NOTE: If the printed form is used, the endorsement will be shown on the back of the last page of the form. It is not necessary to use a backing sheet in that case.

Illustration No. 50, Endorsements of Legal Forms

You are working as stenographer for MADDOX AND WOODBURN, Attorneys-at-Law, San Francisco, California. The following legal papers are typical of the dictation given in the offices of these lawyers.

THE REMINGTON STANDARD TYPEWRITER

In the table of machine parts the first number for each part is the number assigned to that part in the discussion and in the illustration. The second number is the number by which that part is indicated in the charts published by the typewriter company.

1. 13—Left Carriage-Release Lever
2. 29—Right Carriage-Release Lever
3. 30—Thumb Piece
4. Cylinder
5. 17—Paper Guide
6. Paper Table
7. Margin Scale
8. 23—Carriage Frame Pointer
9. 22—Type-Bar Guide
10-11. 10-31—Marginal Stops
12. 16—Line-Space Regulator
13. 28—Right Cylinder Knob
14-15. Paper Clamps (See G and H)
16. 24—Paper Release
17. 1—Space Bar
18. 12—Line-Space and Carriage-Return Lever
19. 20—Line Scale
20-21. 2-33—Shift Keys
22. 5—Tabular Keys
23. Tabular Rack (Not shown on this illustration)
24. 18—Tabular Stops
25. Tabular Scale (Not shown on this illustration)
26. 8—Margin Release
27. 4—Back-Space Key
28. 3—Shift Lock
29. 15—Variable Line Spacer
30. 14—Left Cylinder Knob
A. 6—Ribbon Position Indicator
B. 7—Stencil Lever
C. 9—Left Ribbon-Spool Door
D. 11—Pressure Gauge
E. 19—Plunger and Rebound Check
F. 21—Ribbon Carrier
G. 25—Paper-Bail Roll
H. 26—Paper-Bail Shaft
I. 27—Front-Bail Latch
J. 32—Right Ribbon-Spool Door

THE REMINGTON NOISELESS TYPEWRITER

In the table of machine parts the first number for each part is the number assigned to that part in the discussion and in the illustration given at the left. The second number is the number by which that part is indicated in the charts published by the typewriter company.

1. 11—Left Carriage-Release Lever
2. 11—Right Carriage-Release Lever
3. Thumb Piece (Not used on this machine)
4. Cylinder
5. 15—Paper Guide
6. 16—Paper Table
7. Margin Scale
8. Carriage-Frame Pointer (Not used on this machine)
9. 20—Type-Bar Guide
10. Left Marginal Stop (Not shown on this illustration)
11. Right Marginal Stop (Not shown on this illustration)
12. 10—Line-Space Regulator
13. 8—Right Cylinder Knob
14. Left Paper Clamp
15. 22—Right Paper Clamp
16. 13—Paper Release
17. 1—Space Bar
18. 6—Line-Space and Carriage-Return Lever
19. 18—Line Scale
20-21. 2—Left and Right Shift Keys
22. 27—Tabular Bar
23. Tabular Rack (Not shown on this illustration)
24. Tabular Stops (Not shown on this illustration)
25. Tabular Scale (Not shown on this illustration)
26. 24—Margin Release
27. 4—Back-Space Key
28. 3—Shift Locks
29. 9—Variable Line Spacer
30. 8—Left Cylinder Knob
A. 5—Automatic Ribbon-Reverse Shaft
B. 7—Left and Right Ribbon Spools
C. 12—Cylinder Ratchet Release
D. 14—Release Screws to Remove Cylinder
E. 17—Card Pressure Attachment
F. 19—Ribbon Holder
G. 21—Paper Bail and Scale
H. 23—Ribbon Position Indicator
I. 25—Pressure Indicator
J. 26—Tabulator Set Key
K. 28—Tabulator Clear Key

Exercise 132

Last Will and Testament

DIRECTIONS: Type one copy of the will double space. Use the current date. Your completed copy should be similar to that shown in Illustration No. 51. Type the endorsement given in the illustration on page 152. Bind the pages with the backing sheet and fold for filing.

LAST WILL AND TESTAMENT

KNOW ALL MEN BY THESE PRESENTS:

I, HARRIET D. LESLIE, of the City and County of San Francisco, State of California, being of sound and disposing mind and memory, and not acting under fraud, duress, menace, or the undue influence of any person whatsoever, do make, publish, and declare this my last Will and Testament, in the manner following, that is to say:

FIRST: I hereby revoke, annul, and cancel all other and former wills and codicils by me at any time made.

SECOND: I give and bequeath to my children, ROY C. LESLIE, HELEN R. LESLIE, and JAMES P. LESLIE, all of San Francisco, California, to be equally divided among them, share and share alike, all of my right, title, and interest in and to those certain lots, pieces, or parcels of land situated in the City and County of San Francisco, State of California, and which were distributed to me under a decree of distribution made by the Superior Court of the State of California, in and for the City and County of San Francisco, in the matter of the Estate of Peter Michel, also known as Peter Michael, deceased.

THIRD: I give and bequeath to my husband, DONALD C. LESLIE, the sum of one dollar.

FOURTH: I give, devise, and bequeath to my said children, ROY C. LESLIE, HELEN R. LESLIE, and JAMES P. LESLIE, all the rest and residue of my estate, including my interest in community property, both real and personal, and wheresoever situate.

FIFTH: I hereby nominate and appoint my daughter, HELEN R. LESLIE, sole executrix, without bond, of this my

1

last Will and Testament, and I hereby authorize my said executrix to sell, hypothecate, or otherwise dispose of any or all of my said estate, without any order of or return to any court.

IN WITNESS WHEREOF, I have hereunto set my hand and seal this _____ day of _____, A. D. 19___.

_____(Seal)

The foregoing instrument, consisting of one (1) page, besides this, was, at the date thereof, by the said HARRIET D. LESLIE signed, sealed, and published as, and declared to us, and each of us, to be her last Will and Testament, in the presence of us and each of us, who, at her request and in her presence, and in the presence of each other, have hereunto subscribed our names as witnesses thereto.

ATTEST:

_____   _____

Residence _____   Residence _____

_____   _____

2

Illustration No. 51, Last Will and Testament

Know all men by these presents: (P) I, Harriet D. Leslie, of the City and County of San Francisco, State of California, being of sound and disposing mind and memory, and not acting under fraud, duress, menace, or the undue influence of any person whatsoever, do make, publish, and declare this my last Will and Testament, in the manner following, that is to say: (P) First: I hereby revoke, annul, and cancel all other and former wills and codicils by me at any time made. (P) Second: I give and bequeath to my children, Roy C. Leslie, Helen R. Leslie, and James P. Leslie, all of San Francisco, California, to be equally divided among them, share and share alike, all of my right, title, and interest in and to those certain lots, pieces, or parcels of land situated in the City and County of San Francisco, State of California, and which were distributed to me under a decree of distribution made

THE UNDERWOOD STANDARD TYPEWRITER

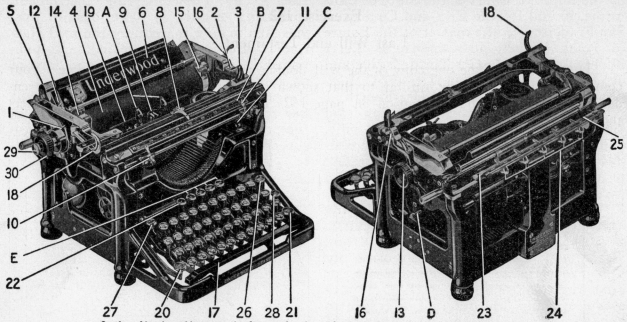

In the table of machine parts the first number for each part is the number assigned to that part in the discussion and in the illustrations. The second number is the number by which that part is indicated in the wall charts published by the typewriter company.

1. 35–Left Carriage-Release Lever
2. 12–Right Carriage-Release Lever
3. 13–Thumb Piece
4. 4–Cylinder
5. 1–Paper Guide
6. 8–Paper Table
7. 15–Front or Margin Scale
8. 9–Carriage-Frame Pointer
9. 7–Type Bar Guide
10. 32–Left Marginal Stop

11. 16–Right Marginal Stop
12. 2–Line-Space Regulator
13. 23–Right Cylinder Knob
14. 3–Left Paper Clamp
15. 10–Right Paper Clamp
16. 11–Paper Release
17. 27–Space Bar
18. 18–Line-Space and Carriage-Return Lever
19. 5–Line Scale

20. 28–Left Shift Key
21. 24–Right Shift Key
22. 30–Tabular Key
23. 21–Tabular Rack
24. 20–Tabular Stops
25. 19–Tabular Scale
26. 26–Margin Release (For writing outside the right margin)
27. 29–Back-Space Key
28. 25–Shift Lock

29. 34–Variable Line Spacer
30. 33–Left Cylinder Knob
A. 6–Left and Right Card-Holding Points
B. 14–Margin Release (For writing outside the left margin)
C. 17–Ribbon-Shift Lever
D. 22–Ribbon-Spool Ratchet Handle
E. 31–Decimal Tabular Keys

THE UNDERWOOD NOISELESS TYPEWRITER

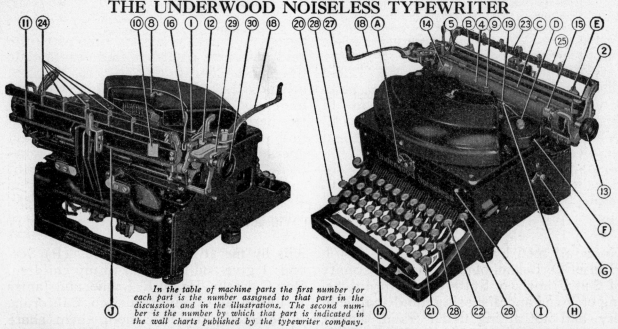

In the table of machine parts the first number for each part is the number assigned to that part in the discussion and in the illustrations. The second number is the number by which that part is indicated in the wall charts published by the typewriter company.

1. 6–Left Carriage-Release Lever
2. 25–Right Carriage-Release Lever
3. Thumb Piece (Not used on this machine)
4. Cylinder
5. 16–Paper Guide
6. Paper Table (Not used on this machine)
7. Margin Scale (Not numbered in these illustrations)
8. 4–Carriage-Frame Pointer
9. 18–Type-Bar Guide

10. 3–Left Marginal Stop
11. 1–Right Marginal Stop
12. 7–Line-Space Regulator
13. 26–Right Cylinder Knob
14. 15–Left Paper Clamp
15. 23–Right Paper Clamp
16. 5–Paper Release
17. 35–Space Bar
18. 10–Line-Space and Carriage-Return Lever
19. 19–Line Scale

20. 11–Left Shift Key
21. 34–Right Shift Key
22. 32–Tabular Key
23. 21–Tabular Rack
24. 2–Tabular Stops
25. Tabular Scale
26. 31–Margin Release
27. 13–Back-Space Key
28. 12-33–Shift Locks
29. 8–Variable Line Spacer
30. 9–Left Cylinder Knob

A. 14–Pressure Indicator
B. 17–Left Marginal Stop Plunger
C. 21–Overhead Paper Bail and Scale
D. 22–Ribbon-Spool Cover
E. 24–Right Marginal Stop Plunger
F. 27–Ribbon Spool
G. 28–Ribbon-Shaft Crank
H. 29–Line-Scale Card Lever
I. 30–Ribbon-Position Indicator
J. 36–Carriage Rail

by the Superior Court of the State of California, in and for the City and County of San Francisco, in the matter of the Estate of Peter Michel, also known as Peter Michael, deceased. (P) Third: I give and bequeath to my husband, Donald C. Leslie, the sum of one dollar. (P) Fourth: I give, devise, and bequeath to my said children, Roy C. Leslie, Helen R. Leslie, and James P. Leslie, all the rest and residue of my estate, including my interest in community property, both real and personal, and wheresoever situate. (P) Fifth: I hereby nominate and appoint my daughter, Helen R. Leslie, sole executrix, without bond, of this my last Will and Testament, and I hereby authorize my said executrix to sell, hypothecate, or otherwise dispose of any or all of my said estate, without any order of or return to any court. (P) In Witness Whereof, I have hereunto set my hand and seal this _____ day of _____, A. D. 19__.

(Seal) (P) The foregoing instrument, consisting of one (1) page, besides this, was, at the date thereof, by the said Harriet D. Leslie signed, sealed, and published as, and declared to us, and each of us, to be her last Will and Testament, in the presence of us and each of us, who, at her request and in her presence, and in the presence of each other, have hereunto subscribed our names as witnesses thereto. (P) Attest:

_____

Residence_____

_____

_____

Residence_____

_____

Exercise 133

Agreement

DIRECTIONS: Type one copy double space. Provide a backing sheet, and an endorsement similar to the illustration on page 152.

Agreement. (P) This Agreement, made this _____ day of _____, 193__, between John Parsons, hereafter called the first party, and Wilson Howell, hereafter called the second party, both of Biggs, California, (P) Witnesseth: (P) Whereas, said first party is at the present time engaged in the operation of an Automobile Stage Line for the transportation of passengers between Biggs, California, and East Biggs, California, said operation having been started prior to May 1, 1917; and (P) Whereas, said first party desires to sell said operative rights in said Stage Line, and said second party desires to purchase said operative rights; (P) Now It Is, Therefore, Agreed that said first party will sell to said second party the said operative rights in said Automobile Stage Line, subject to the authorization of the Railroad Commission of the State of California, a petition for which authorization has this day been filed by said parties with said Railroad Commission. (P) And said second party hereby agrees to purchase of said first party the said operative rights in said Automobile Stage Line, and to pay therefor the sum of One ($1.00) Dollar. (P) It is expressly understood and agreed between the parties hereto that the assignment from said first party to said second party of said operative rights, executed contemporaneously herewith, shall not be valid until said Railroad Commission has made its order authorizing the said transfer. (P) In Witness Whereof: The said parties have hereunto set their hands the day and year first above written.

_____(Seal)

_____(Seal)

Signed, Sealed, and Delivered in the Presence of

_____

_____

Exercise 134

Transcript of Testimony

DIRECTIONS: Type one copy with double spacing. The correct arrangement for the first page is shown in Illustration No. 52.

Illustration No. 52, Transcript of Testimony

In the Court of Common Pleas of Allegheny County, Pennsylvania, County of Allegheny, State of Pennsylvania, ss., William F. Boyd, Plaintiff vs. Sidney R. Hastings, Defendant, suit for damages. Appearances J. S. Radcliffe, Esq., for the Plaintiff, A. W. Weir, Esq., for the Defendant. (P) Martin Denison, having been called and duly sworn on the part of the Plaintiff, testified as follows: Direct Examination By Mr. J. S. Radcliffe.

Q. What is your name?
A. Martin Denison.

Q. Where do you live, Mr. Denison?
A. I live at 2632 Fifth Avenue.

Q. Are you acquainted with William F. Boyd, the plaintiff in this case?
A. I am.

Q. How long have you known him?
A. For the past five years.

Q. Did you see him on the second day of July, last year?
A. I did.

Q. Where did you see him?
A. I first saw him at the corner of Fifth Avenue and Craig Street.

Q. What was he doing when you first saw him?
A. He was talking to a friend.

Q. Which way was he facing with reference to the street?
A. He had his back turned toward the street. He was facing southwest.

Q. Where were you at the time you first saw him?
A. I was on the sidewalk going toward him.

Q. On Craig Street or Fifth Avenue?
A. On Craig Street.

Q. Did you see Mr. Boyd injured in any way at that place?
A. I did.

Q. You may state just what you saw.
A. A truck came around the corner from the south, loaded with steel construction material of some kind. Part of the steel stuck out from the truck a ways, and as the truck rounded the corner, this struck Mr. Boyd and knocked him down.

Q. Was he standing on the sidewalk at the time?
A. He was.

Q. Did he get up by himself or was he helped up?
A. He lay on the walk until picked up.

Q. Did you know to whom the truck, that you spoke of, belonged?

CONTENTS

A. I did not, except that painted on the truck was the sign, "Sidney R. Hastings, General Contractor."

Q. Did you know the driver of the truck?

A. No, sir; I did not.

Q. Who picked Mr. Boyd up after he was injured?

A. The friend to whom he was talking. I do not know his name.

Q. How far were you away when the accident occurred?

A. About twenty feet, I should judge.

Q. Who went with him to his home?

A. The friend to whom he was talking.

CROSS EXAMINATION

By Mr. A. W. Weir

Q. Where were you standing at the time of the accident?

A. I wasn't standing. I was walking toward the corner of Craig Street and Fifth Avenue.

Q. How far down the street were you when you first saw Mr. Boyd and his friend?

A. Forty or fifty feet, I should judge.

Q. And the accident occurred when you first saw them? That was what made you see them, was it not?

A. No, sir; I had walked about half the distance after seeing them when the truck came around the corner.

Q. About half of the fifty feet?

A. About half of the forty or fifty feet. I couldn't say exactly as to the distance.

In Instructional Block III, the major emphasis is placed upon raising the level of typing skill. One-syllable words of two, three, and four letters each are given for practice. This drill will lead from the letter-recognition level of typing to the word-recognition level. Paragraphs in which each letter of the alphabet is used provide for timed writing practice periods of varying length. Corrective drills based on an analysis of more than 60,000 errors are given. From these, corrective drills to meet individual needs are to be selected by each student. The plan for analyzing individual errors challenges the student to assume responsibility for his own progress. Each student learns to isolate a major weakness in technique; then he chooses the corrective drill which will help to eliminate that weakness. The drill may be a carriage-throw and tabular-key control drill (page 18); or it may be the practice of a line of corrective drill words to establish the reach to a particular key (pages 53 and 54). The point of emphasis in the text is that the student shares with the teacher the responsibility for isolating the difficulty and for choosing the corrective practice. This corrective drill is not concerned with keyboard errors alone; it includes all of the manipulative drills as well. It includes work habits, too.

In Instructional Block IV, emphasis upon straight-copy skill is continued through five-minute timed writing practice material, but the real challenge of this instructional block is the use of the developed straight-copy speed in the typing of simple business letters. Sufficient practice in typing the double-space and the single-space letters is given so that the first semester typist can begin to make effective use of his typing skill. Thus typing instruction becomes functional and typing exercises become meaningful to the student.

Typing has personal-use value. The problems in Instructional Block V are suggestive only. The typing of themes, personal letters, history outlines, etc., should be done under the supervision of the typing teacher. Even though the emphasis in this block is upon the use of skill in the typing of personal problems, the development of higher skill is not to be neglected. Thus it is that drills for typing power are given at the beginning of the instructional block.

PART II. OFFICE PROBLEMS

An analysis of the duties of an office typist shows that more than one-half of the work is the typing of letters. The study of business letters therefore assumes a place of major importance in the work of Part II. In Instructional Block VI, practice is given in the typing of letters in the most frequently used styles. In Instructional Block X, special problems in the typing of business letters are singled out for study and for practice. This emphasis upon the development of the business letter is in keeping with the place the letter holds in office work.

Problems in tabulation are common to most office work. The experienced worker can place tabulated material on the page through judgment and eye measurement. The inexperienced typist needs definite instructions for the setting up of tabulation problems. The check list for the mathematical placement of tabulated problems given in Instructional Block VII eliminates guess work and gives that exactness in placement which comes from the use of a workable plan.

The typing of manuscripts, telegrams, legal forms, invoices, and other office forms helps to give to the student an understanding of office forms and office procedures. Emphasis upon skill is never relaxed in the work of this text; but through timed writing practice material and trait analysis information, constant emphasis is given to the development of the qualities which make for successful use of skill. The student is thus challenged to appraise himself as well as the worth of his typing.

It is not possible to make specific acknowledgment to all teachers and students who have contributed to the work of this revision. General acknowledgment is gratefully made for helpful suggestions and criticisms which have been given. Special credit is due to the following teachers who have tried out the material in their classrooms or who have given generously of time and thought in criticizing the manuscript: Miss Jane Church, of Illinois State Normal University, Normal, Illinois; Mr. Ray Wall Fisher, of Merritt Business School, Oakland, California; Miss Fannie B. Harrington, of Bowling Green Business University, Bowling Green, Kentucky; Miss Eliza Johnson and Miss M. Gertrude Miller, of Peabody High School, Pittsburgh, Pennsylvania; Mr. R. L. Montgomery, of Tilghman High School, Paducah, Kentucky; and Miss Julia Myers, of Iowa State Teachers College, Cedar Falls, Iowa.

D. D. LESSENBERRY

INDEX

PREFACE

*I*N the study of typewriting, the primary aim is the development of typing power for personal or vocational use. This is an all-inclusive aim. It must be broken up into its elements in order that materials of instruction and teaching procedures through which the aim is to be realized can be correctly evaluated. Some of these elements, which may well be ranked as secondary aims because of their contribution to the development of the whole boy or girl, may be summarized as follows:

1. The development of fundamental techniques of keyboard and machine parts control.
2. The development of the habit of accuracy in typing and in proof reading material.
3. The development of the use of judgment in the placement of typed material.
4. The development of a familiarity with common office forms and office procedures.
5. The development of a feeling for the correct spelling and syllabication of words.
6. The development of personal qualities, such as accuracy, responsibleness, dependability, courtesy, initiative, judgment, and tact.
7. The development of the attitude of self-appraisal. This means appraising the sincerity of effort as frequently as the worth of production.

The problem of developing typing power is thus seen to begin with the techniques of typing; but along with this development of skill must go the development of the individual in order that there may be intelligent *use* of skill. This broadened scope of typewriting instruction calls for teaching which will stimulate, guide, and challenge each student; it also calls for a text which will provide carefully planned and organized drills and problems through which typing power may be achieved. Thus typewriting text revision keeps pace with progressive school philosophy.

In the revision of 20TH CENTURY TYPEWRITING, certain basic principles are retained from the former edition. A definite lesson plan with a technique guide for special emphasis is provided. The thought content of the paragraphs used for practice will commend the text to all who appreciate the importance of developing attitudes as well as habits, of stimulating the growth of qualities as well as the growth of skill.

Certain features in this revision are new in typewriting text construction. The organization of the teaching materials into specific blocks of work and the giving of an overview of the problem of each block are features which will make for greater ease in motivating student practice. The student knows what outcomes to expect from the completion of the work of each block. This makes for self-motivated practice. After the keyboard has been introduced, each letter of the alphabet is used in each paragraph of practice material. This daily use of all letters of the alphabet provides for a steady improvement in the stroking of all letters, and quickly leads from letter recognition to word recognition.

PART I. THE FUNDAMENTALS OF TYPEWRITING

Typing skill is built on the development of fundamental techniques of keyboard and machine parts control. These fundamental techniques are initiated in Instructional Block I and followed up in Instructional Block II in order that the habits may be made permanent.

Letters of the alphabet are, for the most part, introduced in the order of frequency of use. This has made possible the use of complete sentences from the beginning. The lesson plan provides for a brief review practice at the beginning of each day's work. This reconstruction material makes limited use of letter-combination reaches to reconstruct the finger pathway; then the application of the reach is immediately made to the writing of words, phrases, and sentences. An exercise provides the testing material for each day's work. In each exercise, all the letters previously taught are used. Beginning with Lesson 6, paragraphs using all the letters previously taught are used. To complete the lesson, new reaches are initiated through the fixation practice.

The development of the use of judgment in the placement of typed material is stressed beginning with the first lesson. Instructions are given for the correct length of line for the drill or the exercise. The student adjusts the marginal stops to give the length of line called for; this is horizontal centering. Vertical centering is taught from the first by having the drill or the exercise centered as to top and bottom margins. Centering thus becomes a daily routine, not an occasional drill.

20th CENTURY TYPEWRITING

...*Second Edition*...

BY

D. D. LESSENBERRY

Director, Courses in Commercial Education
University of Pittsburgh

COPYRIGHT
1933

Published By

SOUTH-WESTERN PUBLISHING COMPANY

CINCINNATI   NEW YORK   CHICAGO   SAN FRANCISCO

PRINTED IN U.S.A.

Francis Perrone
Enlisted as 43
Home Room
Miss

Frances Perrone

R